Writing the Incommensurable

Literature & Philosophy

A. J. Cascardi, General Editor

This new series will publish books in a wide range of subjects in philosophy and literature, including studies of the social and historical issues that relate these two fields. Drawing on the resources of the Anglo-American and Continental traditions, the series will be open to philosophically informed scholarship covering the entire range of contemporary critical thought.

Already published:

J. M. Bernstein, *The Fate of Art: Aesthetic Alienation from Kant to Derrida and Adorno*

Robert Steiner, *Toward a Grammar of Abstraction: Modernity, Wittgenstein, and the Paintings of Jackson Pollock*

Peter Bürger, *The Decline of Modernism*

Writing the Incommensurable

KIERKEGAARD, ROSSETTI,
and HOPKINS

Mary E. Finn

The Pennsylvania State University Press
University Park, Pennsylvania

Princeton University Press has granted permission to quote from Søren Kierkegaard's *Fear and Trembling/Repetition, Either/Or,* and *The Concept of Anxiety.*

Library of Congress Cataloging-in-Publication Data

Finn, Mary E.
  Writing the incommensurable : Kierkegaard, Rossetti, and Hopkins / Mary E. Finn.
      p.   cm.
  Includes bibliographical references and index.
  ISBN 0-271-00854-7 (alk. paper)
  1. English poetry—19th century—History and criticism.
  2. Christian poetry, English—History and criticism.   3. Hopkins, Gerard Manley, 1844–1889—Religion.   4. Rossetti, Christina, 1830–1894—Religion.   5. Kierkegaard, Søren, 1813–1855—Religion.
  6. Immanence of God in literature.   I. Title.
  PR595.R4F56   1992
  821'.809382—dc20   91–40859
                                                                                          CIP

Published by The Pennsylvania State University Press,
Suite C, Barbara Building, University Park, PA 16802-1003

It is the policy of The Pennsylvania State University Press to use acid-free paper for the first printing of all clothbound books. Publications on uncoated stock satisfy the minimum requirements of American National Standard for Information Sciences— Permanence of Paper for Printed Library Materials, ANSI Z39.48–1984.

Contents

For Margaret and John Finn, and Mary Linn

Acknowledgments

This project was originally funded by a dissertation fellowship from the American Association of University Women, to whom I am indebted. At Bryn Mawr College, Jane Hedley, Sandra Berwind, and Susan Dean read and improved this work in its first version, and to them, special thanks. At the University of Alabama, Harold Weber, Pat Hermann, and Elizabeth Meese continued in the task of improving the manuscript. Bill Ulmer, senior colleague extraordinaire, also read and read, advised and advised, and more than anyone has helped me with my writing. My research assistant, Mark Drew, and the editorial staff at Penn State Press have helped improve the manuscript in small and large ways. To Tony Cascardi, the editor of this series, I owe thanks and gratitude for his help and his faith as we worked together toward a final product. Jack Hall has been a good friend from start to finish, and I will remember his example when I am in the position to help a new scholar. My friends and family have been great boosters throughout this project, and I appreciate their love and, especially, their humor. Finally, am I just lucky, or have things evolved enough that a not-particularly-young new scholar can name many professional female role models? I will single out just two right now. Claudia Johnson, Chair of the English Department at the University of Alabama, has my deepest respect, and I thank her for making this project's completion possible. And to Carol Bernstein, Chair of the English Department at Bryn Mawr College, I owe the largest debt of all for the successful beginning, middle, and, now at last, end of this endeavor.

1

Introduction:
"Aesthetic Writers"

[For Plato] [w]hat is measurable or commensurable is graspable, in order, good; what is without measure is boundless, elusive, chaotic, threatening, bad.
—Martha Nussbaum, "Plato on Commensurability and Desire"

One must still have chaos in oneself to be able to give birth to a dancing star.
—Nietzsche, *Thus Spake Zarathustra*

In the "Advertisement" to the section of Søren Kierkegaard's *Stages on Life's Way* entitled " 'Guilty?/Not Guilty?': A Passion Narrative," the narrator, Frater Taciturnus, describes a fishing expedition that yields him a box. He tells how as he struggled with some intransigent object at the end of his line he had "the strangest feeling":

> ... and yet I did not have the remotest notion what sort of a find it was I had made. Now when I reflect upon it I know all, I understand it, I understand that it was a sigh from below, a sigh *de profundis*, a sigh that I had wrested from the lake its treasure, a sigh from the shy and secluded lake from which I had wrested its secret. ... Wrapped in oilskin and provided with many seals was a rosewood box. The box was locked, and when I opened it by force the key lay inside—thus it is that morbid reserve always is introverted. In the box was a manuscript written with a very careful and clear hand upon thin paper. There was orderliness

and neatness in it all, and yet an air of solemn consecration as if it had been written before the face of God.[1]

The recovered manuscript contains "Quidam's Diary," a tortured account of a love affair aborted in the interest of a religious commitment. From the element of *de profundis* to the "air of solemn consecration" this passage both delves deep and reaches high to memorialize the moment and object of discovery. And yet in spite of his name, Frater Taciturnus publishes what has clearly been deliberately well hidden, and no amount of rationalization (of which he provides much) can disguise the fact that he ransacks a box whose key is *inside* and exposes its contents to the world in the form of an advertisement to its owner. The theme of the aborted love affair pervades Kierkegaard's pseudonymous works, but the rosewood box, whose key becomes available only after the box has been opened, is one of the most evocative motifs in the Kierkegaardian oeuvre and extends far beyond Quidam's dilemma in its significance and in the significance of its discovery.

Kierkegaard's name for his pseudonymous texts reflects the complicated task he sets for those texts, which from their fictional authorship to their mode of exposition hide and reveal simultaneously. Each "aesthetic" work is another rosewood box, drawn out of the depths of a fictional psyche in trouble, the key to understanding locked up inside. In *The Point of View for My Life as an Author,* one of his last works, Kierkegaard explains the need for duplicity in the work he sets for himself, and the need for what he has famously called "indirection." The rosewood box signals both. It plays duplicitously with the purpose of a key, which should be the cause of an entrance into a locked space, not the result; a forced entry into a locked space only to find the key is ordinary chronology gone awry, confrontation (breaking the box open) as indirection (first the break-in, then the key). Like the British Tractarians who in the increasingly secularized nineteenth century saw the time for direct religious exhortation as past, Kierkegaard holds that "the religious writer, whose all absorbing thought is how one is to become a Christian, starts off rightly in Christendom [a pejorative term in Kierkegaard's lexicon for nineteenth-century institutionalized religion] as an aesthetic writer."[2] Why? Because "in all eternity it

---

1. Søren Kierkegaard, *Stages on Life's Way,* trans. Walter Lowrie (Princeton: Princeton University Press, 1940), 182–83.

2. Søren Kierkegaard, *The Point of View for My Life as an Author / A Report to History and Related Writings,* trans. Walter Lowrie, ed. Benjamin Nelson (New York: Harper and Row, 1962), 30.

is impossible for me to compel a person to accept an opinion, a conviction, a belief. But one thing I can do: I can compel him to take notice" (35).

Kierkegaard's pseudonymous works appeal to contemporary critics because of their rejection of the exhortative mode for the aesthetic, and their commitment to non-authoritative discourse. Read in context, "I can compel him to take notice" promises a speech act of persuasion, the success of which will depend upon the artistry of what is noticed: "[Kierkegaard's] writings offer not ideas about the thing—certainly not clear and distinct ideas—but, through the resplendence of images and the refraction of indirect communication—a way to the thing itself."[3] Again we have both confrontation ("I can compel him . . . ," and "a way to the thing itself") and indirection ("resplendence" and "refraction"). The strategies of indirection—fissures in logic, deliberate silences, and repetition—enable a non-authoritative discourse that is nonetheless seductively readable: "This is why 'silence' is such an important aspect of what we will argue is a particularly Kierkegaardian rhetoric: it does not impose the authority of assertion and conceptualization, but rather creates the occasion, as literature does, for the drama of interpretation—in a word, an occasion for *reading*."[4] As we shall see, however, speakers or characters within Kierkegaard's texts, as well as Christina Rossetti's and Gerard Manley Hopkins's, also have such occasions for reading, but unlike conventional drama, the drama produced is fraught with a tension unrelieved. In *Fear and Trembling*, Johannes de Silentio articulates the problem silence poses for interpretation: "If I go further [than the understandable tragic hero], I always run up against the paradox, the divine and the demonic, for silence is both. Silence is the demon's trap, and the more that is silenced, the more terrible the demon, but silence is also divinity's mutual understanding with the single individual."[5]

Reading and misreading can become difficult to distinguish authoritatively. Just so, in his study, *Points of View*, Mackey reevaluates Kierkegaard and restates his own earlier evaluations in bleaker terms: "Failure is all the success there is: the oblique purpose of the Kierkegaardian text is to take itself out of the way and thereby facilitate its displacement and

3. Louis Mackey, *Kierkegaard: A Kind of a Poet* (Philadelphia: University of Pennsylvania Press, 1971), 269.

4. Ronald Schleifer and Robert Markley, eds., *Kierkegaard and Literature: Irony, Repetition, and Criticism* (Norman: University of Oklahoma Press, 1984), 5.

5. Søren Kierkegaard, *Fear and Trembling / Repetition*, trans. and ed. Howard V. Hong and Edna H. Hong (Princeton: Princeton University Press, 1983), 88.

replacement by the discourse of the Other."[6] Chapter 3 explores in detail this complex web of failure and success that is woven in the writer's attempt at self-effacement, but for now Mackey's restatement itself needs revision. "Displacement and replacement by the discourse" of Kierkegaard's particular Other can never really happen because that Other is divine. Its discourse, like Abraham's life in *Fear and Trembling,* is "a book under divine confiscation and never becomes *publice juris"* (*Fear and Trembling,* 77). Failure may be all the success there is for a religious writer trying to engage the reader with a divine Other, but the failure comes in the text's attempt to "take itself out of the way." No written work can obtain this oblique purpose. The vexing success is the text left standing, stubbornly unobliterated. The objects of inquiry in this study are various versions of that success, the problems they explore, and the problems they pose.

Heidegger rewrote Kierkegaard; Theodor Adorno began his career with a study of his aesthetics; in some accounts existentialism begins with his works; a scholarly series has been devoted to him and postmodernism.[7] He has been compared to Marx, to Freud, to Foucault, to Barthes, to Sterne, to Derrida.[8] When writing of incommensurability he belongs in philosophical dialogue with philosophers like Thomas Kuhn, Richard Rorty, and Martha Nussbaum. In such company, he appears very cosmopolitan indeed, more like his pseudonymous man-about-town Constantius Constantin than the brooding Danish gadfly on Christendom's back that he was in his time. To ally him philosophically with Christina Rossetti and Gerard Manley Hopkins is to rob him of some of this urbanity, although in some current scholarship these two writers have been cast as secularized moderns themselves, Hopkins as an only half-

6. Louis Mackey, *Points of View: Readings of Kierkegaard* (Tallahassee: Florida State University Press, 1986), xxii.

7. See Martin Heidegger, *Being and Time,* trans. John MacQuarrie and Edward Robinson (New York: Harper and Brothers, 1962); Theodor W. Adorno, *Kierkegaard: Construction of the Aesthetic,* trans. Robert Hullot-Kentor, Theory and History of Literature, vol. 61 (Minneapolis: University of Minnesota Press, 1989); and the series edited by Mark C. Taylor, Kierkegaard and Post Modernism published by Florida State University Press.

8. See Paul Bové, "The Penitentiary of Reflection: Søren Kierkegaard and Critical Activity," in Schleifer and Markley, *Kierkegaard and Literature,* 25–57, for the comparison to Marx and Foucault; Schleifer and Markley's introductory essay, "Writing Without Authority and the Reading of Kierkegaard," in *Kierkegaard and Literature,* for a comparison to Derrida. See also John Vignaux Smyth, *A Question of Eros: Irony in Sterne, Kierkegaard, and Barthes* (Tallahassee: Florida State University Press, 1986), and J. Preston Cole, *The Problematic Self in Kierkegaard and Freud* (New Haven: Yale University Press, 1971).

hearted priest, Rossetti as a protofeminist. One purpose—or perhaps result—of this study is to restore to all three writers their historical context, by defining as my area of inquiry the province of nineteenth-century religiosity.

Kierkegaard meets Christina Rossetti and Gerard Manley Hopkins in the maelstrom that is nineteenth-century subjectivity. Kierkegaard, "whose aim was the communication of subjectivity, had to become a poet" (Mackey, *Kierkegaard,* 261), and so did Hopkins and Rossetti. The year 1844 saw the publication of Kierkegaard's *Philosophical Fragments, The Concept of Anxiety,* and four sets of *Edifying Discourses;* it also saw the birth of Nietzsche and Hopkins. At one end of the spectrum of nineteenth-century belief we have "God is dead. God remains dead. And we have killed him." At the other end is Hopkins's bleak self-appraisal: "The Incarnation was for my salvation and that of the world: the work goes on in a great system and machinery which even drags me on with the collar round my neck though I could and do neglect my duty in it."[9] The first statement betrays itself as a gesture of belief inscribed in a gesture of incipient atheism: for God to be killed He must have lived. It simultaneously vitiates the traditional power of God, since He can be killed. The second statement betrays itself as belief in a state of reluctance, allowable (or inevitable) only when the "great system and machinery" of the divine cosmos shows its strings. In *The Gay Science* Nietzsche revels in the murder of the "old god": "At long last the horizon appears free again to us, even if it should not be bright; at long last our ships may venture out again, venture out to face any danger; all the daring of the lover of knowledge is permitted again; the sea, *our* sea, lies open again; perhaps there has never yet been such an 'open sea' " (280). For Hopkins these same "open seas" hide the instrument of death. "Into the snows she sweeps / Hurling the haven behind . . ."; so the *Deutschland* and the *Eurydice* are destroyed, and the objectively verifiable belief in a God whose benignity should be seen in his acts is left to flounder.[10]

Either God is dead, or he has disappeared behind an array of unpalatable material realities.[11] Kierkegaard's pseudonymous texts work out the

9. Friedrich Nietzsche, *The Gay Science,* trans. Walter Kaufmann (New York: Random House, 1974), 181; Gerard Manley Hopkins, *The Sermons and Devotional Writings of Gerard Manley Hopkins,* ed. Christopher Devlin, S.J. (London: Oxford University Press, 1959), 263.

10. Gerard Manley Hopkins, *Gerard Manley Hopkins,* ed. Catherine Phillips (New York: Oxford University Press, 1986), 113, lines 97–98).

11. See Mark Taylor, *Erring: A Postmodern A/theology* (Chicago: University of Chicago Press, 1984), for his view on the Nietzschean death of God and its consequences for the modern—or postmodern—experience. In his "Prelude" he claims: "Postmodernism opens

only possibility left: to choose belief as an act of the human will in the face of incomprehensibility. From *Either/Or* to *Concluding Unscientific Postscript* (on the margin of pseudonymity, "written" by Johannes Climacus but "edited" by Søren Kierkegaard), art and artifice serve "a special kind of madness," the pursuit of the question posed by Climacus in the *Postscript*: "How may I, Johannes Climacus, participate in the happiness promised by Christianity?"[12] The profoundly personal expression of the question ("How may *I*") posed by him who is supposedly *not* a Christian (as Johannes claims in *Philosophical Fragments*) yields art as the answer not to the question itself, but to the problem of expressing the process that results from asking the question:

> . . . [T]he subjective thinker will from the beginning have his attention called to the requirement that this form should embody artistically as much of reflection as he himself has when existing in his thought. In an artistic manner, please note; for the secret does not lie in a direct assertion of the double reflection [the reflection of inwardness]; such a direct expression of it is precisely a contradiction. (*Postscript*, 68–69)

In a Rossetti poem recommended by Hopkins to his friend Dixon, just this strategy of indirection operates literally to reflect, through poetry, the preeminent subjective experience.[13] "Mirrors of Life and Death" begins:

> The mystery of Life, the mystery
> Of Death, I see
> Darkly as in a glass;
> Their shadows pass
> And talk with me.[14]

---

with the sense of irrevocable loss and incurable fault. This wound is inflicted by the overwhelming awareness of death—a death that 'begins' with the death of God and 'ends' with death of ourselves" (6). His first two chapters then derive from this claim: the first being on the death of God, and the second, on the disappearance of the self, with the two ideas presented as cause and effect.

12. Søren Kierkegaard, *Concluding Unscientific Postscript*, trans. David F. Swenson (Princeton: Princeton University Press, 1974), 20. A "special kind of madness" is an allusion to the "divine madness" of the poet in Plato's *Phaedrus*.

13. Gerard Manley Hopkins, *The Correspondence of Gerard Manley Hopkins and Richard Watson Dixon*, ed. Claude Colleer Abbott (London: Oxford University Press, 1935), 62.

14. Christina Rossetti, *The Complete Poems of Christina Rossetti, A Variorum Edition*, 3 vols., ed. R. W. Crump (Baton Rouge: Louisiana State University Press, 1979–90), II, 75, lines 1–5.

From "Darkly as in a glass" the poem progresses entirely as a list of similes, each stanza introduced by an anaphoric "as": "As the flush of a Morning Sky... As the Sun... As the Moon... As Roses...", etc." The impetus for the list is as personal as "How do I, Johannes" (The mysteries *"I* see"); the list itself catalogues signs lifted from nature by the artistic project and stands in for the incommunicably personal. To the limited extent that a purely subjective experience can be expressed, it is done with mirrors.

As Rossetti's poem indicates, the mirrors permit vision only "darkly," and the allusion to Paul (1 Corinthians 12) signifies both not much light and only qualified hope. "Hope is the counterpoise of fear" goes another Rossetti poem, "While night enthralls us here" (*Complete Poems,* II, 250). This counterpoise is the fragile balance struck by Hopkins and Rossetti in their poetry. The will to belief exacts the price of chronic vigilance, necessary to keep fear from overcoming hope. Rossetti's work thus shares with Hopkins's, and Kierkegaard's, a pervasive melancholy. The inexplicability of the actions attributable to the God in which they choose to believe has its consequences for a subjective religious vision. "[Rossetti] never felt sure she was damned," writes Dorothy Margaret Stuart, "she only felt that she *might* be" (author's emphasis).[15] Hopkins and Rossetti have both been described as suffering from *Acedia,* the Deadly Sin of sloth and melancholy.[16] The description—or charge—is apt, as a "favorite ecclesiastical word, applied primarily to the mental prostration of recluses, induced by fasting and other physical causes."[17] Epistemologically it breaks down into "not caring," the paramount religious attitude toward the material world, exemplified, for instance, by the Ignation principle of *quasi-cadaver* (the body stripped of personal will) that Hopkins would have

15. Dorothy Margaret Stuart, *Christina Rossetti* (London: Macmillan and Co., 1930), 127.

16. See Jerome Bump's "Medievalist Poet of Acedia," which emphasizes the predisposition toward paralyzing melancholy that is displayed overtly in Hopkins's prose writings, and that is the basis for most discussions of his "Terrible Sonnets," in *Gerard Manley Hopkins* (Boston: Twayne Publishers, 1982). In a monograph celebrating Rossetti's centenary ("Christina Rossetti" [The English Association, pamphlet no. 78, 1931]), Dorothy Margaret Stuart describes Rossetti as suffering from the same predisposition toward Acedia:

> She was not temperamentally fitted to take part in any strenuous movement, aesthetic, intellectual, or even moral; for if one of the Seven Deadly Sins found harbourage in the soul of this mid-Victorian Virgin Saint it was *Accidia.* The word is usually mistranslated "Sloth," but the thing is... "a form, or at least a corruption, of Melancholy." *Accidia*... leads to a sort of mournful apathy..., to distrust of self, and to distrust of God. (5)

17. From the *Oxford English Dictionary,* under "accidie."

been indoctrinated to follow as a Jesuit. *Acedia* is the sin of caring too much about not caring.

According to Kierkegaard, "the Hegelian philosophy [against which he wrote] assumes no justified hiddenness, no justified incommensurability" (*Fear and Trembling*, 82). The works of Kierkegaard, Rossetti, and Hopkins all assume a justified hiddenness, a justified incommensurability. What is hidden? God. What is incommensurable? Subjective, personal religious belief with its means of expression. Two "secret agents" thus demand an account in their philosophies of faith—a Pascalian hidden God and the believing subject. No such account is possible, only aesthetic and therefore fictional approximations. Because of their fictionality, these approximations permit relationships of incommensurability to proliferate in spite of an apparent fundamental contradiction: if two things are truly incommensurable, they cannot be in relationship. Throughout this study, two such sets of "two things" receive attention, the "relationship" between a hidden God and the believing subject, and the "relationship" between the believing subject as writer and her or his audience. By understanding how Kierkegaardian incommensurability signals both surplus and relation, we prepare ourselves for recognizing the fragility and tenuousness—the fictionality—of these "relationships."

In articulating his notion of faith, Kierkegaard devalues containment, measurement, and quantification. A scholar of Plato, he leaves Plato behind:

> Faith is namely this paradox that the single individual is higher than the universal. . . . For if the ethical—that is, social morality— is the highest and if there is in a person no residual incommensurability in some way such that this incommensurability is not evil . . . , then no categories are needed other than what Greek philosophy had or what can be deduced from them by consistent thought. (*Fear and Trembling*, 55)

Positing this "residual incommensurability," Kierkegaard severs a critical connection forged by Greek philosophy, "between number and order, between the ability to count or measure and the ability to grasp, comprehend, or control, [which] runs very deep in Greek thought about human understanding."[18] From Plato to Rorty's epistemologists, theorists of

---

18. Martha Nussbaum, *Love's Knowledge* (New York: Oxford University Press, 1990), 107.

commensurability defend against its lack as the danger of irrationality.[19] To the extent that Kierkegaardian incommensurability is residual, it has a quality of chaotic excess that anticipates theories of slippage in language between signified and signifier, notions of *sous rature,* of *mise-en-scène,* of *mise en abyme,* of the usurping power of the supplement, all threats to the heretofore rational relationship between a linguistic sign and its external referent.

If in Greek thought, however (and in the thought of modern apologists for referential language), that which "is without measure is boundless, elusive, chaotic, threatening, bad," Kierkegaard would make a substitution: that which is without measure is boundless, elusive, chaotic, threatening, or good, or God. This can be made sense of tautologically— "God is the sign of the unknown."[20] Or it can be understood as itself a paradox: "It is the measure of the unknown which lends to the experience of God—or of the poetic—their great authority. But the unknown demands in the end sovereignty *without partition*" (my emphasis).[21] Such formulations, however, help little in finding how "this incommensurability is not evil" or how it is related to the paradox of faith. One way is by recognizing how incommensurability operates not only as surplus but simultaneously as a fiction of relation. There is much at stake in arguing this relational function in any philosophy of faith. Theodicies, doctrines of atonement, the myth of Original Sin, leaps of faith—most of the apparatus of theology—all attempt to mitigate the threat of what in a system of benevolent Godhood seems evil but must be called "good." Working through a series of incommensurables, Kierkegaard's, Rossetti's, and Hopkins's texts interrogate these strategies of belief and the contradictions they must accommodate: failure as success; innocence as proleptic guilt; self-effacement as self-promotion; imitating the good only to perform the bad; sensuality as a necessary, if negative, component of asceticism; and artistic opportunism inherent in the expression of human tragedy.

As a term that establishes grounds for relation, incommensurability

19. Richard Rorty, *Philosophy and the Mirror of Nature* (Princeton: Princeton University Press, 1979). Rorty's version of the epistemological project helps in an understanding of Kierkegaard's appropriation of "incommensurability." But the hermeneutical project Rorty describes as displacing the epistemological one must not be confused with Kierkegaard's, because of the element of surplus, and the role of religious faith in Kierkegaard's use of the term.

20. Mark C. Taylor, *Tears* (Albany: State University of New York Press, 1990), 182.

21. Georges Bataille, *Inner Experience,* trans. Leslie Anne Boldt (Albany: State University of New York Press, 1988), 5.

resembles the "operating table" ("where the umbrella encounters the sewing machine") Foucault has Borges take away, "the mute ground upon which it is possible for entities to be juxtaposed."[22] Subjectivity and actuality are incommensurable—they have that difference with each other in common. In pitting the incommensurable—the individual, interiority, subjectivity, and, especially, faith—against actuality, infinite resignation, the ethical, and the universal, Kierkegaard establishes relationships of immeasurability, but relationships nonetheless. But always at the same time, unaccountable, unknowable excess threatens to dismantle these tenuous relationships that allow at least provisional expression. Once we understand the dual nature of incommensurability, we see that it permeates the Kierkegaard lexicon. Four terms from that lexicon organize this study: anxiety, lyric voice, repetition, and choice. They are interrelated, here no less than in the pseudonymous works from which they come. Each chapter thus erects a theoretical framework based on a Kierkegaardian pseudonymous text within which to read closely poems by Hopkins and Rossetti.

In *Either/Or,* the first narrator, called "A," depicts (modern) Antigone as "hurled . . . into the arms of anxiety" because of the knowledge she possesses about her father. In modern tragedy, "anxiety is the vehicle by which the subject appropriates his sorrow and assimilates it."[23] Sorrow is experienced as a result of the vacillation between guilt and innocence, what A calls "tragic guilt" (154). We must read A's multigenre presentation of the aesthetic (vs. the ethical) as provisional and highly suspect. Nonetheless, his selection of Antigone, an appropriately secular figure for his secular agenda, usefully begins an analysis of religious anxiety. As Mark Taylor notes, Kierkegaard's Antigone is the keeper of a secret, "the transgression of the father," thus "[t]he secret of the father becomes the secret of the child" (*Tears,* 194). The state of anxiety probed in certain poems by Rossetti and Hopkins and by Kierkegaard's *The Concept of Anxiety* derives directly from Original Sin, the event that in the Judeo-Christian story results in family genealogy as being predicated upon inherited guilt. As we will see, this genealogy joins innocence to that guilt in a cause-and-effect relationship. Innocence is guilty of engendering guilt.

---

22. Michel Foucault, *The Order of Things: An Archaeology of the Human Sciences* (New York: Vintage Books, 1973), xvii.

23. Søren Kierkegaard, *Either/Or,* trans. Howard V. Hong and Edna H. Hong (Princeton: Princeton University Press, 1987), I, 154.

Read within the context of Kierkegaard's *The Concept of Anxiety,* dramatic monologues and apostrophes by Hopkins and Rossetti reveal their speakers' dilemmas as guilty believers. As "authors" the speakers in the dramatic monologues cannot script for themselves a redemptive version of their own story. And the speakers in the apostrophes must project their voices onto the hiddenness of silence, uncertain, like Johannes, whether they address the demonic or the divine. The dilemmas of all these speakers are played out dramatically, and like good drama, end tragically, in expressions of religious anxiety, the tragedy of heresy. Implicitly asked but left unanswered by an analysis of anxiety is to what extent and in what way is this threat of heresy an inevitable consequence of authorship, both in the poems and of the poems.

Answering that question requires attention to the means and limitations of poetic expression itself. In *The Concept of Irony,* Kierkegaard writes: "For a doubt that despairs of communication there is only the role of repressed silence ... —or the desperate search for concealment, for masks and other voices with which to speak out of hiding as it were, the impulse to play with language, consciously structuring it into a fabric vibrant with meaning, to make his peace with the fickle echo that formerly mocked his own fullness."[24] Language as repressed silence gets at the burden of lyric expression. Johannes de Silentio's self-imposed obligation in *Fear and Trembling* to give voice to the voiceless Abraham frames the discussion of lyric voice in poems by the two poets that draw attention to the "selfhood" of that voice, even when this "selfhood" is at odds with its first devotional task—the removal of itself from the spectacle of worship. The second task, to define in language a subject that eludes definition as that speaker understands it, only compounds the dilemma.

De omnibus dubitandum est, goes the motto of the eponymous Johannes Climacus, and doubt is the silent partner in all contracts of faith.[25] If language is repressed silence, or if language *represses* silence, then lyrical expressions of religious faith always stand threatened by the silent doubt they repress. This threat is managed, though barely, by one of the most conventional strategies of poetry, repetition. We see this in operation as *Fear and Trembling* opens: four attempts to tell the story of Abraham, the main elements repeated, altered only by perspective. All

24. Søren Kierkegaard, *The Concept of Irony: With Constant Reference to Socrates,* trans. Lee M. Capel (London: Collins, 1965), 28.

25. Søren Kierkegaard, "Johannes Climacus: De Omnibus Dubitandum Est," an unfinished work, and the first appearance of Johannes Climacus.

are attempts to manage—make sense of—Abraham's willingness to kill his son; all reveal the doubt one brings to the efficacy of this central story; all fail: "One cannot weep over Abraham. One approaches him with a *horror religiosus,* as Israel approached Mount Sinai" (61).

If Abraham's story poses extraordinary difficulties for a believer because of what Abraham must be willing to do, Job's story literalizes the confusion between the demonic and the divine to confound "rational" faith. Job, argumentative victim of a wager between God and Satan, is finally "blessed and has received everything *double,"* writes the young poet in Kierkegaard's *Repetition:* "This is called a *repetition"* (212). But Job's old life, wife, and family are not restored to him; he receives *new* versions of the elements in his old life. This restoration that is not a restoration exposes the fictionality of repetition. As a device to manage anxiety, it imposes linearity and narrative logic on what one can just as easily describe as arbitrary or random. Kierkegaard's *Repetition,* with its multiple generic reprisals, introduces a discussion of Hopkins's shipwreck poems and Rossetti's sonnets of sonnets, all of which query *and* exploit the role of repetition in lyric expression.

Combining Kierkegaard and Heidegger, William Spanos defines repetition as "a circularity that repeats the same to disclose, retrieve, deepen, and extend the cultural and sociopolitical implications of the unnameable Ontological Difference repressed or concealed by the sedimented archival representations of being."[26] If we substitute God for the "unnameable Ontological Difference" and believing subject for "being," we have a definition that reinforces repetition's role in managing anxiety and enabling lyric expression, and brings us to the final element in the fiction of incommensurability, the concept of choice. Anxiety manifests itself as a tenacious concern over that which remains hidden to or repressed by the believing subject. Religious representation—lyrical expression—inevitably becomes self-expression, occluding the divine subject it purports to render. Repeating this process again and again— the complete canon of a religious writer—incrementally exposes not what is concealed, but that something is concealed. Believing that the concealed something is divine is an act of radical choice. In Kierkegaard's use of it, choice is non-Hegelian, not historically progressive but dualistic, with any synthesis or dialectical resolution infinitely deferred. To attribute this meaning to Kierkegaard, and to Rossetti and Hopkins, is

26. William Spanos, *Repetitions: The Postmodern Occasion in Literature and Culture* (Baton Rouge: Louisiana State University Press, 1987), 4.

to court charges of Manicheanism or simplistic dualism on behalf of all three authors. But the *description* of radical choice as a literary strategy is quite complex and sophisticated, for it risks lacunae and the unwriteable where one might expect authorial or narrative assistance, it must describe not only what is chosen but what is not, and it maintains stern fidelity to the necessity of consequences resulting from the free act of radical choice. The poems of Hopkins and Rossetti are concerned if not obsessed with a religious vision that is harsh in its demands and strictures and precludes mediating away the difficulties and doubts one faces as a believer, particularly in a world where such mediations seem to be available to the written enterprise. Yet, to describe what must not be chosen requires that all three authors "be party to the devil," suspiciously talented in rendering material or sensual temptation in sophisticated and provocative language.

In *Philosophical Fragments,* Johannes Climacus claims:

> I have disciplined myself and kept myself under discipline, in order that I may be able to execute a sort of nimble dancing in the service of Thought, so far as possible also to the honor of the God [Guden], and for my own satisfaction. For this reason I have had to resign the domestic happiness, the civic respectability, the glad fellowship, the *communio bonorum,* which is implied in the possession of an opinion.[27]

Johannes pays unwitting etymological homage here to the word "asceticism" (from the Greek *askein*), in which are buried the notions of discipline and exercise. In connecting discipline to artistic execution (nimble dancing), he reminds us that asceticism in its strictest, oldest sense has as much to do with activity—disciplined exercise—as it does with austerity. Rossetti and Hopkins can be called ascetic in the most commonplace sense, but the combination of discipline and execution more accurately defines the nature of their asceticism. Perhaps suffering from *Acedia,* undoubtedly austere in their private lives, nonetheless, they produce work of stunning sensuality. They are paradigms of Kierkegaard's "aesthetic writer." The uneasy alliance of the aesthetic and the

27. Søren Kierkegaard, *Philosophical Fragments, or A Fragment of Philosophy by Johannes Climacus,* trans. David F. Swenson, rev. Howard V. Hong (Princeton: Princeton University Press, 1974), 6.

ascetic in their works has kept modern readers interested in both of them, but the interest remains as uneasy as the alliance. A preliminary examination of this alliance and the purpose it serves in a well-known poem by each poet sets the scene for the multiple balancing acts revealed in all the poems analyzed in this study.

Hilary Fraser cites Hopkins's "The Habit of Perfection" as a poem where the aesthetic pleasure of a poem shares center stage with and does not yield to ascetic austerity: "In . . . 'The Habit of Perfection,' ascetic renunciation of the sensuous world is couched in language which could itself scarcely be more sensuous."[28] "The Habit of Perfection" borrows the courtly technique of *effictio*, in which the lover poetically catalogues the features of a beloved. Here, instead of a beloved, there are the parts of the self: ears, lips, eyes, palate, nostrils, "feel-of-primrose hands," feet. All are being instructed not to do what they are meant to do. The lips should be "lovely-dumb," the eyes, "shelled," the palate, fasting, hands and feet, resisting "plushy sward."[29] By stating what the organs of the senses should not do, this poem that vouches commitment to "Elected Silence" and sensual deprivation is itself an event of the senses. Hopkins's poem inventories what must be shut down to achieve the "habit of perfection" because, like yet another "book under divine confiscation," that habit cannot be made available to the reader in any other way.

Rossetti's most famous poem, "Goblin Market," offers an extended version of the poetic dynamic that simultaneously scorns or condemns material pleasure or beauty, while creating a poetic event of great sensuality. Whether "Goblin Market" is read as a Christian cautionary tale or a lesbian love story, it mounts scenes of resistance to material pleasure that nonetheless enact seductions.[30] However it is read, the poem can only work if the goblin men's wares seem irresistible; hear them advertise:

28. Hilary Fraser, *Beauty and Belief: Aesthetics and Religion in Victorian Literature* (New York: Cambridge University Press, 1986), 68.

29. Hopkins, *Gerard Manley Hopkins*, 80–81.

30. Studies of "Goblin Market" include Ellen Moers, "The Female Gothic," in her *Literary Women: The Great Writers* (New York: Anchor Books, 1977); Sandra Gilbert and Susan Gubar's *Madwoman in the Attic: The Woman Writer and the Nineteenth-Century Literary Imagination* (New Haven: Yale University Press, 1979), 564–75; Germaine Greer's introduction to Christina Rossetti, *Goblin Market* (New York: Stonehill Publishing, 1975); Ellen Golub, "Untying Goblin Apron Strings: A Psychoanalytic Reading of 'Goblin Market,' " *Literature and Psychology* 23, no. 4 (1975): 162–64; Maureen Duffy, *The Erotic World of Faery* (London: Hodder and Stoughton, 1972); D.M.R. Bentley, "The Meretricious and the Meritorious in *Goblin Market*: A Conjecture and an Analysis," in *The Achievement of Christina Rossetti*, ed. David A. Kent (Ithaca: Cornell University Press, 1987), 57–58.

Come buy, come buy:
Our grapes fresh from the vine,
Pomegranates full and fine,
Dates and sharp bullaces,
Rare pears and greengages,
Damsons and bilberries,
Taste them and try:
Currants and gooseberries,
Bright-fire-like barberries,
Figs to fill your mouth,
Citrons from the South,
Sweet to tongue and sound to eye;
Come buy, come buy.
(*Complete Poems*, I, 11, lines 20–31)

The poem opens as an extravaganza of taste, sight, and sound, all of which must be resisted by the poem's characters. Laura fails, Lizzie succeeds, but the presentations of their respective actions share the quality of sexual precocity the poem's plot wants to eradicate. At the precise moment before Laura's seduction, her innocence has already been compromised by her desire, which was aroused by the legend she has already learned:

Laura stretched her gleaming neck
Like a rush-imbedded swan,
Like a lily from the beck,
Like a moonlit poplar branch,
Like a vessel at the launch
When its last restraint is gone.
(81–86)

And at the moment when Lizzie repels her seducers, she is sexually assaulted nonetheless:

Tho' the goblins cuffed and caught her
Coaxed and fought her,
Bullied and besought her,
Scratched her, pinched her black as ink,
Kicked and knocked her,
Mauled and mocked her,
Lizzie uttered not a word;

Would not open lip from lip
Lest they should cram a mouthful in:
But laughed in heart to feel the drip
Of juice that syruped all her face,
And lodged in dimples of her chin,
And streaked her neck which quaked like curd.

(424–36)

"Goblin Market" ends with both sisters grown into motherhood, passing on the cautionary tale of the goblin men to their children. But if the poem wants to shut down avenues leading to wanton sexuality—to caution effectively—it must itself explore those avenues and their dangers. So must the sisters in their telling of their tale. Both of them can bequeath to their children the story of the goblin men only because both have experienced it, albeit differently. Furthermore, they themselves had been warned, to no avail for either of them. The poem ends with no real closure. Cautioning children about the goblin men requires explicit description; such description produces knowledge that immediately compromises innocence, preparing yet another generation to fall. This endlessly repetitive cycle exposes the dynamic of the poem: the work of the cautionary tale is to condemn unrestrained sensuality by conjuring up for its audience horrific avatars of the material world, the goblin men; the work of the poem is to lay out the terrain of that world as precisely and as *interestingly* as possible. These dual and contradictory acts of labor proceed simultaneously, and in "Goblin Market," everything (material) is given up and nothing is given up.[31]

Of any writer who has examined Rossetti's poetry, Virginia Woolf is the most attuned to the role religion plays in Rossetti's writerly avocation. For Woolf,

> . . . something dark and hard, like a kernel, had already formed in the centre of Christina Rossetti's being. It was religion, of course. . . . The pressure of tremendous faith circles and clamps together these little songs. Perhaps they owe to it their solidity. Certainly they owe to it their sadness—[here she addresses Rossetti] your God was a harsh God, your heavenly crown was set

---

31. To answer the question asked about "Goblin Market": are we to read it as a cautionary tale about "the dangers of erotic passion" (Antony Harrison's words about "The World"), or are we to luxuriate in its sensuality and not very covert sexuality? The answer is, yes.

with thorns. No sooner have you feasted on beauty with your eyes than your mind tells you that beauty is vain and beauty passes.[32]

Woolf gets to the "centre" of Rossetti, and also of Hopkins. On the spectrum bordered on either side by a Nietzschean dead God and Hopkins's collaring Incarnation, religious belief has only a narrow space to locate itself. Kierkegaard's aborted love affair, Hopkins's "Terrible Sonnets," his self-excoriation, Rossetti's adolescent self-denials (of chess and the theater, for instance) and her later refusal to read anything that would undermine her faith, all point to the instability of this location, too close for comfort on either side to substantial challenges. Their "aesthetic writings" map out this unstable terrain, ignoring neither the encroaching threats on either side, nor the fault lines within it.

32. Virginia Woolf, "I am Christina Rossetti," in *The Second Common Reader* (New York: Harcourt Brace Jovanovich, 1960), 216–20.

2

Concepts of Anxiety:
Sin in Hopkins and Rossetti

*Certainly, those tapestries and the stained glass dealt with
the same theme. In both were the same musical instru-
ments—pipes, cymbals, long reed-like trumpets. The story,
indeed included the building of an organ, just such an instrument, only on a larger scale, as was standing in the old
priest's library, though almost soundless now, whereas in
certain of the woven pictures the hearers appear as if transported, some of them shouting rapturously to the organ music. A sort of mad vehemence prevails, indeed, throughout
the delicate bewilderments of the whole series... connecting, like some mazy arabesque, the various presentations of
one oft-repeated figure, translated here out of the clear-
coloured glass into the sadder, somewhat opaque and
earthen hues of the silken threads. The figure was that of the
organ-builder himself.... What is it? Certainly, notwithstanding its grace, and wealth of graceful accessories, a suffering, tortured figure.*

—Walter Pater, "Denys L'Auxerrois"

The first aphorism in the "Diapsal-
mata" section of *Either/Or* evokes a commonplace: "What is a poet? A
poet is an unhappy being who conceals profound anguish in his heart,
but whose lips are so formed that as sighs and cries pass over them, they
sound like beautiful music."[1] This characterization risks being a carica-

1. Søren Kierkegaard, *Either/Or,* 2 vols. trans. and ed. Howard V. Hong and Edna H. Hong
(Princeton: Princeton University Press, 1987), I, 19.

ture of the tormented Romantic artist, and we know enough about A, the writer of the "Either" part of *Either/Or,* to receive it with skepticism. Yet A's aphorism renders axiomatically the portrait of the artist emerging from the tapestry in Pater's "imaginary portrait" of the doomed Denys. The "suffering, tortured figure" of the artist stands in stunning contrast (over and over again, as the "oft-repeated figure" throughout the tapestry) to the listeners, who "appear as if transported, some of them shouting rapturously to the organ music." Imagine A's aphorism as a caption for Pater's moving tapestry, and it resonates with truth (as all caricatures do); it also anticipates a particularly modern way of understanding poetry. The aphorism emphasizes not simply a fissure between content (profound anguish) and form (beautiful music), but the loss incurred, the actual fleeing of content, and the lack of significant communication at the moment of poetic expression. The poem presents itself as a pathology, "strangely formed"—beauty is a deformation of suffering.[2] As we have seen, Hopkins and Rossetti tended toward self-lacerating melancholy, so that each was accused of being too scrupulous. This melancholy, characterized as a Deadly Sin, paradoxically stems from an acute awareness of being sinful.[3] A discussion of "secret sufferings" and the perversely "beautiful music" they engender must begin, therefore, in the discourse of "sin." Once we find the right terms in this discourse, we can usefully reexamine the notion of poetry as pathology. These terms can be found in Kierkegaard's *Concept of Anxiety,* beginning with anxiety, and with what that book's pseudonymous author implicitly claims for himself, "psychological-poetic authority."

The Concept of Anxiety expounds a theory that reflects its own historical context, since its concept of anxiety is self-consciously post-Romantic and *un*self-consciously pre-Freudian. In addition, the work, subtitled, not so simply, "A Simple Psychologically Orienting Deliberation on the Dogmatic Issue of Hereditary Sin," links the term "angst" with psychology, but also with the heterodox "hereditary sin."[4] This linkage allows it to criticize the Hegelianism of its time via a rigorous analysis of the Fall and the

2. De Man's article, "Shelley Disfigured," in *Deconstruction and Criticism,* ed. Harold Bloom et al. (New York: The Seabury Press, 1979), 39–74, and Tilottama Rajan's book, *Dark Interpreter: The Discourse of Romanticism* (Ithaca: Cornell University Press, 1980), are two examples of a way of reading poetry that finds a fracture beneath the surface (de Man) or, even more extreme, a void (Rajan).

3. Acedia, the Deadly Sin of Sloth, is discussed in Chapter 1.

4. The original Danish title of *The Concept of Anxiety* is *Begrebet Angest.* The first translation, by Walter Lowrie, was called "The Concept of Dread." In his biography of Kierkegaard Lowrie himself explains that "dread" does not suffice, although he does not explain why he did not use "anxiety." See his *Kierkegaard* (New York: Oxford University Press, 1938), 73.

consequent existence of sin and sinfulness, related but distinct: "The present work has set as its task the psychological treatment of the concept of 'anxiety,' but in such a way that it constantly keeps *in mente* [in mind] and before its eye the dogma of hereditary sin."[5] Rather than employing dialectical concepts such as *aufhebung* (simultaneous annulment and preservation), reconciliation, and mediation, *The Concept of Anxiety*, like all of Kierkegaard's works, establishes and defines its own terms. Their eccentricities and quirkiness do not inhibit the book's narrator from lodging the ultimate insult against Hegelianism: ". . . what Mme Staël-Holstein has said of Schelling's philosophy, namely, that it makes a man clever for his whole life, applies in every way to Hegelianism" (13).

My reading of *The Concept of Anxiety* will set up an analytical framework, first for the dramatic monologues, and second for the apostrophic sonnets, of Hopkins and Rossetti. Each dramatic monologue is clearly concerned with "sin," "sinfulness," and the anxiety they produce. The fiction a dramatic monologue must perpetrate—that the speaker really authors his or her own story—plays off that story's inevitable escape from its "author"; as readers we feel the tension between what the fictional author tells us and what the poem tells us. If a poet is "an unhappy being" with concealed "profound anguish" who makes "beautiful music," then reading dramatic monologues poses the additional challenge of understanding two "poets"—the fictional and the "real"—and two kinds of suffering, with only *one* end result, the beautiful music of the monologue.

Each sonnet apostrophizes God, apparently to complain to or "contend" with Him. While a dramatic monologue has an implied auditor, often identified, it is the speaking persona that distinguishes a monologue from other genres. The second generic mode, the apostrophe, seems the reverse of a dramatic monologue in its formal characteristics; an apostrophe is an apostrophe because of an identifiable and emphasized auditor residing outside the poem. In both kinds of poems the relationship between speaker and auditor matters greatly, though the difference in emphasis between the "I" and the "Thou" of the poems' fictions distinguishes them. This shift in emphasis obscures a more profound affinity between the two genres that Hopkins and Rossetti use as vehicles for anxiety.[6]

5. Søren Kierkegaard, *The Concept of Anxiety*, trans. and ed. Reidar Thomte in collaboration with Albert B. Anderson (Princeton: Princeton University Press, 1980), 14.

6. Patricia Ball's *The Central Self: A Study in Romantic and Victorian Imagination* (London: Athlone Press, 1968) provides a good discussion of the affinities between the Romantic short lyric and the Victorian dramatic monologue.

Kierkegaard's *Concept of Anxiety* is about anxiety's relationship to sinfulness. It's narrator, Vigilius Haufniensis, the Watchman of Copenhagen, has an erudite grasp of pre- and post-Reformation Christianity, but Vigilius is not interested in a formula for a doctrinal understanding of Adam and Eve's story. In fact, though overtly orthodox, he flirts knowingly with heresy (27). Vigilius really wants to claim for himself a particular kind of expertise in understanding human beings, what he calls a "true psychological-poetical authority." "It is not my intention," says Vigilius,

> to write a learned work or to waste time in search of literary proof texts. Often the examples mentioned in psychologies lack true *psychological-poetical authority*. They stand as isolated *notarialiter* [notarized facts]. . . . One who has properly occupied himself with psychology and psychological observation acquires a general human flexibility that enables him at once to construct his example which even though it lacks *factual authority* nevertheless has an authority of a different kind. The psychological observer ought to be *more nimble than a tightrope dancer in order to incline and bend himself to other people and imitate their attitudes, and his silence in the moment of confidence should be seductive and voluptuous,* so that what is hidden may find satisfaction in slipping out to chat with itself in the artificially constructed nonobservance and silence. Hence he ought also to have a *poetic originality* in his soul. (54, my emphasis)

After he runs through the history of doctrinal attempts to understand "the Fall," Vigilius finally eschews interest in them. *The Concept of Anxiety* explores "anxiety" by attending to language and history (or temporality), and by using the synecdochic principle, *unum noris omnes,* to know one is to know all. The *unum* (at least initially), is Adam. His sexuality results *from* his sin and results *in* history, nothing more than the progression of begotten generations, and *in* temporality, the fact of death; and all of this happened because of language in the forms of a prohibition followed by a judgment. At issue is human freedom, what it means to have free will when burdened with the fate of sinfulness inherited from Adam. In question is where Adam actually stands in what we call "history"—the passing on of that inheritance. Exactly where Adam fits in "history" vexes Vigilius, as do dogmatic (that is, systematic theological) theories to explain his place. Vigilius has his own way of narrating Adam's story. God told Adam not to eat from a certain tree, and threatened him with death if he disobeyed. But this threat meant nothing to Adam, who could not understand the word "death," since only eating from the tree could give the word meaning. "Nothing," a void of experience and language, is replaced with "enigmatic words." Enigmatic, but not meaningless, because in their utterance they create, not the understanding of "death," but its possibility, giving Adam a choice, albeit an unequal one: "The prohibition induces in him anxiety, for the prohibition awakens in him freedom's possibility" (44). An innovation in Paradise, choice is the beginning of anxiety. For Vigilius, there are three constitutive parts to the story of anxiety's origin: a central character, Adam; a central event, the Fall; and a central cause, Sin.

Though dissatisfied with available explanations of Adam and history, Vigilius swerves from stating absolutely either that Adam stands outside of human history as its "creator" in his Fall, or he stands within its boundaries, though at the utmost edge as its progenitor. Since he begins the story of the Fall with God's threat as the discourse of possibility before Adam sins, however, then the concept of death exists, though only in this state of possibility. Human history as the progressive, linear movement of birth to death begins as *potentia* in prelapsarian Eden. This implied view of history matters very much, because Vigilius wants to establish both the difference *and* the relationship between *peccatum originans* and *peccatum originatum,* Adam's original sin and hereditary sin, the inheritance of all human beings from Adam. Such a distinction contributes to the continuing discussion of free will: subsequent generations are not history-burdened *victims* of an ahistorical Adam, passive recipients of sins, for a sin must be committed in order to be a sin. On the other hand, Adam's sin dooms all generations to sinfulness, making the committing of (and commitment to) sin each individual's inevitable history. Every person thus moves from innocence, which is also potential sinfulness, to sin; the time spent between is time spent in the state of anxiety. "In anxiety," says Vigilius, "[innocence] is related to the forbidden and to the punishment" (45). Innocence is so radically compromised by Adam's Fall that it almost becomes something other than itself, not an absolute state, but a prolegomenon to the state of sinfulness. Similarity and difference are posited at the same time in Adam's relationship to all other individuals; the grammatical subtlety of the Latin highlights simultaneous distance and relationship between original and hereditary sin.

This issue of human freedom to choose is not new, either to theology or to literature; Milton's "[s]ufficient to have stood, though free to fall" (*Paradise Lost,* III, 99) perhaps most famously captures the paradox of free will vs. God's omnipotence. But Vigilius renders the ancient knotty problem in the language of anxiety, and does the reverse as well: renders human anxiety in the language of sin and freedom. I use "rendering" deliberately, in order to emphasize the evocative, *non*dogmatic quality of *The Concept of Anxiety*, the result of a "psychological" study by one with "psychological-poetic authority." Vigilius's evocations often take the shape of uncanny axioms and aphorisms, hitting home as exactly correct on first glance, yet slyly indeterminate upon further examination: Anxiety "is a sympathetic antipathy and an antipathetic sympathy" (42), "belongs to woman more than to man" (47), is "the dizziness of freedom" (61), "is the psychological state that precedes sin" (92), "is the final psychological state from which sin breaks forth in the qualitative leap" (93). "The relation of freedom to guilt is anxiety" (109) and, most darkly, "No matter how deep an individual has sunk, he can sink still deeper, and this 'can' is the object of anxiety" (113). Most of these axiomatic descriptions rely upon the concepts of relation or of movement, logical dependencies invoking the postlapsarian fate of generational relation and temporality. As the discussion turns toward the poets, it relies upon the following key terms: anxiety, sin, sinfulness, possibility, *peccatum originans, peccatum originatum,* psychological-poetical authority, and *indeslutthede* (a Danish term translated by Walter Lowrie as "reservedness," and later by Reider Thomte as "inclosing reserve").

Rossetti's "The Iniquities of the Fathers Upon the Children" and Hopkins's "Pilate" both feature speakers struggling against figures who dominate their stories as the actual source of, or reasons for the monologue, and who therefore seem not to be present in it. How each speaker proceeds in this struggle constitutes each poem's narrative progression; how each narrates in an acute state of Kierkegaardian anxiety, the artistic tension. Rossetti's Margaret and Hopkins's Pilate both suffer acutely in this state of anxiety, as each poem prepares in its telling for its teller to "fall." Neither dramatic monologue quite falls into religious or devotional categories. Though "Pilate" is biblically inspired, foreshadowing Hopkins's later fascination with *The Spiritual Exercises* of Ignatius Loyola, the poem reveals more pre-Raphaelite sensationalism than religious fervor. "The Iniquities of the Fathers," with its biblically derived title, takes its story from the social arena, and stigma seems to matter more than sin. In their search for psychological-poetic authority, however, Margaret and Pilate manifest against their own narrative intention the symptoms of Kierkegaardian anxiety.

From its title to its melodramatic end, Rossetti's "The Iniquities of the

Fathers upon the Children" offers sin, sex, and suffering.[7] It is a long
poem, but limerick-like in its short lines and easy end-rhymes. The naïveté of its form suits Margaret, its late-adolescent narrator, who tells of
being born "under the rose," and then abandoned to her Nurse by her
mother. Deserted by both parents (her father having previously abandoned the mother), she goes with her Nurse to "somewhere by the sea"
where "men [speak] a foreign tongue," and where she spends her childhood in unchildlike reticence and reserve ("I never cared to play / With
the village boys and girls; / And I think they thought me proud, / I found
so little to say" [32–35]), and in precocious awareness of her power
over the opposite sex ("Boys would hang about me / In sheepish
mooning wise" [41–42]). In her youth she and the Nurse move, and she
meets the "Lady" of her new home, a grave and distant figure, usually
veiled and on horseback. After giving Margaret a gold ring, Nurse dies.
Margaret is brought by the Lady to the Manor, where she is treated as
"almost her child." Now, at this narrative moment when she tells her
story, Margaret has been convinced for some time that the Lady is her
mother. She knows that others suspect her shame, and she seethes in
secret at her mother's failure to acknowledge her. Included in those who
suspect are suitors, of which she has no lack, since she possesses great
beauty: "I'm the fairest in the country," and then parenthetically, "(For so
I've heard it said / Tho' I don't vouch for this)" (436–38). Courted and
wooed though she is, therefore, as a beauty with a large dowry, by the
poem's end Margaret has vowed to remain unmarried, determined not to
replace her namelessness with "any man's good name."

The question of abstemious, ascetic Rossetti's ability to write convinc-
ingly about a bastard was raised by her brother, Dante, himself no
stranger to "social matters" in art. Rossetti defends herself in words that
speak intriguingly *about* her poem and *to* the point of this chapter. In
response to Dante's criticism of her naïveté, she seems at first to endorse
the "much-to-be desired unreality of woman's work on many social matters." She counterargues nonetheless:

> I yet incline to include within female range such an attempt as this:
> where the certainly possible circumstances are merely indicated
> as it were in skeleton, where the subordinate characters perform
> (and no more) their accessory parts, where the field is occupied by
> a single female figure whose *internal portrait* is set forth in her

---

7. Christina Rossetti, *The Complete Poems of Christina Rossetti, A Variorum Edition,* 3
vols., ed. R. W. Crump (Baton Rouge: Louisiana State University Press, 1979–90), I, 164–78.

own words. Moreover the sketch only gives the girl's own deductions, feelings, semiresolutions; granted such premises as hers, and right or wrong it seems to me she might easily arrive at such conclusions: and whilst it may truly be urged that unless white could be black and Heaven Hell my experience (thank God) precludes me from hers, I yet don't see why "the *Poet mind*" should be less able to construct her from its own inner consciousness than a hundred other unknown qualities.[8] (My emphasis)

Rossetti does not often discuss abstractly or theoretically the business of writing poetry, so this reference to "the Poet mind" stands out as a rare commentary by the author on her work, characterized by Dolores Rosenblum as intertextual and repetitious: ". . . her poems are deliberately echoic, reflecting each other and other texts."[9] Here Rossetti defends her poetic "portrait" as a reflection of a social milieu from which her brother would shelter her. And in the apology we hear the distinct echo of Wordsworth's *The Prelude,* which is subtitled *Or Growth of a Poet's Mind.*

If the tale of Margaret reminds us in its deceptive simplicity of such Wordsworth poems as "Michael" and "The Idiot Boy," "The Iniquities . . ." suggests a revision of "The Thorn" as it tells the story of a young girl left by her unwed mother in the care of the mother's old nurse, who takes the child to foreign lands and then back to where the more-than-suspected real mother lives. But the poem is narrated by Margaret, the child born under "the rose of keenest thorn," and with this revision, the "Poet mind," or author, has constructed a narrative of Old Testament suffering told by a poetically constructed "mind" that exposes its "inner consciousness" as damaged, and eventually doomed.[10] In its garrulity, the poem enacts the state of anxiety that is "the psychological state preced-[ing] sin." For all signs, from its title to its conclusion, point toward the fall of Margaret. The subtler, more critical point about Rossetti's poem is that Margaret's ambivalent feelings toward her "mother," the center of

---

8. Janet Camp Troxell, ed., *Three Rossettis: Unpublished Letters to and from Dante Gabriel, Christina, and William* (Cambridge: Harvard University Press, 1937), 143.

9. Dolores Rosenblum, *Christina Rossetti: The Poetry of Endurance* (Carbondale: Southern Illinois University Press, 1986), 2.

10. See also "The Feast of the Annunciation," in *Complete Poems,* II, 238. The second stanza begins: "Herself a rose, who bore the Rose, / She bore the Rose and felt its thorn." The name Margaret reminds us of Wordsworth's "Margaret," another story of abandonment, this time of a widowed mother by her son.

critical discussion of this poem, disguise her real anxiety over the simultaneous distance and similarity between her and her iniquitous father.[11]

In the 1866 edition of *The Prince's Progress and Other Poems*, "Under the Rose" was the poem's title, with the famous biblical passage as its motto. In the 1875 reissue of her poems under the title *Goblin Market, The Prince's Progress, and Other Poems in 1875*, the motto became the title. This change repays attention, because it is one of movement away from Romantic and Pre-Raphaelite influences (in the painterly evocativeness of "Under the Rose"); the poem now had a characteristic Rossettian title, an unidentified but easily identifiable passage from the Bible. Georgina Battiscombe describes the second version of the poem as "clumsily retitled";[12] on the contrary, the title is effectively elliptical, omitting a word few readers would fail to supply: "*Visiting* the Iniquity of the Fathers Upon the Children."[13] Syntactically implacable and static, without even a gerund to give it movement, the 1875 title becomes an inescapable moral pronouncement. It inscribes in itself the whole story of the Fall, *peccatum originans* and *peccatum originatum*, and the unnegotiable eventuality of the second because of the first, played out in generations of sinners. Against this title that decrees Margaret's fate stands the poem, Margaret's attempt to revoke the effects of her father's sin by narrating her life into the defiant shape of a celibate, unmarried, and solitary woman: "I'll not blot out my shame / With any man's good name; / But nameless as I stand, / My hand is my own hand, / And nameless as I came / I go to the dark land" (536–41). But Margaret the narrator certainly did not name the poem (not even the less judgmental "Under the Rose"), and the disjunction between title and poem puts unbearable pressure on the narrative's authoritative presentation of a vow to remain chaste.

Margaret, the (unreliable) narrator, reveals her own "Poet mind" as she pieces together her autobiography out of precious few fragments of "truth." It is against charges of unreliability that Rossetti defends the abilities of the "Poet mind." Dante Rossetti asserts that she knows nothing about such "social matters" (and shouldn't); Rossetti claims psychological-poetic authority to disclose an "internal portrait" of one who could only be like her if Heaven were Hell. The strongest argument for Rossetti's reliability in the realm of the mind is the fragility of *Marga-*

---

11. See, for instance, Rosenblum, *Christina Rossetti,* 166, and Georgina Battiscombe, *Christina Rossetti: A Divided Life* (New York: Holt, Rinehart, and Winston, 1981), 61.

12. Battiscombe, *Christina Rossetti: A Divided Life,* 95.

13. The phrase "visiting the iniquities of the Fathers upon the children" appears in the following books of the Bible: Exodus 20:5, Exodus 34:7, Numbers 14:18, and Deuteronomy 5:9.

ret's narrative construction. Margaret, short on the facts, is nonetheless a Kierkegaardian proto-psychologist like Vigilius, Constantius Constantin, or Frater Taciturnus, "more nimble than a tightrope dancer," whose "silence at the moment of confidence" is "seductive and voluptuous." The Kierkegaardian proto-psychologist invokes personal authority to "make" a case, little concerned with verifiable data. What Margaret "knows" lacks "factual authority," but she "knows" nonetheless, so that in the second stanza, after describing her shameful birth and her mother's abandonment—the "facts"—she describes a poignant farewell scenario between her infant self and her mother, ending with "Whether I know or guess, / *I know this not the less*" (my emphasis). Authentically childlike, "knowledge" here is the act of inventing a loving mother, fallen but contrite. In a world where the iniquities of the father are visited on the children, however, knowledge signifies the loss of innocence, not because you "fall," but because you find out what it means to be "fallen"— the ubiquitousness of "sinfulness," and the inevitable event of your own "sin." Against that inevitability Margaret's nurse and later her mother rally nobly, intent upon Margaret's not "knowing": "Nurse never talked to me / Of mother or of father, / But watched me early and late / With kind suspicious cares: / Or not suspicious, rather / Anxious, as if she knew / Some secret I might gather / And smart for unawares" (115–23). Later "my Lady" will keep her in her room whenever any "gentleman / Is staying at the Hall." The anxiety manifest here belongs to the Nurse and "my Lady," who want to keep Margaret ignorant, respectively, of the sin of sex of which she is the yield, and of her own inherited proclivity toward that same sin.

This anxiety, however, does not compare with Kierkegaardian anxiety; it just describes the typical fears a mother once had for her daughter. If the poem is rife with tension, it is not because of the two women's nervous vigilance. They (and Margaret) know she is pretty with her "longest curls," "largest eyes," and "teeth like small pearls," and they simply fear her attractiveness and attraction to the wrong kind of man. In his litany of nearly oxymoronic aphorisms, Vigilius describes a state of mind less straightforward, more contradictory and ambivalent. By turning again to what he has to say about the state of innocence we can locate the connection between knowledge in "The Iniquities...," already suspect by the poem's second stanza, and the real anxiety in the poem, obscured but not annulled by Margaret's own description of her Nurse as "anxious." "This is the profound secret of innocence," claims Vigilius, "that it is at the same time anxiety" (41). The profound compro-

mise innocence makes in the postlapsarian world is its direct, proleptic
connection to guilt:

> But he who becomes guilty through anxiety is indeed innocent,
> for it was not he himself but anxiety, a foreign power, that laid
> hold of him, a power that he did not love but about which he was
> anxious. And yet he is guilty, for he sank in anxiety, which he
> nevertheless loved even as he feared it. There is nothing in the
> world more ambiguous; therefore this is the only psychological
> explanation. (43)

Its protagonist entrapped in this dilemma, Margaret's narrative is of-
fered as the only possible "psychological explanation." The full stanza
containing the Nurse's "anxiety" inventories all of the components of
this dilemma:

> I often sat to wonder
> Who might my parents be,
> For I know of something under
> My simple-seeming state.
> Nurse never talked to me
> Of mother or of father,
> But watched me early and late
> With kind suspicious cares:
> Or not suspicious, rather
> Anxious, as if she knew
> Some secret I might gather
> And smart for unawares.
> Thus I grew.
>   (111–23)

"Know," "simple-seeming state," "suspicious," "secret," and "unawares":
these words turn that stanza into a synopsis of the poem's dynamic. The
activity of knowing is already suspect by line 26, and tied to the activity
of guessing ("Whether I know or guess"). Her "simple-seeming state" is
virtually synonymous with the radically compromised state of postlapsarian innocence described by Vigilius. Margaret's insight about
Nurse's worry that she should "smart . . . unawares" for a "secret," gathered but not yet known, exposes her state of incipient guilt, connected
to innocence via anxiety. "Gather" reminds us of the instability of "knowledge" in the poem, of Margaret's piecing together a life from what she

literally "gathers," inferring it even as she convenes its events in a narrative. But as the "psychological explanation" of Margaret, the narrative explains best when it is out of her control; only then does the audience get a sense of the real source of anxiety, obscured by worry about her sexuality, and by her resentment against the Lady for not acknowledging the true nature of their relationship.

Margaret's story consistently escapes her control. She tells about discovering her illegitimate identity, meeting her mother and silently rebuking her, and consequently opting for a solitary life, stoic "witness" to her own victimization.[14] The story tells these same events, but points to the untold narrative of the iniquitous father. If "knowing" the events of her mother's abandonment is willful invention, not knowing her father is equally willful, equally invented. Perhaps nowhere else does Margaret assert so strongly her psychological-poetical authority than in this not-knowing:

> I do not guess his name
> Who wrought my Mother's shame,
> And gave me life forlorn,
> But my Mother, Mother, Mother,
> I know her from all other.
>
> (4–8)

"Whether I know or guess, / I know this not the less" follows in the next stanza. The two uses of "guess" begin and end a tripartite pattern later to be reversed: first, an apparently dismissive reference to the father; second, the obsessional, overdetermined chant-like repetition of "Mother." The third part of the pattern undoes this protestation of respective indifference and obsession. "Whether I know or guess, / I know this not the less" implicates "guessing" in the suspect act of "knowing" (Margaret "knows," whether she obtained her knowledge redundantly from "knowing," or from the act of guessing).[15] Retroactively challenging the dismissive tone of "I do not guess his name," burdening it with the import of "I refuse to *try* to guess his name" or "I do not *choose* to guess his name," Margaret deliberately avoids the most important but most dangerous chapter of her life story.

---

14. "Witness" is the "exemplary figure" in Rossetti's poetry according to Rosenblum (6). In this chapter and in the next, I dispute that broad characterization by focusing on figures of action and voice in Rossetti's poetry.

15. See sonnet 4 of "Monna Innominata": "I loved and guessed at you, you construed me / And loved me for what might or might not be—" (*Complete Poems*, II, 88, lines 6–7).

How do we know this and why does she do it? We know it quite
simply because guessing, gathering, knowing are what Margaret *does* as
she defines herself ("Now I have eyes and ears / And just some little
wit..." [364–65]). Not to do it is uncharacteristic and therefore suspicious. She even has a possible lead to her father's identity: the Lady of the
Hall spins a tantalizing theory about the ring the Nurse gave her: "... she
should infer / The ring had been my father's first, / Then my mother's,
given for me / To the nurse..." (325–28). Inferring fits with Margaret's
detective activities, but she drops the clue. At the end of the stanza
Margaret says "Then she was silent, and I too" and abruptly changes the
subject: "I hate when people come." According to the Lady's theory, the
ring provides a generational link that Margaret seems determined to
ignore. And again, Margaret busily pieces the clues of the Hall's gossip
and the Lady's blushing demeanor, but still refuses to speculate about
her father:

> Oh, keep your counsel close,
> But I *guess* under the rose,
> In long past summer weather
> When the world was blossoming,
> And the rose upon its throne:
> I *guess not* who he was
> Flawed honour like a glass
> And made my life forlorn,
> But my *Mother, Mother, Mother,*
> Oh, I know her from all other.
>   (373–82, my emphasis)

Why Margaret avoids "knowing" her father in any of the ways available
to her according to her own epistemology supplies the key to the poem.
Rossetti claims to provide an "internal portrait" of an unfortunate girl
"set forth in her own words," and indeed she does. But the "internal
portrait" is not a sociological study of a victim, but a glimpse of a woman
self-trapped in the pattern of a father upon whose actions she, in an
unsuccessful attempt at self-defense, refuses to speculate. Her refusal pits
itself against the obsessive desire to "know" that generates the real anxiety in "The Iniquities...," Margaret's anxiety (her hate-love, fear-desire,
her temptation, her glimpse of freedom, her glimpse of just how deep
she can sink) that she will reenact her father's sin. As I have said, Margaret asserts her "psychological-poetical authority" most emphatically in
her strong declarative statements of negativity ("I do not guess his

name"; "I guess not who he was"). A vivid picture of her father, at least in his role of seducer and the cause of her mother's ruin, emerges nonetheless in a stanza that describes what Margaret says she could say, but will not:

> So my Lady holds her own
> With condescending grace,
> And fills her lofty place
> With an untroubled face
> As a queen may fill a throne.
> While I could hint a tale—
> (But then I am her child)—
> Would make her quail;
> Would set her in the dust,
> Lorn with no comforter
> Her glorious hair defiled
> And ashes on her cheek:
> The decent world would thrust
> Its finger out at her,
> Not much displeased I think
> To make a nine days' stir;
> The decent world would sink
> Its voice to speak of her.
>   (395–412)

Above all, this stanza makes explicit what has been suggested throughout the whole narrative—Margaret is not just a naïve, docile victim. By the time this stanza occurs, Margaret has already shown: sexual precocity ("The girls might flout and scout me, / But the boys would hang about me / In sheepish mooning wise"); a proclivity for the symbols of seduction ("In time of primroses, / I went to pluck them in the lane . . ."); and a strong propensity for illicit freedom ("It's charming to break bounds, / Stolen waters are sweet . . . Give me a long tether, / Or I may break from it"). These tendencies reproduce at least in type her father: sexually attractive, drawn "under the rose" to conduct his seduction, and willing to abandon his consequent responsibility. Margaret says she could "hint" (a companion to "guess"—if you hint, I'll guess) a tale but does not ("But then I am her child," said in protestation of loyalty); yet the tale does get told, elaborate in sordid detail and in a tone of vengeful enjoyment. And in its telling, this "untold" tale reveals itself to be a rehearsal of the same threat of exposure her father caused her mother. At her birth

Margaret had to be left "under the rose" to free her mother from the narrative of her disgrace, for an illegitimate child tells the story of sin.[16] Margaret's legacy, her inherited sin, is the seductive desire to destroy her mother, the temptation to use her psychological-poetical authority to reiterate her father's sin.

Grown to adolescence, Margaret makes a vow "Never to speak, or show / Bare sign of what I know." We know, however, that she has lavished detail on what she "knows" ("Her glorious hair defiled / And ashes on her cheek"), and this vow of silence will be impossible to maintain. She shores up her resolution with her intention of living unmarried, alone, and "nameless." Although the penultimate stanza ends with further proof of her resolution not to tell her and her mother's secret ("And nameless as I came / I go to the dark land" [540–41]), several lines earlier, we see how fragile and tenuous Margaret's resolutions are:

> But I could almost curse
> My father for his pains;
> And sometimes at my prayer
> Kneeling in sight of Heaven
> I almost curse him still . . .
> (519–23)

Tempted to expose her mother, tempted to curse her father, Margaret ends her narrative with a prayer. But the poem ends with the hint that the prayer will not suffice to prevent the inevitable procession of sin passed on as surely as her gold ring. Harold Bloom coins a Vigilius-like axiom that seems meant for "The Iniquities . . .": "A poem is not an overcoming of anxiety, but is that anxiety."[17] Margaret's monologue is an anxiously garrulous attempt to defer what the title announces as inevitable, that the sins of the father (*peccatum originans*) will be visited on the children (*peccatum originatum*).

If Bloom has little regard for Hopkins and never mentions Rossetti, his

---

16. One of the most famous examples is Pearl in *The Scarlet Letter.* For instance, early in the novel Hester Prynne and Pearl have an exchange that informs the protocol of catechism with the import of Hester's sin. Hester asks Pearl, "Tell me, then, what thou art, and who sent thee hither?" Pearl responds, "Tell me, Mother!" Hester's unconvincing "Thy Heavenly Father sent thee" prompts Pearl to touch the scarlet letter and claim, "He did not send me! I have no Heavenly Father!" Nathaniel Hawthorne, *The Scarlet Letter* (New York: New American Library, 1980), 99–100.

17. Harold Bloom, *The Anxiety of Influence: A Theory of Poetry* (New York: Oxford University Press, 1973), 94.

Anxiety of Influence is, nevertheless, particularly indebted to *Fear and Trembling* and *Repetition*. Though Bloom himself would not apply his revisionary ratio to Hopkins and Rossetti, who are absent from his roster of strong poets, their work nonetheless belongs in "the ruminative line, the poetry of loss" (*Anxiety of Influence,* 33). In a postlapsarian world, loss, of course, is the whole story, and latecomer-status the only kind available. "A poem," says Bloom, "is a poet's melancholy at his lack of priority" (96). Margaret feels this lack as she fails to escape from her own history. Pilate will fail similarly as a result of his relationship with Christ in Hopkins's "Pilate." Vigilius provides a religious version of the melancholy Bloom describes, as he identifies the human condition of anxiety: "Christianity has never assented to giving each particular individual the privilege of starting from the beginning in an external sense. Each individual begins in an historical nexus..." (*Concept of Anxiety,* 73). All men and women come after Adam—the definition of history. All men and women inherit Adam's sin—the condition of Hereditary Sin. There is no such thing as priority after the Fall—"after" is the human temporal state. To challenge such inevitability by attempting a radical revision of events yields first anxiety, then failure.

The argument for reading "The Iniquities..." as a postponement strategy revises a reading of Rossetti's poetry as a commentary on deferral and postponement. "Hope deferred" is a Rossetti leitmotif, *self-*postponement a tendency attributed to Rossetti herself by her brother.[18] As either self-abnegating Christian or self-effacing woman, she is seen as using strategies of deferral or postponement to articulate an ethos of self-denial or, more extremely, self-punishment. I agree with critics like Kathleen Blake and Dolores Rosenblum that strategies of deferral abound in Rossetti's poetry, but I account for them differently.[19] Since her poetry is often about fear of the future (the other side of hope in many of her

---

18. Christina Rossetti, *The Poetical Works of Christina Georgina Rossetti, with Memoir and Notes by William Michael Rossetti* (London: Macmillan and Co., 1914), lxvii. William writes: "She was replete with the spirit of self-postponement."

19. Rosenblum's use of the notion of endurance is very useful, particularly since it relies on the Christian belief that earthly life is to be endured in all its misery before receiving one's just reward after death. I believe she relies too heavily on it, however, and her commitment to it as the explanation for Rossetti's poetry disregards many of that poetry's complexities. Kathleen Blake has a chapter on Rossetti in her book, *Love and the Woman Question in Victorian Literature: The Art of Self-Postponement* (Totowa, N.J.: Barnes and Noble, 1983). She employs "self-postponement" as the presiding description of Rossetti's poetry. While Blake's treatment of Rossetti is, I believe, one of the most thoughtful and least polemical of modern studies, it still ignores the other way strategies of deferral must be understood in Rossetti's poetry, that is, as self-*interested* attempts to defer future punishment for sins.

poems) as the result of being fallen and sin-ridden, it gives literary expression to the impulse to stave off an inevitable fate. Such poems are strong expressions of self-survival, not self-denial. Another monologue called "A Martyr," the obsessive narrative of a young woman the night before she is to die for her religious beliefs, overwhelms one with the sense that talking, telling, expostulating, begging, bargaining may not change God's mind about the morning when it comes, but may postpone that coming at least as long as the young woman talks—that is, for the length of the poem.[20]

Though no one can understand Hopkins's poetics without having read St. Ignatius Loyola's *Spiritual Exercises,* Hopkins wrote poetry before he was a Jesuit. The religiosity that led him to the Catholic margins of Protestant England remained marked by that English Protestantism he rejected. Geoffrey Hartman notes how the two strains mix in Hopkins: "The Protestantism into which he was born had come to regard poetry as the most viable and open aspect of religion, its vernacular as it were; while the Catholic faith to which he converted recalled him to the mystery, discipline, and tradition indispensable for a real presence of the spirit."[21] Kierkegaardian anxiety offers a way of hearing Hopkins's pre-Jesuit artistic voice and locating that voice's later "authentic cadence" in the Ignatian protocols for prayer.[22] The poem "Pilate" records an imaginary denouement to the story of Christ's trial and crucifixion. Not the first to speculate about Pilate, Hopkins appropriates the Roman Consul

20. Todorov understands the power and suggestiveness of this narrative strategy of deferral and how it manipulates time. If all we get of the martyr is her deferring story, then within the context of the poem (all we have) the deferral is endless, even though the poem ends. Says Todorov in his *Poetics of Prose,* trans. Richard Howard (Ithaca: Cornell University Press, 1977):

> There are, then, so many reasons for narrative never to stop that we cannot help wondering: What happened before the first narrative? And what will happen after the last? *The Arabian Nights* have not failed to provide an answer, ironic though it may be, for those who want to know the "before" and the "after." The first story, Scheherazade's, begins with these words, meaningful on every level . . . "It is told . . ." No need to search out the origin of narrative in time—it is time which originates in narrative. (78–79)

21. Geoffrey Hartman, "Hopkins Revisited," in his *Beyond Formalism: Literary Essays 1958–1970* (New Haven: Yale University Press, 1970), 233. Also see Alison Sulloway, *Gerard Manley Hopkins and the Victorian Temper* (New York: Columbia University Press, 1972), and G. B. Tennyson, *Victorian Devotional Poetry: The Tractarian Mode* (Cambridge: Harvard University Press, 1981), for thorough discussions of the religious and intellectual influences on Hopkins before and beyond his conversion and his ordination.

22. The sestet of "Let me be to Thee" begins: "The authentic cadence was discovered late" (*Gerard Manley Hopkins,* ed. Catherine Phillips [New York: Oxford University Press, 1986], 75).

to write a poem about sharp remorse firmly in the Christian tradition.[23] His perhaps naïve appropriation, however, results in a spectacularly troubled psychological profile. Hopkins draws an "internal portrait" of a sufferer beset by Kierkegaardian anxiety in its most radical form. "No matter how deep an individual has sunk," we have heard Vigilius say, "he can sink still deeper, and this 'can' is the object of anxiety." In her story Margaret is suspended in the moment of that first plunge from innocence to guilt, reprieved for the length of her story, and then doomed. Pilate has already sunk far deeper than the young Margaret, but in Hopkins's dramatic monologue Pilate, too, is suspended for the moment of the poem before an even greater plunge. Seemingly as low as one can get, Hopkins's Pilate really can and does "sink still deeper."

One of two early, unfinished attempts at dramatic monologue (along with "Soliloquy of the Spy in the Wilderness") "Pilate" reveals an inclination toward gritty, sometimes grotesque realism that resembles some of Rossetti's poetry (specifically, the poems that earned her the reputation for being "morbid") and also anticipates *The Spiritual Exercises,* whose commitment to realism earned *it* the label of "revolting crudity."[24] Written two years before his religious conversion in 1864, while Hopkins was still an undergraduate, its final arrangement is unclear, its state of completion unknown. Hopkins does mention it, however, in a letter describing a particularly fertile period in his life.[25] "I have written a lot of my *Pilate,*" he writes, and

> I am thinking of a *Judas,* but such a subject is beyond me at present. . . . I have nearly finished an answer to Miss Rossetti's *Convent Threshold,* to be called *A voice from the world,* or something like that, with which I am at present in the fatal condition of

23. Mt. Pilatus in Lucerne, Switzerland, for instance, is so named from the legend that Pilate exiled himself there to die, or to kill himself. Clarkson Stanfield did an engraving of Mt. Pilatus to illustrate an edition of Sir Walter Scott's *Anne of Geierstein.*

24. Roland Barthes, *Sade, Fourier, Loyola,* trans. Richard Miller (Berkeley and Los Angeles: University of California Press, 1989), 63. Barthes is quoting Ernest Renan here. To read further about Ignatius, and Barthes's remarkable essay on him, see Chapter 3. Renan's comment about Ignatian "crudity," however, is apt because of how Barthes himself invokes Renan—in the middle of a discussion of the Ignatian goal of "go[ing] beyond the signified of the image . . . to its referent, the material Cross. . . . This upward movement toward matter . . . is conducted in the manner of a conscious fantasy." Hopkins's Pilate surely is a proto-Jesuit in Barthes's reading of the exercitant's duty (and pleasure).

25. Gerard Manley Hopkins, *Further Letters of Gerard Manley Hopkins,* 2d ed., ed. Claude Colleer Abbott (New York: Oxford University Press, 1956), 213.

satisfaction. I have written three religious poems which however you would not at all enter into, they being of a very Catholic character.[26]

The grouping here is intriguing: Pilate and Judas, types of traitors; three devotional lyrics; and in the middle a fictional plea to a cloistered woman to stay in and of the secular world and to love the speaker.[27] At the end of this same letter Hopkins mentions that he has been "introduced to Miss Rossetti [Maria, the eldest sister] and Miss Christina Rossetti." Nothing further is mentioned about this meeting, either by Hopkins or Rossetti, but Hopkins's array of poetic subjects lends credence to Jerome Bump's speculation about Rossetti's influence:

> Hopkins may never have had much personal contact with this woman who was to inspire some of his best poetry in the 1860's, but like Beatrice in Dante's poetry, Christina Rossetti became in his poetry the lady who is spiritually more advanced, clearly superior in holiness. Much as Beatrice intervened to save Dante in Hell, Hopkins's meeting with Christina Rossetti in 1864 apparently interrupted his more worldly poetic endeavors and called upon him to pursue higher ideals.[28]

Yet Hopkins's "best poetry in the 1860's" consisted of not much more than he describes in his letter. This small early output shares with Rossetti what Elisabeth Schneider calls a general "nineteenth-century religious medievalism," the same tendency that fueled the pre-Raphaelite artistic flame. Schneider demonstrates Hopkins's early medievalism by assuming that Pilate speaks from Hell and suffers the torments of the damned. In doing so, according to Schneider, Pilate seems very much like Rossetti's Cherubim and Seraphim in "The Convent Threshold," who were "Racked, roasted, crushed, wrenched limb from limb" in their time on earth.[29]

Schneider and Alan Heuser both assume that the narrator of "Pilate"

---

26. See Chapter 6 for a discussion of "A Convent Threshold" and "A Voice from the World."

27. Devotional, that is, if Abbott is correct in guessing the identity of the three poems. He speculates in his footnote to the passage quoted that they are "Thou who on Sin's wages starvest," "New Readings," and "He hath abolished the old drouth."

28. Jerome Bump, "Hopkins, Christina Rossetti, and Pre-Raphaelitism," *The Victorian Newsletter* 57 (1980): 4.

29. Elisabeth W. Schneider, *The Dragon in the Gate: Studies in the Poetry of G. M. Hopkins* (Berkeley and Los Angeles: University of California Press, 1968), 9–10.

suffers in Hell. "The pang from Tartarus, Christians hold," moans Pilate, "Is this, from Christ to be shut out." In the third and fourth editions of Hopkins's poetry, Gardner follows Humphrey House's editorial decision to place the stanza begun by these two lines at the beginning of the poem. In Hopkins's notebooks where it first appears, this stanza follows the six stanzas Hopkins numbered 2 through 7 to begin what I call the second part of the poem. Phillips has reproduced the poem exactly as it appears in manuscript; thus in her edition the poem begins: "Unchill'd I handle stinging snow . . ." The experiences of reading "Pilate" in either the third or fourth edition (Schneider and Heuser would have read the third edition), and reading Phillips's version differ radically; the chief difference is how quickly or assuredly one can assume that Pilate literally speaks from Hell. Nonetheless, Tartarus is a compartment of Hades, a prefiguration of Hell, and whether Hopkins meant for these lines to begin the poem or not, they imply residence in a hellish place, the "this" of the second line forging a link between Pilate's state and Christian Hell.

The rendering of Pilate as a persona fighting desperately for "psycho-logical-poetical authority" alters the assumption that the fiction actually occurs in Hell. The external environment, so powerfully evoked, clearly contributes to Pilate's understanding of his predicament ("This outer cold, my exile from of old / From God and man, is hell no doubt"). Traditionally, however, in Hell anxiety yields to despair.[30] Heuser ac-knowledges Pilate's real dilemma, though he contradicts his own assump-tion that Pilate is in Hell: "[Pilate] hover[s] in response between two worlds, flesh and spirit, earth and heaven . . . while over them stands a judgment, the judgment of spirit upon the body of sense."[31]

The stanzas Hopkins himself numbered two through seven undoubt-edly describe a *place.* Stanza 2 contains details concerning weather conditions ("stinging snow," "afflictive heat," "fierce skies are blue to black"), stanza 4, mention of the "dead lake." Pilate cannot leave this place: "Whatever time this vaporous roof, / The screen of my captivity" (29–30). Together the six stanzas constitute an Ignatian *composición*

---

30. Walker Percy's exploration of the complexity of despair in his novel *The Moviegoer* (New York: Avon Books, 1961) is instructive in this discussion. The novel has as its epigraph a quotation from Kierkegaard's *The Sickness Unto Death* (a later, non-pseudonymous work): "[T]he specific character of despair is precisely this; it is unaware of being despair." Binx Bolling, Percy's protagonist, is like Margaret and Pilate as his own story testifies against him. His definition of despair, "Not to be on to something is to be in despair" (18), is helpless against the weight of the epigraph.

31. Alan Heuser, *The Shaping Vision of Gerard Manley Hopkins* (London: Oxford Univer-sity Press, 1958), 16.

viendo de lugar, the introductory injunction of every individual exercise in the *Exercises*—"Composition, seeing the place" (with which Hopkins was not yet familiar). Pilate makes the place vivid and horrifying, the better to communicate the desperateness of his own state in its perverse immunity to the elements. Pilate is not "racked, roasted, crushed, wrenched limb from limb," but suffers the punishment of absolute physical insensitivity:

> Unchill'd I handle stinging snow,
> The sun whose vast afflictive heat
> Does lay men low with one blade's sudden blow
> Cleaves not my brain, burns not my feet,
> When the fierce skies are blue to black, albeit
> The shearing rays contract me with their blaze
> Most *dead-alive* upon those days.
>   (Stanza 2, my emphasis)

The last line provides the key to "Pilate." The contradictory "dead-alive" captures the indeterminate, apparently impossible position a man occupies when he feels nothing, yet feels intensely the pain of feeling nothing. From this position of indeterminacy Pilate nonetheless strongly asserts his claim of psychological-poetical authority. If we look at stanza 2 again, we realize that Pilate's power of description remains uncompromised after his loss of feeling. "Stinging snow," "vast afflictive heat," "fierce skys," "shearing rays": these are powerful descriptions from a man who must imagine rather than experience them. In these descriptive stanzas, we meet another "Poet mind." Margaret pieces together a story about and for herself with no recourse to facts; Pilate describes a landscape in its tactile diversity without recourse to his sense of touch.

If Hopkins was not yet reading Ignatius, he was reading Milton, whose Satan knows that "[t]he mind is its own place, and in itself / Can make a Heav'n of Hell, a Hell of Heav'n" (*Paradise Lost,* I, 254–55).[32] These lines derive their pathos from their succinct expression of Satan's suffering, but they derive their power from their more subversive claims for

---

32. See Gerard Manley Hopkins, *The Journals and Papers of Gerard Manley Hopkins,* ed. Humphrey House, completed by Graham Storey (New York: Oxford University Press, 1959), 38. This passage of his early diaries (1864) begins "The poetical language lowest." Hopkins takes the position of the young iconoclast, describing as "Parnassian" the poetry of his antecedents, including Milton's.

the imagination. One finds echoes of Satan's words in Pilate's, in whose imagination even an apocalypse would be "sweet to taste" in comparison to his present state:

> The day of doom!
> I cry 'O rocks and mountain make me room'
> And yet I know it would be better so,
> Ay, sweet to taste beside this woe.
> (Stanza 7, lines 39–42)

Just as Milton's Satan defines the mind as its own *place,* Hopkins's Pilate describes neither hell nor hell-on-earth, but the grim landscape of his own mind. Rossetti also read Milton and Blake, and must have recognized the sly allusions to *Paradise Lost* and "The Marriage of Heaven and Hell" in her elliptically expressed assurance to her brother that heaven would have to be hell before she could share in the experience of a woman like Margaret. Vigilius elaborates on what it means to have the "poetic originality of the soul" necessary for psychological-poetical authority. With such originality, one need not venture far nor experience much: "... he should sit entirely composed in his room, like a police agent who nevertheless knows everything that takes place. What he needs he can fashion at once. ... To that end [achieving freshness and the 'interest of actuality'] he imitates in himself every mood, every psychic state that he discovers in another" (*Concept of Anxiety,* 55). We have already seen how for Margaret imitation is a trap, the unavoidable repetition of her father's sin. She traps herself with her own imaginative powers, as will Pilate. In the second part, Pilate recreates the event of his personal fall; in the third he attempts the ultimate imitative act in what he hopes is appropriate atonement.

The second section rehearses the trial of Christ, as Pilate describes how each year on the anniversary of Christ's sentence he regains physical sensation: "There is a day of all the year / When life revisits me, nerve and vein" (50–51). This section gives a past to Pilate, who in the first section has no identifying history (without a title there are no reasons to assume the speaker is Pontius Pilate). Told in the present tense, however, the description of the trial is not a memory but a rehearsal in the poem's present. "I try the Christus o'er again," says Pilate, and he actually speaks to Christ—"Sir! Christ! against this multitude I strain"—and hears the crowd, "And all in one say 'Crucify!' " (53–56). In the next stanza Pilate gasps his way through his story:

Before that rock, my seat, He stands;
And then—I choke to tell this out—
I give commands for water for my hands;
And some of those who stand about,
(57–60)

Loath to tell, Pilate turns abruptly to a more neutral event: "Vespillo my centurion hacks out / Some ice that locks the glacier to the rocks / And in a bason [sic] brings the blocks" (61–63). Reminiscent of Margaret's abrupt turn from a discussion of her ring, this stanza contains in its ellipses the part of the story Pilate avoids, or for which he does not (any longer) possess language—the moment he orders the death of Christ. In the next stanza, in graphic detail, his sensory loss returns:

I choose one; but when I desire
To wash before the multitude
The vital fire does suddenly retire
From hands now clammy with strange blood.
My frenzied working is not understood.
Now I grow numb. My tongue strikes on the gum
And cleaves, I struggle and am dumb.
(64–70)

The clarity with which Pilate can communicate the experience of total *in*articulateness distinguishes him here from Margaret, whose saying of the unsaid signals her loss of control over her narrative. In this stanza where Pilate ironically makes quite clear the experience of not being understood ("My frenzied working is not understood"), he is at his authorial best as he lucidly reiterates a horrifying moment of frenzy. In sections 1 and 2 Pilate manages to keep a grasp of his psychological-poetical authority, but the last fragment of "Pilate" moves from the graphic to the gruesome; in it we see through Pilate's narrative to his real dilemma as a sinner.

In the third existing section Pilate imaginatively projects a future. This projection is grounded in his memory of his role in the crucifixion of Christ, about which, in the second section, he is so obsessed that it returns once a year to plague him as his present. This confusion of past, present, and future is symptomatic of Pilate's fundamental miscomprehension of his predicament. The third section begins, "I have a hope if so it be" (like anxiety, hope is not an emotion experienced in hell), but the stanza continues ominously:

> A hope of an approved device;
> I will break free from the Jews' company
> And find a flint, a fang of ice,
> Or fray a granite from the precipice:
> When this sought trees will be wanting not,
> And I shall shape one to my thought.
>   (77–82)

Shaping a tree to his thought with the "approved device," Pilate continues commanding subservience to his authorial activity from the environment. But that activity reveals itself finally to be, both literally and figuratively, suicide. "This shall I make a cross," Pilate continues, telling us why he needs a device to shape wood. He will affix himself on the cross, and he imagines details, from the footrest to tying his left hand to achieving immobility. Finally, in what is probably an incomplete stanza, he imagines nailing himself:

> I'll take in hand the blady stone
> And to my palm the point apply
> And press it down, on either side a bone,
> With hope, with shut eyes, fixedly;
> Thus crucified as I did crucify.
>   (90–94)

This bizarre twist on an "imitatio christi" signals the utter breakdown of Pilate's authority. Vigilius says to imitate, "to incline and bend himself to other people and imitate their attitudes"; the Christian tradition demands that its followers imitate the ways of Christ, and Pilate himself speaks of hope here. But to rehearse literally the crucifixion of Christ is to kill onself, a sinful act in its imitation of the good. A "sinner" has a complicated and potentially dangerous relationship to a standard of divine goodness. Margaret and Pilate are doomed; their narratives, meant to alter this doom, fail. What should we make of poems so firmly grounded in the Christian tradition that nonetheless eschew the most basic conventional doctrine, that human sin is forgivable as a consequence of the crucifixion? And how does any answer to this question relate to a literary strategy of creating a character who authors her or his own life?

As atonement, Pilate's plan is disastrous. As a narrative, Pilate's rehearsal of the crucifixion is a travesty of pious "imitatio christi" in its attempt at imitation. In demonstrating his ability to reiterate imaginatively Christ's experience, Pilate makes strong claims for his ability as author; as claims belonging to the man who "authored" Christ's death, they beg to be suspected. (There is rich ambiguity in the words Pilate remembers Christ saying to him: "Take courage; this shall need no further art.") We are in an enormously ambitious "Poet mind" who asserts authority to preempt a sacrosanct image in Christian tradition, Christ on the cross: "Thus crucified as I did crucify." Like Margaret, Pilate tells us his most diabolical thoughts while postponing them to the indeterminate future. A remnant of the poem not included in published editions of Hopkins's poetry, however, suggests the strain under which Pilate labors to rectify his past, and the paradoxical inevitability, in the not-too-distant future, of his further degradation: "But if this overlast the day / Undone, and I must wait the year, / Yet no delay can serve to grate away / A purpose desperately dear" (*Journals and Papers*, 49). At the precise moment when Pilate imagines himself committing the one truly irreparable act (killing himself like Judas, also on Hopkins's mind at this time), he profoundly misunderstands that act's implications, still harboring a hope of redemption. He, like Margaret, narrates to save himself, but the narration dictates both his future damnation and his concomitant fate as an author, the complete loss of psychological-poetical authority to his enemy. Margaret's father is her enemy, and Christ is Pilate's. Like Adam for man in general, these adversaries constitute the inescapable beginnings of our narrators' stories, and such beginnings dictate the stories' ends. There is no possibility for preemption or revision, only postponement; that period of postponement is the poem, an exposé of the narrator's helpless implication in future sin.

In *The Concept of Anxiety*, Vigilius writes a section called "The Anxiety About the Good," subtitled "The Demonic." He defines the demonic as "anxiety about the good," (123) and dismisses its traditional associations: ". . . every fantastic notion of entering into a pact with evil etc., whereby a person becomes entirely evil, must be abandoned" (122). For Vigilius, the demonic really has to do with the problem of language; muteness and communication play off each other in his many examples: "The demonic is *inclosing reserve* [*det Indesluttede*] *and the unfreely disclosed*. . . . [I]nclosing reserve is precisely the mute, and when it is to express itself, this must take place contrary to its will. . . . [I]t is the individual who in anxiety betrays himself against his will" (123, translator's emphasis and interpolation). Muteness and involuntary communication as the definitions of Vigilius's concept correspond to an everyday understanding of reservedness. His antidote makes sense also: "Language, the word, is precisely what saves, what saves the individual from the empty abstraction of inclosing reserve" (124). At first glance inclosing reserve is the state of isolation from which Margaret and Pilate have saved themselves. But Vigilius implicates their very method as the discourse of inclosing reserve: "... monologue is precisely its [inclosing reserve's] speech, and therefore we characterize an inclosed person by saying that he talks to himself." And a few lines later: "What the inclosed person conceals in his inclosing reserve can be so terrible that he does not dare utter it, not even to himself, because it is as though by the very utterance he commits a new sin or as though it would tempt him again" (128). Vigilius's model inclosed person is another, more famous Dane; Hamlet's increasing isolation as he draws more and more inward is marked by ever-increasing self-colloquy. The corollary is that fewer and fewer want to listen to him. Similarly, no one wants to talk to Margaret about what worries her, and in her monologue she describes furtively that which she says she will not reveal. Pilate's monologue has no sense of furtiveness only because he is already so solitary and isolated that sanity is at stake or already surrendered to a hostile, nonresponsive silence. Although desperately garrulous, both Margaret and Pilate know events in their histories that they cannot bring themselves to say; these events paradoxically are the reasons for their present dilemmas.

Like Hamlet, Margaret and Pilate are inclosed persons, and the main impression given by their narratives is that language fails them drastically. But like Hamlet, they are not unsympathetic characters, precisely due to that failure of language to redeem them. Their monologues index that failure. Attention to Vigilius's notion of the good, its relation to anxiety, and its role in the involuntary expression of the inclosed or reserved person helps us understand its inevitability. In Vigilius's scheme, an inclosed person expresses himself in an act of self-betrayal because of anxiety about the good. Using the analogy of the "obdurate criminal," Vigilius tells us that the most effective means to coerce an inclosed person into speech is to match silence with a more powerful silence: "If an inquisitor has the required physical strength and the spiritual elasticity to endure without moving a muscle, to endure even for sixteen hours, he will succeed, and the confession will burst forth involuntarily. A man with a bad conscience cannot endure silence" (125). Soon after, he tells us the good is "absolutely able to keep silent" (125). The most successful inquisitor is the "good"; the exemplar of the good in religious terms is God; Vigilius's chapter on the demonic, therefore, depicts God as simultaneously silent and as a Jesuitical Grand Inquisitor. (The pejorative "Jesuitical" is quite to the point, since on the same page as the silence of the good, the Jesuit Order is a prominent example of a

"higher demon" capable of great manipulation of the weak [125].) In
their silence, God and the good test the speakers in the following apostrophes, because private colloquy with God offers the only evidence of
His existence, making silence an unbearable non-response.

The excruciating detail with which Margaret's and Pilate's predicaments
unfold testify to an ability, or a compulsion, to examine the corrupt yield
of human sinfulness—but not without tension, because in the face of
evidence of God's absence, sin and sinfulness become the strongest
evidence of his presence. In the apostrophes "Justus Quidem Tu Es,
Domine" and "Have I Not Striven, My God?" the poetic admission of
sinfulness doubles as a testimony to the existence of God. If we call sin
an act that breaks God's law, by its commission it bears witness to that
law, and to that God. If no act is sinful, if there is no distinction between
good acts and evil ones, if there are no clear dualisms completely resistant to obliterating mediation, then probably there is no God. As the
bridge between innocence and guilt, therefore, Kierkegaardian anxiety
is not a totally undesirable state for a believer, for while it bridges it does
not reconcile. From the time of the Fall guilt implicates innocence, but
the two are never identical. The event of hereditary sin, *peccatum originatum,* imitates Adam's original sin, *peccatum originans,* but is not
explained away by it, nor are its consequences mitigated by its inevitability. In their unsuccessful struggle for psychological-poetical authority,
Margaret and Pilate each is his or her "author's alias," and their failures
are inversely proportionate to the poets' successful mining of their own
"Poet mind."[33] In the move to lyric apostrophes, the aliases disappear;
without a specific "Margaret" or "Pilate," the poet can keep her or his
distance only by disappearing behind the much more transparent
"speaker." The issue of power, below the surface of a dramatic monologue, breaks through the surface in a first-person lyric.

If a monologue bespeaks inclosing reserve, it would seem that a poem
directly addressing God must be the monologue's direct opposite. But
the strategy of poetical direct address discloses speakers no more successful than the reserved speakers of monologues. In her application of
the principle of apostrophe, Barbara Johnson defines that trope in its use
from Sidney to Gwendolyn Brooks:

33. I borrow the phrase "author's alias" from Gayatri Spivak's article, "Sex and History in
The Prelude," Texas Studies in Literature and Language 23, no. 3 (Fall 1981): 324–60, where
she argues for an inverse relationship between Vaudracour's descent into insanity (in book 9)
and Wordsworth's return to artistic health after his relationship with Annette Vallon.

Apostrophe is thus both direct and indirect: based etymologically on the notion of turning aside, of digressing from straight speech, it manipulates the I/Thou structure of direct address in an indirect, fictionalized way. The absent, dead, or inanimate entity addressed is thereby made present, animate, and anthropomorphic. Apostrophe is a form of ventriloquism through which the speaker throws voice, life, and human form into the addressee, turning its silence into mute responsiveness.[34]

Turning the apostrophizer into a ventriloquist, someone who invents respondent and response, brings that speaker closer to monologue, whose involuntary self-colloquy indicates not greater isolation, but perhaps greater authorial naïveté. In its ability to throw its own voice into a void of silence, the speaker in an apostrophe possesses a sophisticated weapon in the pursuit of psychological-poetic authority. What does this voice achieve versus what it discloses?

The last sonnet Hopkins wrote before eleven years of literary silence, "Let me be to Thee," is Herbertian and joyful; ironically it describes the discovery of poetic voice: "I have found my music in a common word." The speaker blissfully apostrophizes God, asking to serve as poet. The sestet marries poetry and piety: "The authentic cadence was discovered late / ... I have found the dominant of my range and state— / Love, O my God, to call Thee Love and Love." In its optimism about a felicitous relationship between work and worship, this sonnet differs remarkably in tone from other, grimmer poems written in 1865, one year before his conversion to Roman Catholicism. "Myself Unholy," "My prayers must meet a brazen heaven," and "Trees by their yield" preview the mental torture to which Hopkins would later subject himself, but "Let me be to Thee" appeals apostrophically to a God from whom the speaker anticipates a response. Twenty-three years later, Hopkins has written almost all the poetry he will write, is living miserably in Dublin, and is questioning everything about his life and work. In a letter to Robert Bridges during this period, he offers a bleak view of this work: "It is now years that I have had no inspiration of a longer jet than makes a sonnet, except only in that fortnight in Wales: it is what, far more than direct want of time, I find most against poetry and production in the life I

34. Barbara Johnson, "Apostrophe, Animation, and Abortion," in her *World of Difference* (Baltimore: The Johns Hopkins University Press, 1989), 185. See also Jonathan Culler's discussion on apostrophe in *The Pursuit of Signs: Semiotics, Literature, Deconstruction* (Ithaca: Cornell University Press, 1981), 135–54.

lead."[35] This same letter contains the famous passage of despair, the main proof for those who argue that Hopkins's religious devotion oppressed and finally ruined his poetic talent: "All impulse fails me: I can give myself no sufficient reason for going on. Nothing comes: I am a eunuch—but it is for the kingdom of heaven's sake" (270). His writings for himself are even grimmer. In "Retreat Notes," written in the same month as his letter to Bridges, Hopkins describes the painful problem of his accomplishments in Ireland (it has much to do with being a loyal Englishman serving a hostile people) and then turns his view inward:

> I was continuing this train of thought this evening when I began to enter on that course of loathing and hopelessness which I have so often felt before, which made me fear madness.... I could therefore do no more than repeat *Justus es, Domine, et rectum judicium tuum....* What is my wretched life? ... I am ashamed of the little I have done, of my waste of time, although my helplessness and weakness is such that I could scarcely do otherwise. And yet the Wise Man warns us against excusing ourselves in that fashion. I cannot then be excused; but what is life without aim, without spur, without help? All my undertakings miscarry. I am like a straining eunuch. I wish then for death: yet if I died now I should die imperfect, no master of myself, and that is the worst failure of all.[36]

"Eunuch," an arresting word that appears again in "Thou art indeed just," deserves the careful attention it has received in most critical studies of Hopkins.[37] Christopher Devlin, the editor of Hopkins's *Sermons and Devotional Writings,* offers an intriguing gloss on what Hopkins calls here "the worst failure of all." "There may be a symptomatic confusion of thought here," writes Devlin:

35. Gerard Manley Hopkins, *The Letters of Gerard Manley Hopkins to Robert Bridges,* ed. Claude Colleer Abbott (London: Oxford University Press, 1935), 270.

36. Gerard Manley Hopkins, *The Sermons and Devotional Writings of Gerard Manley Hopkins,* ed. Christopher Devlin, S.J. (London: Oxford University Press, 1959), 262.

37. As an example, Michael Sprinker straightforwardly plays out the implications of "eunuch" in the language of the poet as progenitor of his own text ("... textual production is a kind of procreation, the writer's text his progeny" in *A Counterpoint of Dissonance: The Aesthetics and Poetry of Gerard Manley Hopkins* (Baltimore: The Johns Hopkins University Press, 1980), 79. This kind of analysis, taken with Hopkins's own comments about the "male gift" necessary to write poetry, makes Hopkins a prime target for Sandra Gilbert and Susan Gubar in *The Madwoman in the Attic,* which begins its revisionary task by discussing Hopkins as exemplary phallocentric poet.

The state of perfection which the profession of a religious enjoins is a constant *striving* for perfection; the complete attainment of it is not possible in this life. . . . [S]elf-mastery is a means to a closer union with Christ; it is not an end in itself. *Perfect* self-mastery is an academic rather than a religious ideal. (319, Devlin's emphasis)

Academic, or perhaps authorial: Devlin plays it straight as a Jesuit editor, but his "symptomatic confusion of thought" can serve as an ambiguous characterization of both Hopkins and Rossetti as religious poets. We have seen this confusion about perfect self-mastery already, in the characters of Margaret and Pilate, and we will see it in William Rossetti's description of his sister. The idea for "Justus Quidem Tu Es, Domine" germinates throughout 1888, but the tension between a desire for self-mastery and an almost groveling belief in powerlessness manifests itself in the sonnet in a way not entirely predicted by the letters and journal entries always cited to explain the poem.

"If apostrophe is the giving of voice," writes Barbara Johnson, "the throwing of voice, the giving of animation, then a poet using it is always in a sense saying to the addressee, 'Be thou me' " (*World of Difference*, 188). The first two lines of "Justus . . ." set up a contest between speaker and Lord over the quality of justness, playing off this aspect of apostrophe while maintaining a semblance of propriety: "Thou art indeed just, Lord, if I contend / With thee; but, sir, so what I plead is just." Thou art just, but I have a just cause; not only am I like you, but you must be on my side in order to be just because "what I plead is just" (Or, "I say more: the just man justices" ["As Kingfishers Catch Fire"]). The plea follows as evidence for just cause: "Why do sinners' ways prosper? and why must / Disappointment all I endeavor end?"

In the second half of the quatrain the contest between Thou and I yields to an even fiercer challenge of competing definitions: "Wert thou my enemy, O thou my friend, / How wouldst thou worse, I wonder, than thou dost / Defeat, thwart me?" The speaker still nods to propriety in direct address ("O thou my friend"), but sets it parallel to its direct opposite, hypothetical impropriety ("Wert thou my enemy"). From there the speaker speculatively replaces the conventional definition of friend with that of enemy, so that all propriety of address is negated by the charges of thwarting and defeating. The oppositions accumulate around the speaker: I vs. thou, friend vs. enemy, and then "the sots and thralls of lust" who "more thrive than I that spend, / Sir, life upon thy cause." Finally all of nature stands in contrast to (and in a contest with) the speaker as the sonnet moves quickly toward its climax. Banks and brakes (thickets) are laced with chervil, fecund and prosperous, and "birds build—but not I build; no, but strain, / Time's eunuch, and not breed one work that wakes, / Mine, O thou lord of life, send my roots rain." "O thou lord of life" ends the poem as it began, with a ritualistic address that contains an unseemly challenge to the addressee—to be lord of life you must generate life; my death without generation makes you *not* lord of life, so you had better "send my roots rain." The sonnet studies contradictions, a just lord who does not "justice," a friend who behaves like an enemy, sinners who prevail over a non-sinner, a lord of life who tolerates "time's eunuch." It is also pugnacious, a deliberate provocation instead of a more appropriate invocation.

The prominence of the "Thou" arises because of its unresponsiveness, its silence. For Johnson, an apostrophe turns the "silence [of the addressee] into mute responsiveness." Hopkins writes some apostrophes that match this description: "Nondum," "Peace," "The Habit of Perfection," and, of course, "Let me be to Thee." But in "Justus Quidem Tu Es, Domine," the "Thou" establishes its prominence by an imperturbability that provokes the litany of defiant dichotomies in the poem's structure and story. This sonnet is an apostrophe about the failure of apostrophe's fiction. It tells its story, nevertheless, within the context of religious faith, so the failure can best be described by remembering Vigilius's characterization of the good as capable of absolute silence. The "Thou" is inscrutable in the face of provocation as the "I" discloses its anxious relationship to that inscrutability; the expression of that relationship, one dichotomous pair after the other, is a successful sonnet. This complex interplay between failure and success reiterates the dynamic of "Pilate" (and "The Iniquities . . ."), and comments on that interplay by bringing forward in the apostrophe the "Thou" (Margaret's father and Christ) that remains, not hidden, but beyond the purview of the two dramatic monologues.

To characterize "Justus Quidem Tu Es, Domine" as a successful sonnet about failed apostrophe begs the question implicit in Hopkins's letter to Bridges, where a sonnet is the meager result of the shortest possible "jet" of inspiration. "Jets" of anything, including inspiration, remind us of the eunuch mentioned by Hopkins in all the modes in which he was writing at the time. "Time's eunuch," however, revises the "eunuch" and "straining eunuch" of Hopkins's prose. When Hopkins calls himself a eunuch in his letter he uses the term's sexual meaning just as he does in the sonnet. "Nothing comes," he tells Bridges, and the sonnet's speaker "breed[s] not one work that wakes": predictably, sexual impotence stands in for literary unproductiveness. His retreat notes continue similarly, and "straining eunuch" intensifies the frustration over the gap between attempt and result. But in the sonnet, "eunuch" operates differently as a result of its new modifier, "time's." Powerlessness and self-hatred, for which Hopkins excoriates himself in prose, metamorphose via the identical vehicle of a sexual eunuch into a literary trope for human temporality, powerlessness, and inevitable defeat in any attempt to challenge God. If a sonnet is a poor show for a literary career because of its puniness, that same puniness, the small amount of time it occupies, makes it the perfect symbolic product of "time's eunuch." I will soon argue that Hopkins's (and Rossetti's) use of form willfully (and successfully) transgresses the formal limitations of that form, but "Justus Quidem Tu Es, Domine" performs as the cautionary tale for all of Hopkins's sonnets in its successful demonstration of what it means to be a failure.

As an accomplishment, successfully demonstrating failure does not mitigate the suffering manifest in Hopkins's prose. Rossetti well understood the pathos of self-laceration as artistic theme:

> Each sore defeat of my defeated life
> Faced and outfaced me in that bitter hour;
> And turned to yearning palsy all my power,
> And all my peace to strife,
> Self stabbing self with keen lack-pity knife.
> (*Complete Poems*, II, 124–25, lines 41–45)[38]

If "Justus Quidem Tu Es, Domine" employs apostrophe to cut both ways, toward failure and toward success, Rossetti's "Have I Not Striven, My God?" uses the same method to articulate the sharp outer edge of her poetry. To understand this sonnet's place in the poet's oeuvre is to recognize it as more extreme than other poems written in the same year (1863), especially than poems in which the speaker addresses God.

Rossetti apostrophizes God in her poetry, but it is more characteristic of her to address God or Christ in her dialogue poems. These poems modify the apostrophe form and include a direct, written response from the addressee. "Up-hill" is perhaps the most famous of Rossetti's dialogues, but there are many, as well as several ways of depicting the addressee through its address. The issues raised by Johnson about confusion between direct and indirect address and between the I and Thou become vexing in poems whose fiction makes the deity speak. The dialogue poems, however, more easily meet conventional expectations of a religious poet, because to create a response to one's own appeal is to

---

38. See Chapter 3 for a discussion of "An Old World Thicket."

participate in a fiction that assuages anxiety, at least postpones despair, and does not mark that event of appeal as failure. All indeterminacy, structural and thematic, is resolved by the dialogue poem's last line, invariably spoken by the addressee-deity; that response rebuts any notion of God as silent and hostile. The dialogue poem implies recourse to an earlier world view when God's presence was immanent and verifiable (simply, if one believes, then all things become proof of the correctness of one's belief). The strength of Rossetti's religious belief nonetheless does not preclude, but results in that very anxiety detectable in Hopkins's address to an unresponsive God, and in Vigilius's rendering of the demonic—anxiety's relation to the good. Rossetti's non-poetic writing is much more circumspect than Hopkins's. William Rossetti's Memoir of his sister, however, provides an agnostic's view of Rossetti and where she fits in the context of paradigms of Christianity.

"The Christian believer has before him two things," he writes:

> one, the promise of ecstatic bliss; the other, the decree of excessive misery. Some believers, perceiving themselves to be undoubted Christians in faith, become serenely or perhaps exuberantly happy in their inner selves: it may be said that Maria Rossetti [Rossetti's sister] was of these, for (at any rate in her later years) she felt the firmest confidence of salvation. *Not so Christina, who always distrusted herself, and her relation to that standard of Christian duty which she constantly acknowledged and professed.* In this regard her tone of mind was mainly despondent: it was painfully despondent in the last few months of her life. . . . All her life long she felt—or rather she exaggerated—her deficiencies or backslidings: she did not face religion with that courageous yet modest front with which a virtuous woman, who knows something of the world, faces life. Passages can no doubt be found in her writings in which she is more hopeful than abased; in which her ardent aspirations towards heaven so identify her with its bliss that she seems to be almost there, or on the very threshold. These passages are of course perfectly genuine, *but they are coupled with an awful sense of unworthiness, shadowed by an awful uncertainty.* (*Poetical Works,* liv–lv, my emphasis)

Several times in the Memoir, William attributes much of Rossetti's mental despondency to physical illness (*Poetical Works,* 1); as a "sadly-smitten invalid," Rossetti resembles Hopkins, also plagued by bad health. William offers an astute description, in his second kind of Christian, of both Rossetti and Hopkins. But he also misses the point in his brotherly concern about her "exceeding sensitiveness of conscience" (lxvi) and her major shortcoming in his eyes, her "over-scrupulosity" (lviii).

A worldly man, William Rossetti must have seen Christina Rossetti as the epitome (along with her sister and mother) of Christian virtue and its excesses. He describes Rossetti's pledge at age eighteen to give up the theater (opera and drama) and the pleasures of chess (*Poetical Works,* lxvi).[39] If Rossetti and Hopkins fall into the category of "excessive misery," however, that category must be understood correctly in relation to the concept of sin, which inspires such misery. Unworthiness and uncertainty plague both as believers, the second as a direct result of the first; merely to attribute these concerns to "over-scrupulosity" risks overlooking their importance to both Hopkins and Rossetti as artists. William locates the cause of a modern reader's bewilderment about the poets' intense awareness of sin in their pious, quiet lives; he also identifies the source of that awareness in what he calls the "deeper currents." William Rossetti characterizes his sister's life as "a life which did not consist of incidents: in few things, external; in all its deeper currents, internal" (*Poetical Works,* liv), and again his words fit both poets. Dorothy Margaret Stuart, one of Rossetti's early biographers, restates William's point: "Nothing is more curious in the mentality of Christina Rossetti than her almost complete independence of external stimuli."[40] A change of scenery, be it Hastings or Italy, did not penetrate Rossetti's mental life: "Yet here [Hastings] as elsewhere, her subjectivity dominates" (67). In a brief look at poetry influenced by Rossetti's trip to Italy, Stuart comments on the poet's mind in an insight that recalls Rossetti's defense of the "Poet mind" and Vigilius's poetic agent who sits "entirely composed in his own room": "Yet she who in 'Goblin Market' and 'A Birthday' wove a tapestry that dazzles the eyes of the mind could find no words, did not even attempt to find any words, wherewith to catch and keep something of the characteristic colour of Italy. *She was always better able to suggest realities of which she had no personal knowledge*" (68, my emphasis). There is a cost paid for this dominating subjectivity, and for the strength of an imagination capable of "suggest[ing] realities" possible only if "Heaven [were] Hell." We have seen that both poets can insinuate them-

---

39. Like Dorothea in *Middlemarch,* the depiction of whom conveys the (not intended) pleasure derived from the idea of renunciation: "Riding was an indulgence which [Dorothea] allowed herself in spite of conscientious qualms; she felt that she enjoyed it in a pagan sensuous way, and always looked forward to renouncing it" (George Eliot, *Middlemarch* [New York: Oxford University Press, 1990], 9).

40. Dorothy Margaret Stuart, *Christina Rossetti* (London: Macmillan and Co., 1930), 41.

selves into the psychologies of sinners, "more nimble" than Vigilius's "tightrope dancer." This insinuation itself insinuates that Hopkins and Rossetti risk collusion in a heresy, the unforgivableness of human sin. The dilemma of the believer-poet in the landscape of disbelief that is his or her home plays itself out in Rossetti's "Have I Not Striven, My God?"

Where Hopkins's sonnet proceeds in the language of logic and propriety until it takes a desperate turn in its sestet, Rossetti's "Have I Not Striven, My God?" begins in desperation, as the speaker pleads not for justice, but for an audience. According to Johnson, the opening of Baudelaire's "Moesta et Errabunda" "makes explicit the relation between direct address and the desire for the *other's* voice: 'Tell me: you talk' " (*World of Difference,* 185). Rossetti's speaker sounds frantic with that desire: "Have I not striven, my God, and watched and prayed? / Have I not wrestled in my agony? / Wherefore still turn Thy Face of Grace from me?" (*Complete Poems,* II, 205, lines 1–3). Unlike a dialogue-poem, in this sonnet the "you" will not talk—*that* is what the poem is about; the speaker's questions go unanswered, the tension remains unbroken. Instead the questioning continues, perilously close to blasphemy in its challenge to power: "Is Thine Arm shortened that Thou canst not aid?" The next two lines provide the climax of the sonnet: "Thy silence breaks my heart: speak tho' to upbraid, / For thy rebuke yet bids us follow Thee." This speaker is no antinomian—wanting (desiring) grace in acknowledgement of having striven, watched and prayed, and wanting (needing) grace to aid in winning the wrestle with sin. How do we know it is the temptation to sin that incurs "mine agony"? Because if the appeal is to speak even if only to upbraid, to rebuke, then the speaker acknowledges having sinned. Sinfulness should produce a sign of God's attention in the form of a rebuke. Without even a rebuke, therefore, powerlessness sets in: "I grope and grasp not; gaze, but cannot see." These first seven lines record a complicated confessional by a believer who first itemizes strenuous efforts (striving, watching, praying, wrestling), and then resorts to shortcomings, implied in an appeal for a rebuke, in a frantic attempt to pierce the heartbreaking silence. The second half of the poem projects into the future; a seven-line interrogative sentence, it ends by suggesting daring criteria for "God-ly" success:

> Thou Who for my sake once didst feel the Cross,
> Lord, wilt Thou turn and look upon me then,
> *And in Thy Glory bring to nought my shame,*
> *Confessing me to angels and to men?*
>   (11–14, my emphasis)

After the death of the speaker, in the context of the Second Coming, "Thy Glory" and "my shame" exclude each other; the suggestion, couched in a question, is that if "Thy Glory" does not negate "my shame," the existence of "my shame" threatens "Thy Glory." This exclusionary relationship, like the pairs of oppositions in Hopkins's sonnet, foregrounds the "Thy" in its irresponsiveness. But where Hopkins's sonnet provokes one last time with a demand ("Send my roots rain"), this sonnet ends with its provocative question doubling back on its first seven lines. In the last line the speaker uses the word "confesses" in its traditional sense of expressing faith in, believing: will Christ acknowledge virtue after death? But the real pathos of the sonnet lies in how the other sense of "confess" operates. "Confessing me to angels and to men" could make public "my shame," even as "Thy Glory" cancels it out ("bring[s it] to nought"). In other words, God's act replicates the personal, sacramental confession of sins. If the real tension derives from the suspicion that even sinfulness does not exist, then that tension will be relieved, and the believer (who is also always a sinner) will be vindicated (shame brought to nought) by an acknowledgment of those sins (a rebuke, an upbraiding, as the consequence of an act of confession). The "excessive misery" of William Rossetti's second kind of believer doubles as testimony to God's existence. One's own sinfulness, the anxiety accrued in anticipation of committing an actual sin, and inevitable failure (exposure as a sinner) must suffice as a subjective guarantee of God's responsiveness.

Early in his discussion Vigilius observes that ". . . when sin is brought into esthetics, the mood becomes either light-minded or melancholy, for the category in which sin lies is that of contradiction, and this is either comic or tragic" (*Concept of Anxiety,* 14). In the poetry of Hopkins and Rossetti, the mood is decidedly melancholic, the contradiction tragic. In its progression from Margaret, to Pilate, to apostrophe as successful display of failure, and finally to sin as successful belief, this discussion has flirted with a heresy Vigilius mentions almost immediately, and whose severe implications he disingenuously exiles. Embedded in his compressed history on the theology of Hereditary Sin, Vigilius dismissively mentions that

> a rhetorical concern, with no consideration whatever for thought, makes the most terrifying pronouncement about hereditary sin: *quo fit, ut omnes propter inobedientiam Adae et Hevae in odio apud deum simus* [from which it follows that all of us, because of

the disobedience of Adam and Eve, are hated by God]—*Formula of Concord.* The *Formula* is nevertheless circumspect enough to protest against thinking this, for if one were to think it, *sin would become man's substance* [my emphasis]. (27)

Here is the disingenuous note:

> The fact that the *Formula of Concord* forbade thinking this concept must nonetheless be commended as proof of the energetic passion by which it knows *how to let thought collide with the unthinkable* [my emphasis], an energy that is very admirable in contrast to modern thought, which is all too slack.

We end with a return to beauty as deformation of suffering and poetry as pathology by suggesting that Hopkins and Rossetti let thought collide with the unthinkable in their poetical explorations of their own religious beliefs. The collision is between belief in the efficacy of the crucifixion, on the one hand, and that terrifying pronouncement against which all theology since the record of Adam's fall has had to contend—if God exists, he hates man for Adam's transgression, and man's substance is indeed sin. Out of this collision comes poetry that seems to have ransacked the "Poet mind" for a range of suffering apparently endless, and therefore, ironically, sublime in its testimony to the power of the artist's imagination. The next chapter begins with this irony, the remarkable strength of Hopkins's and Rossetti's poetic egos, even as the poets seem to wield against themselves, obsessively and masochistically, a "keen lack-pity knife" of religious remorse and scrupulosity.

3
Una Selva Oscura:
The Lyric *I*

*But this breaking free, the human voice harvesting echo
where there was silence before, is both miracle and outrage,
sacrament and blasphemy.*
 —George Steiner, "Silence and the Poet"

*Of that place beyond the heavens none of our earthly poets
has yet sung, and none shall sing worthily.*
 —Plato, *Phaedrus*

Kierkegaard's collected private
papers indicate that he considered "Simon Stylita" as a possible pseudonym for his work on Abraham and the problem of faith in his own time.
In a draft of the title page of what eventually would be *Fear and Trembling* Kierkegaard annotated his trial pseudonym: "Simon Stylita: Solo
Dancer and Private Individual."[1] Kierkegaard finally abandoned Simon
Stylita; nonetheless, this reference to Simeon, the fifth-century Syrian
ascetic who spent between thirty to thirty-five years (reports vary)
sitting atop a pillar, provides a link between Kierkegaard and Victorian
England.[2] Tennyson features Simeon in a dramatic monologue ("St. Sim-

---

1. Søren Kierkegaard, *Fear and Trembling / Repetition,* trans. and ed. Howard V. Hong and
Edna H. Hong (Princeton: Princeton University Press, 1983), 243. Recall from the first chapter
Johannes Climacus's commitment to "dance in the service of Thought."
2. See Carol Christ, *The Finer Optic: The Aesthetics of Particularity* (New Haven: Yale
University Press, 1975). The Simeons of Tennyson's, Hopkins's, and Kierkegaard's works provide exemplary instances of what Christ calls "obsessive particularity." Christ maps out the way
in which this Victorian tradition of obsessive particularity evolved out of the Romantic change
in emphasis "from the object portrayed to the mind in the process of perception" (11). Christ

eon Stylites") that Hopkins calls "magnificent," and to which he probably alludes in his own dramatic monologue, "Pilate."[3] Simeon and his imitators, called Stylites (from *stulos,* Greek for pillar), emblematize the principle of asceticism as an interesting aesthetic problem. We see something of this, the ascetic as aesthetic emblem (an early instance of what we now know as performance art), in a Hopkins drawing. In a letter to his friend Baillie, he draws a picture of a Simeon-like figure entitled "Simeon the Stileite" in the crudely penned style of a political cartoon, rife with allegorical items. The drawing depicts an emaciated man with a halo, with one hand holding a newspaper featuring himself, and the other taking some food from a basket raised by a pulley system. The pillar, surrounded by twinkling stars, reaches the heavens. The skeleton-like thinness of the man notwithstanding, Hopkins satirizes the story of Simeon by achieving in his sketch a bizarre sense of drawing-room comfort, the burgher in his armchair, newspaper and food to keep him complacent. So too does Tennyson remark upon the vexatious self-promotion of extreme asceticism in his monologue ("Who may be a saint if I fail here?" asks his Simeon), and so, no doubt, would Kierkegaard if he had actually used a Simeon figure for his pseudonym in *Fear and Trembling,* a work that thrives on the tension between humility and egotism.

In short, Simeon the Stylite calls attention to himself atop his pillar as surely as Oscar Wilde does in his stroll down the street with lily in hand. The humility implicit in self-punishment ("Altho' I be the basest of mankind . . ." begins Tennyson's Simeon) starts to resemble arrogance, and the isolation he imposes on himself—the height of the pillar—only places him more easily in view of a greater number of people. The private act of self-mortification becomes the public act of self-

focuses on Hopkins, Tennyson, and Browning to chart how post-Romantic nineteenth-century poetry both reflects and struggles with the metamorphosis, for example, of Keats's enabling "negative capability" into "infinite possibilities of isolation" (12). She concerns herself with the reflections of isolation in the three poets' works and the sustained attempt by their poetry to transcend that hallmark of an isolated state, an obsessive focus on the particular.

3. Gerard Manley Hopkins, *Further Letters of Gerard Manley Hopkins, Including His Correspondence with Coventry Patmore,* 2d ed., ed. Claude Colleer Abbott (London: Oxford University Press, 1956), 8. Hopkins's drawing of "Simeon the Stileite" is on page 210. Gerard Manley Hopkins, *Gerard Manley Hopkins,* ed. Catherine Phillips (New York: Oxford University Press, 1986), 309. Phillips notes: "G.M.H. may have been influenced by Tennyson's 'St. Simeon Stylites,' which he greatly admired . . . both in choosing to write the poem as a dramatic monologue and for the descriptions of Pilate's sufferings. The imagery suggests that he also had *Prometheus Bound* in mind."

promotion. If by virtue of the distance between him and the ground, he cannot participate in normal discourse, Simeon feels quite at ease (armchair ease) discoursing with the heavens, as Hopkins's twinkling stars suggest.[4] As Tennyson and Hopkins portray him, Simeon is a caricature of what I call hyperbolic self-effacement; his self-denial, his exaggerated attempt to deny the physical self, turns him into a spectacle as he proclaims his presence by imitating absence in the act of physical, but visible, isolation. By installing himself atop his pillar, he creates a unique space for the very self he ostensibly wants to efface in the name of devotion to God.[5]

Tennyson lambasts and Hopkins lampoons a sensibility that, at its most ludicrous extreme, surely invites such treatment. But that same sensibility, in its more moderate and infinitely more poignant form is the sensibility that plagues Hopkins as poet and priest. Similarly, Rossetti's work incites questions about how a woman with a strong artistic drive can genuinely believe in a religion that systematically subdues its followers, especially its female followers, into humble passivity. Hopkins and Rossetti share this dilemma as artists, I argue, as well as a consequent literary strategy in the exploitation of this dilemma as theme and structure in the art itself: in other words, what we have is the artist's dilemma as art. In its formal structure and the substance that structure wants to capture, Kierkegaard's *Fear and Trembling* provides a metatext for this symbiotic pairing.

Simon Stylita's successor to the authorship of *Fear and Trembling,* Johannes de Silentio, also inherits a Simeon-figure's propensity for hyperbolic self-effacement in his appellative pun, because a claim of silence by an author reiterates aurally Simeon's slyly visible gesture of isolation. *Fear and Trembling* is a multigeneric meditation on Abraham, but the business and the *busyness* of the text only partly obscure Johannes's attempt to make a space for himself and to create a forum in which he can speak. But his is a subtler case than Hopkins's and Tennyson's Simeons' (as would have been Simon Stylita if he had "authored" *Fear and Trembling*), because in spite of his text's obscuring function, his overt desire to understand Abraham is not merely a smokescreen for an ulterior, self-focused motive. If a subtly drawn Simeon figure would have

4. Hopkins's Simeon, a middle-class grotesque, revises Tennyson's, who is, as W. David Shaw says, "... a humorless fanatic, always teetering on the edge of absurdity" (W. David Shaw, *Tennyson's Style* [Ithaca: Cornell University Press, 1976], 103).

5. *The Penguin Dictionary of Saints* describes Simeon as increasingly courted by all, including princes, for advice and comfort, over the course of his time on the pillar. In the meantime, the pillar got higher and higher.

inscribed in itself a fight between isolation and obscurity on one side, and an audience and renown on the other, the name Johannes de Silentio also inscribes in itself an unresolvable contradiction, a silent author. These two inscriptions are ultimately interchangeable: isolation and obscurity are courted by the steadfastly silent, audience and renown, by the author. But "Johannes de Silentio" succeeds in a way "Simon Stylita" probably would not have in performing as an introductory marker, an attention-getter, to what becomes the sustained difficulty throughout the text: articulating Abraham. (I use "articulate" in both its most literal sense—identifying and uniting distinct parts—and its ordinary sense of rendering verbally.) One of the first things Johannes must face in his study of Abraham is that Abraham was a non-poet and therefore a non-recorder of his own life: "There is no dirge by Abraham" (*Fear And Trembling,* 17). Furthermore, as Johannes creates his text he always must be in contention with his own name, since, unlike Abraham, he cannot be silent; in fact, this inability exemplifies the dilemma in which Johannes finds himself as an author.

In *Fear and Trembling,* an author attempts to give voice to a subject who is by that author's definition voiceless; even the attempt, therefore, is at best a compromise, and guarantees failure. On the other hand, the obscured but ever-present agenda of authorial self-promotion and artistic display proceeds apace, making *Fear and Trembling* a text in profound conflict with itself. Though this claim of conflict sounds deconstructive, it must be remembered that in *Fear and Trembling* the conflict occurs on the surface, on the text's most literal level, for Johannes is himself a fiction. Kierkegaard's *Fear and Trembling* offers the relationship between Johannes and Abraham as a paradigm for an investigation of the problems inherent in a text's relationship between its "I" and its ostensible subject, when that subject escapes, by its very definition as the "I" understands it, artistic capture.[6]

Fear and Trembling may be one of the most sustained exercises, along with *Either/Or,* in Kierkegaardian "indirect communication." Its epigraph, a quote from Hamann, signals as much: "What Tarquinius Superbus said in the garden by means of the poppies, the son understood but the messenger did not" (3). It confines itself to no one method of discourse, a primary strategy of indirection. Johannes de Silentio introduces himself in the Preface, where he speaks in the third person about the "present author."

6. By using a pseudonym Kierkegaard thrusts the whole paradigm one remove from himself. As the "real" author, therefore, he establishes that same fraught relationship with Johannes-understanding-Abraham, *his* subject.

The next two sections, a four-part Exordium (four attempts to retell the biblical story of Abraham on his way to Mount Moriah) and a Eulogy on Abraham, also refer in the third person to the author of what follows. They provide no clue whether we should distinguish Johannes from "the present author," and though most commentary and criticism on the text refer to the "I" in the text as Johannes, to do so automatically misses the point of such confusion. The last and longest section, called Problemata, consists of a Preliminary Expectoration, and Problemata I, II, and III. These parts of the Problemata do have first-person voices, but the three Problematas-proper begin almost identically: "The ethical as such is the universal. . . . The ethical is the universal. . . . The ethical as such is the universal."[7] I, II, and III can be construed just as easily as alternatives to one another as consequent upon one another, putting into question the continuity of the first-person voice. And it is this putting into question of voice, what I will soon be calling a dialectical-lyric voice, that *Fear and Trembling* accomplishes in its ironic attempt to give voice to the adamantly voiceless Abraham.

Any description of *Fear and Trembling* must first attend to its title page where, in addition to its pseudonymous author's identity, the subtitle "Dialectical Lyric" appears.[8] From the beginning, then, the text plays with the notion of impossibility; one would think that a work cannot be dialectical (two-directional and extensive) and lyrical (one-directional and intensive) at the same time.[9] Johannes plays with the implications of his subtitle throughout the work. In the Preface he describes "the present author": "The present author is by no means a philosopher." In the same paragraph he repeats that negative characterization exactly (*Fear and Trembling,* 7).[10] In the first section, the "Exordium," he introduces

7. The repetition at the beginning of each Problemata resembles the poetic strategy of anaphora, making them like the verses of a long lyric. Later in the chapter I discuss Rossetti's "Thread of Life," a series of palinodic revisions; the same relationship very possibly exists between the three Problemata. Given Kierkegaard's pervasive use of Plato in many of his works, and since Plato depends on the palinode for the progression of speeches in *Phaedrus,* exploring the strategy of the palinode could yield further insight into the elusive *Fear and Trembling.*

8. See page 236 of the Hongs' edition of *Fear and Trembling* for a facsimile of the original Danish title page.

9. See Tillottama Rajan's "Romanticism and the Death of Lyric Consciousness," in *Lyric Poetry: Beyond New Criticism,* ed. Chaviva Hosek and Patricia Parker (Ithaca: Cornell University Press, 1985), for a useful discussion of the "intertextualization of the single lyric with other forms of discourse" (198). Romantic lyric expression, to which *Fear and Trembling* is indebted, is lyric "made interdiscursive," a process very much like what happens throughout *Fear and Trembling.*

10. Chapters 4 and 5 deal with the concept of repetition and with Kierkegaard's *Repetition.* Since *Repetition* deliberately echoes previous Kierkegaard texts and also comments on them, the discussions of it also serve as further discussions of *Fear and Trembling.*

a fiction: "Once upon a time there was a man who as a child had heard that beautiful story of how God tempted (*fristede*) Abraham and of how Abraham withstood the temptation (*Fristelsen*), kept the faith, and, contrary to expectation, got a son a second time" (9). This man, who may or may not be the first-person voice in the later sections of the book, "was not a thinker . . . was not an exegetical scholar" (9). In the last section of the book, however, a voice declares: "But here I stop; I am not a poet, and I go at things only dialectically" (90). Any reader of *Fear and Trembling* recognizes the not very subtle contradiction here, but there is a subtlety to recover, perhaps best explained analogically by an English grammatical commonplace: two negatives make a positive. A protestation in the language of modesty that the voice in a text described as a "dialectical lyric" is neither dialectician nor poet is belied by the existence of the text itself. The impossible "dialectical lyric" exists, because *Fear and Trembling* exists, and its existence in turn posits the existence of an authorial voice that promotes itself as both dialectician and poet. The book claims to be an impossibility, but refutes that claim by existing to make it. That this assertion of an impossibility takes the form of presenting what amounts to a new literary genre matters greatly in understanding *Fear and Trembling*, and in seeing the artistic dilemma in trying to render a recalcitrant subject. Johannes suggests in the Exordium that the "man" obsessed with Abraham has a single-minded goal that has no artistic component: ". . . for what occupied him was not the beautiful tapestry of imagination but the shudder of the idea" (9). But what comes to occupy the text, of course, is precisely the business of weaving "a beautiful tapestry of imagination," because "the shudder of the idea," immediate and inchoate, cannot be sustained by its dialectical-lyric voice.

Fear and Trembling brings to bear the indeterminacy of voice and the proposal of an impossible structure on the text's "subject," Abraham's willingness to sacrifice Isaac. First and foremost, *Fear and Trembling* restores the "full terror" of meaning to the story of a man willing to kill his son, for in its fame the story had become naturalized into the banal stuff of sermons. "There were countless generations who knew the story of Abraham by heart," says the voice in the Preliminary Expectoration, "and word for word, but how many did it render sleepless?" (28). It imagines one of the sleepless, upon hearing the story in church, going out and murdering his son in a fatal misinterpretation of the story (like Pilate, the man imitates the good only to commit the gravest of sins). His minister responds to the act with self-righteous apoplexy, but this tale, as well as the four attempts to retell the Biblical story, recovers the story's complexity and uncovers its contradiction—what Abraham is willing to do is an act of faith, what the man does is murder. The Expectoration's speaker wants to place himself in the company of the sleepless, against the minister: "As for me, I do not lack the courage to think a complete thought" (30). One must recognize Abraham's act as premeditated murder if one does not have faith: "It is only by faith that one achieves any resemblance to Abraham, not by murder" (30). This is merely a reasonable response, however, to the misguided man; it is one the minister could have made. Furthermore, what Abraham is willing to do, he does not in the end need to do, and Isaac is saved. To do something called restoring the "full terror" of meaning requires understanding, the most elusive of conditions in *Fear and Trembling*. From its speaker's boast, the Expectoration plunges into a litany of "I's": "I" am "paralyzed," "I sink down," "I have seen the terrifying face to face." The speaker then says simply, "Abraham I cannot understand; in a certain sense I can learn nothing from him except to be amazed" (37), and presents the first in a series of categorical distinctions that populate the text.

Drawing categorical distinctions (the knight of infinite resignation vs. the knight of faith) and recasting Greek myth, fairy tale, Bible story, and accounts of intellectual heroism (Agamemnon, Agnes and the Merman, Sarah in the apocryphal Book of Tobit, and Socrates), the Problemata approach the Abraham story from every angle—the heroic, the demonic, the doomed—proving only that this time there is no route from point *A* to point *B,* straight or indirect; in other words, a paradox, Abraham's simultaneous faith and fear, cannot be undone into its parts. The silent Abraham (point *A*) with which *Fear and Trembling* begins still dominates the last section of the text (point *B*):

> Speak he cannot; he speaks no human language. And even if he understood all the languages of the world, even if those he loved also understood them, he still could not speak—he speaks in divine language, he speaks in tongues. (114)

There *is* a way for Abraham to gain his voice, but it would cost him his uniqueness:

> At every moment, Abraham can stop; he can repent of the whole thing as a spiritual trial; then he can speak out, and everybody will be able to understand him—but then he is no longer Abraham. (115)

But finally and most revealingly, he is and is not voiceless. By not saying anything, he "speaks worlds":

> First and foremost, he does not say anything, and in that form he says what he has to say. His response to Isaac is in the form of irony, for it is always irony when I say something and still do not say anything. (118)[11]

This last quotation compresses the strategy employed throughout the text, whereby the speaker insinuates himself into an explanation of the unexplainable Abraham. They seem to meet on common ground here, ironists both, but by the end of the work the ground has become the agon on which the "I" pits itself against Abraham, wielding the mode of dialectical lyric as weapon. And if the silent Abraham seems an unlikely adversary, I suggest that this litany of silences sounds very much like another kind of hyperbolic self-effacement, the use of extraordinary taciturnity to draw and keep attention.

Abraham's uncooperative silence could be made no clearer than in Problemata, and yet one more effort, in Problemata II, to relay the import of this silence takes the form of an analogy whose own import will have significance again and again in this chapter: "Nor could Abraham explain further, for his life is like a book under divine confiscation and never becomes *publice juris* [public property]" (77). A version of Keats's unheard melodies and Rossetti's "silences" as "music of an unlike fashioning," this analogy participates in the Romantic conceit that the written text—Keats's "Ode on a Grecian Urn," Rossetti's "The Thread of Life," and now *Fear and Trembling*—is the "public property" available to an audience, but humble in its testimony to the greatness of an unavailable text, silent or unheard.[12] Kierkegaard's use of "confiscated," more-

---

11. Kierkegaard's dissertation and first publication is *The Concept of Irony* and any time he uses the term one must keep that work in mind. Socrates is the central figure in *The Concept of Irony*, and like Socrates (and Abraham), "Irony establishes nothing, for that which is to be established lies behind it. It is a divine madness which rages like a Tamberlane and leaves not one stone standing upon another in its wake" (*The Concept of Irony: With Constant Reference to Socrates*, trans. Lee M. Capel [London: Collins, 1965], 278). "Divine madness" is a direct reference to Plato's *Phaedrus* (see note 8).

12. See Mary Shelley's Introduction to *Frankenstein* for a paradigmatically Romantic articulation of the difference between the imagined and the written. She describes her early attempts at writing: "My dreams were at once more fantastic and agreeable than my writings. In the latter I was a close imitator—rather doing as others had done than putting down the suggestions of my own mind" (*Frankenstein: Or the Modern Prometheus* [New York: New American Library, 1983], vii).

over, adds a sense of taboo, a sense of a text as dangerous as eating from the Tree of Knowledge. The second epigraph to this chapter reveals that Johannes belongs to a tradition that long predates the Romantics. In *Phaedrus,* Plato describes the limitations of the poet in a work that nonetheless resuscitates the reputation of poetry in Plato's oeuvre: "Of that place beyond the heavens none of our earthly poets has yet sung, and none shall sing worthily."[13] None shall sing worthily, but many will sing nonetheless, and though unheard, silent, or confiscated, the song "beyond the heavens" ("under divine confiscation") is *detectable* by and therefore *in* its unworthy, yet available, material stand-ins. In the cases of Hopkins and Rossetti (and Kierkegaard), "beyond the heavens" still means Christian heaven, but by the nineteenth century "beyond the heavens" has become a trope for "beyond the self," an epistemological transformation to which the works of both poets attest. Geoffrey Hartman identifies the question that ensues from this transformation in an essay on Hopkins; his question applies just as aptly to Rossetti: "As a post-Romantic he identified poetry with the '[s]elfyeast of spirit,' and the question was whether poetry could authentically be anything more. Could one pass beyond the self to its other side?"[14] In the same essay, Hartman also describes the enormously difficult "place" from which both poets write their poetry: "He is always on this shadowy ground where personality, free will, and grace intertwine" (237).

Kierkegaard's analogy to a confiscated book reminds us that writers attempt to "pass beyond the self" by writing. This obvious statement reminds us that every written attempt to "pass beyond the self" results in a written text, available to, that is readable by an actively solicited audience. In *Hopkins, the Self, and God,* Walter Ong sees the intricate dynamic operating in Hopkins's poetry. His words also apply equally to Rossetti: "The deeper and deeper penetration of textuality into the psyche . . . has been a major factor in producing the modern solitary self who is also the avid interpersonal communicator."[15] Ong's "solitary self" materializes in

---

13. Plato, *Phaedrus,* trans. Reginald Hackforth (New York: The Liberal Arts Press, 1972), 78.

14. Geoffrey Hartman, "Hopkins Revisited," in his *Beyond Formalism: Literary Essays 1958–1970.* (New Haven: Yale University Press, 1970), 234. Also see George Eliot's *Middlemarch* (New York: Oxford University Press, 1990) for an answer, not to Hartman's question, but to the implications of the question. Dorothea is crying in Rome two months into her marriage, and the narrator tells us: "If we had a keen vision and feeling of all ordinary human life, it would be like hearing the grass grow and the squirrel's heart beat, and we should die of that roar which lies on the other side of silence. As it is, the quickest of us walk about well wadded with stupidity" (159).

15. Walter J. Ong, S.J., *Hopkins, the Self, and God* (Toronto: University of Toronto Press, 1986), 142.

Simeon, alone atop his pillar but making his point nonetheless, and in Johannes de Silentio, the impossibly silent author. In the poetry of Rossetti and Hopkins discussed in this chapter, the pathos of Hartman's question and Ong's contradictory assertion becomes stunningly clear. These poems, however, also assert their right not just to display helplessly a mire of "selfness" and self-referentiality, but to be recognized as discourses *on* the problems they face as written remains of a divinely confiscated text. The four poems discussed at length in this chapter have in common a first-person voice that shares with Simeon and Johannes the trait of hyperbolic self-effacement, whereby egotism and humility confront each other in a rigorous attempt at communication that engenders the consequent poem. The four poems have no identifiable persona, and therefore no identifiable gender. To avoid the confusion of author and lyric voice that would result from assigning gendered pronouns to the speaking "I," therefore, all references to that "I" will use the gender-neutral "it," or "itself." This strategy also insists that a speaking "I" in a poem (or in literature, including autobiography, and Kierkegaard's pseudonymous works) remains always a fiction and cannot be held to the same rules of "behavior" as can a "real" human voice.

Dorothy Margaret Stuart, an early biographer of Christina Rossetti, offers in her chapter on Rossetti's overtly devotional work some statistics that capture a quality about Rossetti's poetry that has eluded subsequent critics. "In [Rossetti's] devotions, as in all things," writes Stuart,

> she was introspective and—after her own peculiar fashion— egotistical. As Mr. Walter de la Mare has pointed out, "She asks, Am I saved? rather than, Are you?" The piety of her brother has preserved more than nine hundred of her English poems, and among them there are seventy-seven beginning with the pronoun "I," and only six with "we"; twenty beginning with "my," only seven with "our." It may be objected that most poets, especially lyrical poets, have an excusable affection for the first person singular. Yet the *Oxford Book of English Verse,* with its eight hundred and eighty-three poems, contains only fifty-four in which "I" is the initial word; Tennyson uses it only fourteen times as a jumping-off point, and Shakespeare in the *Sonnets* only twice. This is a prosaic and insensitive standard to apply, but it gives the measures of Christina's artless egotism.[16]

16. Dorothy Margaret Stuart, *Christina Rossetti* (London: Macmillan and Co., 1930), 140.

Prosaic and insensitive as Stuart's standard may be, it is instructive, and her coinage, "artless egotism," aptly renames the moderated version of hyperbolic self-effacement displayed in Rossetti's poetry. De la Mare identifies a strain of self-interest in her devotional poetry, a strong sample of which we saw in the last chapter, in "Have I Not Striven, My God?" Once one realizes that personal and religious humility is not the whole story of the artistic and religious ethos of Christina Rossetti—and if one is not yet convinced that the other part of the story is always repressed eroticism or female anger—then the " 'I's' have it," for they never fail to catch the eye, either by dominating the visual landscape of a poem through repetition, or by being foregrounded in a grammatical or rhetorical structure. This second strategy is a Rossetti signature, found throughout her hundreds of poems. The loose antimetabole of the love poem "Remember" ("Nor I half turn to go yet turning stay") pulls the "I" through both clauses of the line. Sonnet 8 of "Monna Innominata" quotes Esther, self-sacrificing queen of the Jews: "I, if I perish, perish"; the grammar emphasizes the "I's" strength of action and informs self-immolation with personal will. And in an earlier poem, "A Royal Princess," the identical structure provides the Princess with ego even as she prepares to sacrifice herself: "I, if I perish, perish; they today shall eat and live; / I, if I perish, perish; that's the goal I half conceive . . . ," and finally in the last line: "I, if I perish, perish; in the name of God I go." In "An 'Immurata' Sister" (a cloistered sister), the forceful oddity of a parenthetical (cloistering) remark turns the parentheses into marks of accentuation: "(for I'm a woman, I)." The compression of parallelism and anadiplosis in the "Thy Will I will, I Thy desire desire" of "A Martyr" also compresses to nothing at least the grammatical distance between the "I" and the "Thy"; the line flirts with the Hypostatic Union, joining God and woman, here a double heresy, preempting both man and Christ as the proper mortal half of that Union. Once again, "A Martyr" provides enlightening commentary, for this flirtation evolves into a more serious relationship in the discussion of both poets, beginning with Rossetti's "The Thread of Life," which for now offers one last example of first-person declamation: "But what I was I am, I am even I."

    In all of these examples, either self-effacement or self-sacrifice is literally brought to the page by means of self-assertion. The "I" marks a place for itself on behalf of speakers who seem at first glance to be paradigms of religious and feminine humility. At first glance, and also at second: isolating these particular lines and arranging them together to compose virtually a mantra of the first-person subject pronoun accentuates the self-assertion and subordinates the humility in a useful distortion of the

individual poems. Kathleen Blake argues persuasively that femaleness
and the traditional traits associated with it rehearse tropologically the
paradigmatic Christian, and that attempts to find suppressed eroticism
can be misguided efforts to rescue for a feminist agenda the works of a
poet like Rossetti. She makes an observation critical for my own argument: "I have found that most historians of the nineteenth-century
women's movement deny or denigrate a feminist ascetic trend."[17] What
asceticism means, however, as displayed in art, or as it *displays itself as
art,* she leaves unattended, depending on prior or conventional assump-
tions about the ascetic personality or, in art, the ascetic persona. But an
aesthetic based on asceticism, the event of a keenly perceiving self in the
act of austere "self-curtailment," or equally, the event of the austerely
curtailed self in the act of keen perception, allows the impossible "I, if I
perish, perish" to stand as a rigorously performative utterance, even if its
performance is perishing.[18] (Kierkegaard understands the power of an
aesthetics of asceticism. In *Stages on Life's Way,* the epigraph to
"Quidem's Diary" is "I had perished had I not perished.")[19] More sophisticated avatars of the crude Simeon, the speakers in these poems do know
their places, and take them rightfully, though within the context of, and
therefore in inevitable conflict with, conventional models of humility.

   In an analysis of Rossetti as a poet looking for—and failing to find—
her rightful place in the poetic tradition, Dorothy Mermin banishes
Rossetti (as well as Elizabeth Barrett Browning) from the realm of strong
poetry, describing her failure as "the retreat into feminine submissive-
ness and self-repression represented by Rossetti's devotional poetry."[20]

   17. Kathleen Blake, *Love and the Woman Question in Victorian Literature: The Art of Self-
Postponement* (Totowa, N.J.: Barnes and Noble, 1983), xiv.
   18. I borrow "self-curtailment" as a major factor in an aesthetics of asceticism from Harold
Bloom's introduction to *The Selected Writings of Walter Pater* (New York: Columbia University
Press, 1974), xvii. In more traditional models of asceticism, a keenly perceiving self—a self
vulnerable to things of the senses—is antithetical to the austerely curtailed self, unindulgent of
such things. I use the term "performative" to describe "I, if I perish, perish" in the strict sense J.
L. Austin meant. Esther makes the pronouncement effectively, and her words are acts, like
marriage vows or promises (both relevant examples for her situation). See J. L. Austin, *How to
Do Things with Words* (Cambridge: Harvard University Press, 1975), lecture 1. For a treatment
of the linguistic and philosophical problem of the specific speech act of promising, see Shoshana Felman, *The Literary Speech Act: Don Juan with J. L. Austin, or Seduction in Two
Languages,* trans. Catherine Porter (Ithaca: Cornell University Press, 1983).
   19. Søren Kierkegaard, *Stages on Life's Way,* trans. Walter Lowrie (Princeton: Princeton
University Press, 1940), 187: "Periisem nisi periissem."
   20. Dorothy Mermin, "The Damsel, the Knight, and the Victorian Woman Poet," *Critical
Inquiry* 13 (Autumn 1986): 80. Mermin also claims that "religious poetry reinforced impulses
toward self-effacement" (74–75). I question precisely this assumption about religious poetry.
The poem I quote Mermin quoting is "The Dead City" (see *Complete Poems,* III, 63).

Mermin misrepresents Rossetti's work, which from the start included devotional poetry and was no retreat but a long-term interest. On the other hand, her discussion of "place" as that which the Victorian female poet could not properly establish is helpful: "The Victorian woman poet has to be two things at once, or in two places, whenever she tries to locate herself within the poetic world" (67). But Rossetti's poetry (including the line from a very early poem Mermin herself cites, "What was I that I should see / So much hidden mystery") initiates not a retreat from but a sustained discourse on this very problem of a place from which to speak. Mermin's "Two things at once" is apt, for as I have said, my litany of Rossetti lines tells only part of the story of each poem. Before looking closely at the voice, structure, and subject of two poems, I offer as an analogy to these strands from the "beautiful tapestry" of Rossetti's dualistic imagination two biographical commentaries. In his Memoir, William Rossetti says of his sister: "In Christina's character there was great dignity tempered—or rather indeed reinforced—by modesty."[21] Modesty is a leitmotif in any discussion of either Rossetti or Hopkins. But Simeon-like *im*modesty manifests itself in odd places. In her essay "I am Christina Rossetti," Virginia Woolf extracts from available biographical data (including attention to Rossetti's modesty and shyness) the event of a tea party where from among the sedate tea-drinkers comes forward a woman who says simply, "I am Christina Rossetti," and then sits down.[22]

Woolf entitles and concludes her essay with this line. The modesty of William's sister, enforced and reinforced throughout her life, is itself tempered—or given a temper—by Woolf's Rossetti. In apostrophic homage to Rossetti the poet, Woolf speaks also to lyrical complexity: "Yet for all its symmetry, yours was a complex song" (219).

The two Rossetti poems, "The Thread of Life" and "An Old-World Thicket," follow one another in the edition of Rossetti's poetry called *A Pageant and Other Poems* (1881). Like most of her poetry written after the 1860s, neither poem has a date of composition. How Rossetti arranged her poems in the editions in which they appeared, therefore, provides the most reliable index to her sense of her own work, for she carefully combined secular and religious poems and gathered together

---

21. Christina Rossetti, *The Poetical Works of Christina Rossetti, with Memoir and Notes by William Michael Rossetti* (London: Macmillan and Co., 1914), lxvi.

22. Virginia Woolf, "I am Christina Rossetti," in her *Second Common Reader* (London: Harcourt Brace Jovanovich, 1960), 217. She discovered the incident in Mary F. Sandars's biography, *The Life of Christina Rossetti* (London: Hutchinson, 1930). Both Woolf's essay and Sandars's book were written during the year of Rossetti's centenary.

poems whose composition probably spans two decades.[23] Extant letters indicate that she wielded artistic control over her editions (often in spite of her well-meaning brothers). The following excerpt from a letter to her editor refers to *A Pageant and Other Poems:* "I computed its [*A Pageant and Other Poems*'] prospects by a minute comparison with the pretty old "Goblin Market" edition, and on this basis judged it sufficient for a volume. At any rate I may count (may I not?) on no 2 poems sharing pages or part-pages, and on all sets of sonnets being treated as so many separate sonnets."[24] Poems overtly devotional in title and content follow "The Thread of Life" and "An Old-World Thicket," although they sing a no less "complex song" for being so. "The Thread of Life," a three-sonnet series, and "An Old-World Thicket," a 180-line lyric narrative, straddle the division between secular and devotional by having as their subject the issue of religious salvation. At the same time they feature personae who are profoundly worried about that subject. The first two sonnets in "The Thread of Life" ostensibly pit their speakers against themselves as their own adversaries. The third sonnet then seems to resolve these previous tensions, and the speaking self emerges victorious, that is, saved. A saved self, however, causes a problem for the very theory of Christian salvation it means to prove.

The first sonnet starts by revoking for its speaker the "pathetic fallacy," what Ruskin calls the "falseness in all our impressions of external things," produced by violent feelings such as those manifest here; any comfort derived from believing that nature responds to human needs is denied the speaker:[25] "The irresponsive silence of the land, / The irresponsive

---

23. See Delores Rosenblum, *Christina Rossetti: The Poetry of Endurance* (Carbondale: Southern Illinois University Press, 1986):

> This collection is notable for the inclusion of the two sonnet sequences, "Monna Innominata" (as previously noted, written during the sixties) and "Later Life," which can be dated only as B[efore] 1882. Out of fifty-nine poems, about twenty-two, including "Later Life" as one entry, are specifically "devotional," demonstrating that Rossetti was concerned to keep the same proportion [between secular and religious poetry] as the previous volumes. Out of the total, only one, "Italia, Io Ti Saluto," is dated from before the seventies, and the rest are dated B. 1882, for the most part, which tells us only that they were written after 1866. (57–58)

24. Lona Mosk Packer, ed., *The Rossetti-Macmillan Letters* (Berkeley and Los Angeles: University of California Press, 1963), 137.

25. John Ruskin, "The Pathetic Fallacy," in *The Literary Criticism of John Ruskin,* ed. Harold Bloom (Gloucester, Mass.: Peter Smith, 1969), 63. Rossetti read Ruskin, of course, given his importance in the career of her brother. In a letter to her sister-in-law she expresses her ambivalence about him: "I am not fretting over the Ruskiniana [most probably a reference to his criticism of her poetry], though at the moment I plead guilty to having felt annoyed. Yet my resumed philosophic calm is not based on a contempt for the writer, as I cannot help admiring much of his work" (William Michael Rossetti, ed., *The Family Letters of Christina Georgina Rossetti* [New York: Charles Scribner's Sons, 1908], 137–38).

sounding of the sea, / Speak both one message of one sense to me:— / Aloof, aloof, we stand aloof..."[26] Ruskin, we must remember, does not condemn the use of "pathetic fallacy," but insists that a "spirit of truth" accompany it. The object in nature, first, must remain itself, "how many soever the associations... that crowd around it" (*Literary Criticism,* 66). Second, the poetic liberties taken with it must be warranted by the "violent feelings" expressed through it. Though Rossetti's poetry did not gain Ruskin's approval, her poem nonetheless meets his criteria for an appropriate fallacy, as it turns a Ruskinian pathetic fallacy into a poetic revocation (different from a rejection of the fallacy itself).

Introduced by this revocation, each of the three sonnets shows symptoms of claustrophobia and acute solipsism. The second sonnet starts, "Thus am I mine own prison... ," the third with "Therefore myself is that one only thing..."; nonetheless, taken together, they build to the crescendo of salvation as the last sonnet has God bid the speaker "sing": "O death, where is thy sting? / And sing: O grave, where is thy victory?" Try to take them apart, however, and the sinew of the connecting thread turns out to be the two adverbial conjunctions "thus" and "therefore." What is conjoined, the wily "I," taxes these conjunctions to the fullest extent of their grammatical power. The thread of "The Thread of Life" may seem to fray under its burden as it tries to weave coherence into its three parts, but only if one expects the continuity and progression of one thread weaving together the three parts. The series, however, consists of three competing "threads of life," and logical movement proceeds not through progression but retraction. In the "Thread of Life" we revisit the territory of de Silentio, where voice is indeterminate, and the subject resists capture by evading available means of perceiving it. Like the Exordium's four attempts to tell Abraham's story, like the Problemata's multi-angled desire to do the same, "The Thread of Life" plays out three possible ways to render the "shudder" of an idea. The Abraham of "The Thread of Life" is a redeemable self, able to sing the song that God bids in the face of overwhelming isolation. This comparison to Abraham acts also as a caveat if we consider a singer as a type of poet, and remember that for de Silentio Abraham is the non-poet ("There is no dirge by Abraham").

Why characterize the "I" of "The Thread of Life" as wily, when it never disappears from the poem, and when it seems to move from past to present to future in orderly sequence from sonnet to sonnet? If we remember the inefficacy of progress in *Fear and Trembling,* however,

---

26. Christina Rossetti, *The Complete Poems of Christina Rossetti: A Variorum Edition,* 3 vols., ed. R. W. Crump (Baton Rouge: Louisiana State University Press, 1979–90), II, 122.

the trick "point *B*" plays on the text by being indistinguishable from "point *A*," the narrating "I" can be used as a model of fiction that plays with an irresolvable problem. "No one in his right mind," writes Paul de Man, "will try to grow grapes by the luminosity of the word 'day,' but it is very difficult not to conceive the pattern of one's past and future existence as in accordance with temporal and spatial schemes that belong to fictional narratives and not to the world."[27] It is difficult, but for the fictional narrative itself not impossible, to query this very perception by positing the inscrutable and then spinning itself out, like so many threads in a tapestry, to an "end" (point *B*) no further along than its "beginning" (point *A*). The first sonnet, then, begins with a poetic attempt that engenders two palinodic revisions; one sonnet succeeds coherently to the other only in a pattern of retraction, a relationship of try and try again, one after the other. In a palinode a poet retracts the import of one of his or her previous poems. In the most famous palinode, Stesichorus retracts the "scandal" he has spread about Helen of Troy; his retraction is serious business, because he has been struck blind by his first story, and only by retraction will he regain his sight. Invoking Stesichorus's form emphasizes the serious nature of the pattern of retraction in "The Thread of Life."

The "irresponsiveness" of the first sonnet's land and sea, of course, immediately undergoes interpretation as a response, a "message" of aloofness, and the speaker takes that meaning of aloofness as meant for itself: "Thou too aloof bound with the flawless band / Of inner solitude; we bind not thee; / But who from thy self-chain shall set thee free?" The "self-chain" binding the speaker belongs to a category of utterance that includes Blake's "mind-forged manacles," Tennyson's "abysmal deeps of personality," Pater's "thick wall of personality," and, of course, Hopkins's famous "taste of myself." The "I" in the sonnet tries to modify its self: "And I am sometimes proud and sometimes meek, / And sometimes I remember days of old." But the modifications are tentative (proud or meek?) and unreliable (sometimes). The speaker is left not with the memory of fellowship, relationships of affinity, or the *sharing* of common modifiers, but only of the time "[w]hen fellowship seemed not so far to seek . . ." Perhaps fellowship lies as near as the next sonnet, but without a firm commitment to what the "I" is in the first sonnet, the second sonnet's beginning, "Thus am I mine own prison . . ." may or may not be a new voice, bound by its own "self-chain." This (perhaps new)

27. Paul de Man, *Resistance to Theory,* Theory and History of Literature, vol. 33 (Minneapolis: University of Minnesota Press, 1986), 11.

"I" revokes the revocation of the pathetic fallacy, and anthropomorphizes nature into a "merrymaking crew":

> . . . Everything
> Around me free and sunny and at ease:
> Or if in shadow, in a shade of trees
> Which the sun kisses, where the gay birds sing
> And where all wind makes various murmuring;
> Where bees are found, with honey for the bees;
> Where sounds are like music, and where silences
> Are music of an unlike fashioning.
>
> (1–8)

Again the speaker tries to give itself attributes, now by insinuating itself into this pleasing scene: "Then gaze I at the merrymaking crew, / And smile a moment and a moment sigh / Thinking: Why can I not rejoice with you?" As characteristics, alternating moments of smiling and sighing are as unstable as "sometimes proud and sometimes meek"; the speaker recognizes this, and then retracts even acquisitions of memory as the signature of an identifiable self: "I am not what I have nor what I do; / But what I was I am, I am even I." Within the context of its poem, this line, quoted earlier, tells the other part of its story, the danger of tautology; upon failing to modify itself, the "I" extends itself simply by reiterating its own isolated state. The revocation and retraction in "The Thread of Life" at the end of its second part achieve their effect through *askesis*, the stunning austerity of "But what I was I am, I am even I." The chant-like extension of "I," however, imitates godliness, as it rehearses God's identification of Himself to Moses in Exodus: "And God said unto Moses, I AM THAT I AM" (3:14).[28] *Askesis*, here radical renunciation of self-attributes (self-perishing), performs as the powerful positioning of self, not vis-à-vis the material world, but in imitative relation to God. Such positioning poses enormous problems in its near-blasphemy and must be undone: thus a third try at rendering the redeemable self.

If Hopkins's Pilate figured the danger of misguided imitation of Christ, the figure of Simeon in this chapter caricatures the problem inherent in extreme asceticism. William Rossetti cites Thomas à Kempis's *Imitatio*

---

28. Coleridge's distinction between primary and secondary imagination also resonates in this line. He says: "The primary imagination I hold to be the living Power and prime Agent of all human Perception, and as a repetition in the finite mind of the eternal act of creation in the infinite I Am" (*The Portable Coleridge*, ed. I. A. Richards [New York: The Viking Press, 1978], 516). Rossetti's line goes further; it contains no admission of finitude or limited imitation.

Christi in his list of his sister's reading material (*Poetical Works,* lxix),
and as Jerome McGann notes, her poetry abounds in a "network of
references to more recondite spiritual works like the *Imitatio Christi.*"[29]
The term "vanities" in the title of the *Imitatio*'s book 1, "Of the Imitation
of Christ and Contempt of all the Vanities of The World," pervades Rossetti's poems as thoroughly as the words "modesty and shyness" pervade
biographies of her.[30] In book 3, an ongoing dialogue between Christ and
disciple, one of the "Four Things That Bring Peace" is to "seek the lowest
place, and be submissive to all" (*Imitation of Christ,* 156). The poem
William Rossetti thought characteristic enough to engrave on Rossetti's
tombstone is called "The Lowest Place," and closely follows this formula
for acquiring peace (*Complete Poems,* I, 187).

The chief message of the *Imitation* is boldly stated and often repeated: "If we were perfectly dead to self and not embroiled in the evil
which is in ourselves, then we should be able to taste of divine things
and to have experience of heavenly contemplation" (46). And again:
"But as yet many things trouble and displease thee; for thou art not yet
perfectly dead to self, nor art thou wholly separated from worldly
things" (85). And once again, in the last chapter of the first book: "When
a man attaineth to that estate in which he no longer seeketh the consolation of any created thing, then only doth he begin more perfectly to
know God" (79).

Death to self and disavowal of the material world: such are the means
to knowing God promoted since at least the time of St. Augustine, another religious writer read by Rossetti; but the *Imitatio Christi,* like
spiritual guides in general, problematically purveys those means. A
glance at some of its chapter subheadings tells of that problem:
"Thoughts Pertaining to the Inward Life"; "Of the Proper Consideration
of Oneself"; "On Inward Consolation"; even, early in the work, "Of Having a Humble Opinion of Oneself." In order to follow the "Christian
Pattern" (also the name of an eighteenth-century version of the
Imitatio), one must focus inwardly in a sustained meditation on one's
self. This strategy creates a double-bind, apparent already in Augustine's
ironically self-promoting *Confessions* and in the autobiographical urge

29. Jerome McGann, "Christina Rossetti's Poems: A New Edition and a Revaluation," *Victorian Studies* 23 (Winter 1980): 237–54. McGann mentions that the *Imitatio* was "a book that
enjoyed enormous popularity in the period, for reasons which have never been explored" (240).
30. Thomas à Kempis, *The Imitation of Christ,* trans. George F. Maine (London: William
Collins, 1957). Also important in the title to book 1 is the word "contempt." As I discussed in
Chapter 1, asceticism involves less the giving up of what one wants than giving up what one
holds in some contempt.

of Christian mystics (such as Theresa de Avila), and emblematized by St. Simeon.[31] It resembles the dilemma of the "man" in *Fear and Trembling,* taken with the "shudder of an idea," the idea of death-to-self in an instantaneous comprehension of Abraham. But he can give extension (in time and space) only to a particular subjective imagination (the tapestry). A nineteenth-century reader of the *Imitatio Christi* would find herself in this same bind by unfailingly finding her particular *self,* ineradicable in the consequent attempt to express the process by which one imitates Christ through self-annihilation. This experience, which increasingly becomes the norm (as Pater, for instance, helps begin a modern ethos of art by celebrating this experience), still distresses and puts stress on the poetry of Rossetti, and also of Hopkins. Both belong in the group Carol Christ describes when she writes, "The observation of minute particulars thus comes to signify both the solipsism the Victorians feared and their last attempt to discover a universal order in the world of things" (*The Finer Optic,* 13). "But what I was I am, I am even I" is untenable as a declaration of position, in danger on the one hand of being pure solipsism, of being blasphemy on the other. It declares, nonetheless, the knot in "The Thread of Life" at the end of its second sonnet. Undoing this knot by undoing the second sonnet falls to the third sonnet as its palinodic task.

The third sonnet of "The Thread of Life" immediately signals a shift in strategy by way of a grammatical modification. Where the subjective "I" dominates sonnets 1 and 2, the possessive "mine" (used archaically for "my") determines this sonnet's literal sense:

31. A small example from Augustine's *Confessions:* Immediately after describing his last and most profound conversion experience (remember his conversion was achieved in increments), Augustine tells how he decided to retire from teaching ("making use of my tongue in the talking-shop"). Addressing God, he says, "I had been bought by you and was not going to return again to put myself up for sale." The appropriate passivity of God's servant (God is the actor here, not Augustine the converter) is contained in the same sentence in which Augustine sees himself as a very precious commodity (*The Confessions of St. Augustine,* trans. Rex Warner [New York: New American Library, 1963], 185). In St. Teresa's autobiography, her self-consciousness as a *writer* demonstrates the difficulties of being purely self-effacing. In chapter 10 she first promotes her written record thus far: "I beseech him [her confessor] for the love of the Lord to publish what I have said up to this point about my wretched life." And then she asserts the authorial prerogative *not* to publish, or at least to remain anonymous: "As for what I say from here on, I do not give this permission, nor do I desire, if they should show it to someone, that they tell who it is who has experienced these things, or who has written this" (*The Collected Works of St. Teresa of Avila,* vol. 1, trans. Kiernan Kavanaugh, O.C.D., and Otilio Rodriguez, O.C.D. [Washington, D.C.: ICS Publications, 1976], 76–77). As autobiography, Teresa's work becomes the agon on which fight the passive servant of God and the author, whose self-involvement simply cannot be erased (or there would be no text).

> Therefore myself is that one only thing
>   I hold to use or waste, to keep or give;
> My sole possession every day I live,
> And still mine own despite Time's winnowing.
> Ever mine own, while moons and seasons bring
>   From crudeness ripeness mellow and sanative;
> Ever mine own, till Death shall ply his sieve;
> And still mine own, when saints break grave and sing.
>
> (1–8)

With this shift the sonnet begins its task of undoing, first of all because a possessive modifies by attribution, and gives adjectival extension to a subject or an object ("My sole possession every day I live"). The subject is the speaker's self, the star of the octave ("Therefore myself is that one only thing"). Finally, the elusive self, until now pursued unsuccessfully, yields to possession, ironically enabling the speaker in this sonnet to obey its Christian mandate to dispossess its self of itself: "And this myself as king unto my King / I give, to Him Who gave Himself for me . . ." God bids the speaker to sing "[a] sweet new song of His redeemed set free." God's bidding—His command—becomes an invitation as the speaker speaks the lyrics of this song, and concludes this third sonnet in full voice: "O death, where is thy sting? . . . O grave, where is thy victory?"

The flaw in this sonnet's revisionary attempt at resolution is the disingenuous division between "I" and "mine own," as if "I" could possess itself in the same way it can own a favorite book; but this flaw obscures the tenacious problem "The Thread of Life" still plays out in its third attempt. The octave carefully establishes the worth of "mine own," a self immutable even beyond death. God must be understood to recognize the kingly nature of the offering; thus his command is also an invitation that results in the last two lines of the poem. In this sonnet, to posit a redeemable self, capable of accepting God's invitation to sing the song of salvation from death, is to posit an immutable self, sharing one of God's unique qualities, and in doubtful need of salvation. One can refute this reading by accepting the self-division and attributing the song of salvation to the now worthy "I" who has done the possessing and dispossessing of "mine own," but such a rebuttal compounds the problem by eliciting the question, what is the nature of that "I" if it can own and give away the immutable? And with *that* question we find ourselves, and "The Thread of Life," in the theological domain of "First Causes," which is in fact what the poem's title has hinted from the start. Follow any thread toward an understanding and *articulation* of the mystery of "Life," even a religiously validated one (sonnet 3), and one arrives at the edge of expressibility, as each thread leads inexorably toward an indissoluble knot of selfhood, leaving unrecoverable by that articulation the "shudder" of the original idea, here the idea of an impossibly separate entity, a redeemed self.

This reading of "The Thread of Life" suggests that the answer to the question Hartman poses on behalf of Hopkins, (and I on behalf of Rossetti), "Could one pass beyond the self to its other side?" is no. The next poem, "An Old-World Thicket," appears to second that no resoundingly, but woven into the failed effort is a bravura display of poetic imagination. If Simeon, who over the years built his pillar higher and higher, risked perishing into the heavens or being struck down for his presumption like the tower of Babel, still, as I have said, he made his point. Rossetti's poetic discourse on the redeemable self might finally perish into inexpressibility, but it nonetheless claims its poetic authority. In "An Old-World Thicket" the speaking "I" effaces itself even more thoroughly, at the exact moment when the event of redemption takes place. Again we find the particularities of a self, deeply immured in its own acutely disturbed emotional state, desperate to interpret its suffering as the guarantee of its future salvation. That this interpretation seems to fail does not militate against, but rather testifies to the poem's effectiveness as a probe of that interpretative process.

"An Old-World Thicket" identifies as early as its epigraph the massy confusion characteristic of the "thicket" in its title. It borrows "una selva oscura" from Dante, signaling both the concern of the poem and a not altogether trustworthy clue to the "old world" in which it places itself: "Nel mezzo del cammin di nostra vita / mi ritrovai per una selva oscura / che la diritta via era smarrita."[32] The speaker negotiates a tortuous path through a natural setting that is both busy with life and responsive to the equally torturous process of self-inquiry the speaker undergoes. At the end of the path and the end of the process, nature presents itself harmoniously as an allegory of resurrection, replete with a "patriarchal ram" leading his flock "[s]till journeying toward the sunset and their rest."[33] The first two lines of "An Old-World Thicket" echo the opening of

32. The first two lines of *The Inferno:* "Midway in our life's journey, I went astray / from the straight road and woke to find myself alone in a dark wood" (*The Inferno,* trans. John Ciardi [New York: New American Library, 1954], 28).

33. Both Lona Mosk Packer and William Rossetti read the end of this poem as unproblematically redemptive. See her *Christina Rossetti* (Berkeley and Los Angeles: University of California Press, 1963), 322; and his *Poetical Works of Christina Rossetti,* 463.

Dante's *Inferno*—"Awake or sleeping (for I know not which) / I was or was not amazed within a wood"—but also distort that opening with their equivocations, "Awake or sleeping" and "I was or was not." The poem begins by promising only that what ensues may or may not have happened, presenting itself as both a Dantesque dream-vision and a self-conscious commentary on the efficacy of such a vision. In "An Old-World Thicket," allegory cannot sustain the import of anagogy with the authority of its medieval predecessor; the poem demonstrates its inability to fulfill its deictic function, pointing straight to a redeemed afterlife, in the midst of the "thicket" in which its speaker finds itself. *Fear and Trembling* offers a textual Virgil to the reader's journey through Rossetti's poem in its presentation of a chronically failing exegesis of an unexplainable text (Abraham's story), articulated by a questionably motivated exegete (the indeterminate speaker).

In Problemata II of *Fear and Trembling,* the speaker directly refers to a story from Luke (to which Johannes alludes in his preface [8]): "As we all know, Luke 14:26 offers a remarkable teaching on the absolute duty to God: 'If any one comes to me and does not hate his own father and mother and wife and children and brothers and sisters, yes, and even his own life, he cannot be my disciple' " (72). Exegetical scholars would qualify the harshness of this verse in order to make it more palatable by explanation through euphemistic synonyms for hate: "love less, esteem less, honor not, count as nothing" (72). But Luke 14:28 challenges such diminution of meaning: "For which of you, intending to build a tower, sitteth not down first, and counteth the cost, whether he have sufficient to finish it?" "The close proximity of this story and the verse quoted," claims the Problemata's speaker, "seems to indicate that the words are to be taken in their full terror in order that each person may examine himself to see if he can erect the building" (72). There is a way of understanding counter to the exegete's: "It is easy to see that if this passage is to have any meaning it must be understood literally" (73). How a loving God can demand such hatred does not allow itself to be rationally explained; it only keeps its full meaning as an undissected paradox, the contradictory parts of which must be comprehended simultaneously. In *Allegories of Reading,* over a hundred years later, Paul de Man suspects rhetorical language of doing what the Problemata's exegete does. In Yeats's "Among School Children," " 'How can we know the dancer from the dance?' " yields many figural readings but "here, the figural reading, which assumes the question to be rhetorical, is perhaps naive, whereas the literal reading leads to greater complication of theme and statement."[34] For de Man, an allegory is built out of the "structural interference of two distinct value systems" (206); in Luke, the vexatious demand for love and hate at the same time. Problemata II restores the full import of the most difficult aspects of religious faith, the *horror religiosa,* reminding us what a terrifying place the Dantean "selva oscura" must be for a believer.

The equivalent to the second Problemata's exegete in Problemata III is "aesthetics," "a courteous and sentimental branch of knowledge that knows more ways out than any pawnshop manager" (*Fear and Trembling,* 85). "Aesthetics" can depend upon coincidence to arrive at resolution—the happy ending against all odds, or the tragic one, the accumulation of unfortunate coincidences. It also rewards hiddenness (86), thereby enabling dramatic tension (coincidences abound but remain hidden) and endless possibilities for undisclosed but more palatable meaning. ("Hate" can mean "love less," etc., because one assumes interpretations proliferate behind the literal harshness of "hate." Abraham's intent to kill can be understood as something else.)

If one "goes through hell," suffers greatly in this world, one will achieve salvation, the reliable outcome of suffering in a system where God's plan makes sense through deductive logic (there is a God; therefore all things prove His existence). In other words, the other, "hidden" meaning of suffering is salvation, which mitigates the harshness of that suffering. This two-tiered definition of suffering characteristic of Christianity exists side by side with, and is helped along by, the exhortation to "be dead" to oneself, a futile exercise, as we have already seen in "The Thread of Life." "An Old-World Thicket" worries the meaning of suffering, tugs at it, toys with it, gnaws at it, to find for itself—in order to believe—its esoteric significance. Rossetti makes this extraordinarily difficult, moreover, by crowding the poem's surface with intertextual presences that either have made art out of the process of worrying (and worrying about) the same problem without resolution, or have thrown the whole process into question.

"An Old-World Thicket," then, announces its debt to Dante in its epigraph, but like the beginning of "The Ballad of Boding," an earlier poem in *A Pageant* . . . ("There are sleeping dreams and waking dreams; / What seems is not always as it seems" [*Complete Poems,* II, 79]), the first two lines of the poem proper question that debt by accentuating the state of uncertainty in which one has a dream vision, and consequently,

34. Paul de Man, *Allegories of Reading* (New Haven: Yale University Press, 1979), 11.

the unreliable nature of that vision. Coleridge resides as the genius of this place, the "woods" where the speaker may or may not be, not simply as the purveyor of dream-poems read by Rossetti: in his work can be found the extreme example of Romantic fragmentation, whereby a poem perishes and yet does not perish into its own state of incompleteness.[35] "An Old-World Thicket" is a finished poem; nonetheless, it incorporates fragmentation into its resolution.

After the second line of "An Old-World Thicket" the speaking "I" disappears for fifteen lines behind a two-stanza paean to nature governed by anaphora and totally visual images, and then emerges only weakly, as part of "we" and "our": "They seemed to speak more wisdom than we speak, / To make our music flat / And all our subtlest reasonings wild or weak" (18–20). After providing this visual tour of nature's beauty and energy, the "I" finally emerges completely enervated: "But I who saw such things as I have said, / Was overdone with utter weariness . . ." (36–37). The speaker identifies itself as the scene's center ("But I who saw such things"), even as it describes its own response to the fullness of nature as self-punishing *askesis:*

> Sweetness of beauty moved me to despair,
>   Stung me to anger by its mere content,
>   Made me all lonely on that way I went,
>   Piled care upon my care,
> Brimmed full my cup, and stripped me empty and bare:
>
> For all that was but showed what all was not
> But gave clear proof of what might never be;
>   Making more destitute my poverty,
>   And yet more blank my lot,
> And me much sadder by its jubilee.
>
>   (46–54)

The "I" shuts down its visual faculty ("And closed mine eyes: for wherefore see or hear?") but cannot block out sounds, having no "shutter to mine ear." And sounds assault that vulnerable ear, the sounds of weeping, sobbing, crying, clanging:

---

35. To identify Coleridge as a genius of this place, the "wood" in which the speaker may or may not be, is to do no more than has already been done by critics and biographers. See Packer, *Christina Rossetti,* 321–24; Stuart, *Christina Rossetti,* 107; and Rosenblum, *Christina Rossetti: The Poetry of Endurance,* 129.

Such universal sound of lamentation
I heard and felt, fain to feel or hear;
Nought else there seemed but anguish far and near;
Nought else but all creation
Moaning and groaning wrung by pain or fear,
Shuddering in the misery of its doom:
                                        (71–76)

Nature's first appearance in this poem bespeaks harmony; now, like the first and second groans of misery by nature in book 9 of *Paradise Lost,* this extended lamentation seems to implicate the human presence as its cause. Unlike the chronology in *Paradise Lost,* however, the overt act of rebellion does not precipitate, but follows nature's groans, as the stanza ends: "My heart then rose a rebel against light, / Scouring all earth and heaven and depth and height, / Ingathering wrath and gloom, / Ingathering wrath to wrath and night to night."

This rewritten reference to Milton provides a second identity for the *selva oscura,* now not only the Wood of Error, but also Eden after the Fall. Important for what follows, it signals a postlapsarian world from the perspective of the one who lapses.[36] For the next fifty-nine lines the speaker describes itself as experiencing virtually the entire repertoire of human suffering: powerlessness ("All impotent, all hateful, and all hate, / That kicks and breaks itself against the bolt / Of an imprisoning fate"); despair ("Why should I breathe whose breath was but a sigh?"); and acute awareness of mutability ("The pleasure I remember, it is past; / The pain I feel, is passing passing by") and mortality ("All things that cannot last / Have grown familiar, and are born to die"). But this microscopic examination of its self in radical misery does not inspire the speaker to long for its own death; being the mourner is difficult to bear but being the mourned is impossible to imagine: "Mourning grows natural to us who mourn / In foresight of an end, / But that which ends not who shall brave or mend?" "That which ends not," the eternity of death, inspires only fear, and holds no promise of relief: "I, trembling, cling to dying life; for how / Face the perpetual Now? / Birthless and deathless, void of start or stop . . ." These lines especially communicate the state of the speaker's distress if we recognize their reference, again rewritten, to Thomas Carlyle's everlast-

36. Rossetti also read Milton, but according to her brother's Memoir, she did not like his work very much: "Another great thing she disliked was Milton's *Paradise Lost*" (*Poetical Works,* lxx).

ing Now of *Sartor Resartus,* because within the context of that reference
it becomes clear that the distress is *not* the prolegomenon to salvation.[37]
Herr Teufelsdröckh, the putative writer of the "edited" text *Sartor Resar-
tus,* recounts passing through the stages of "The Everlasting No" (no to
Satan), "The Center of Indifference" ("the first preliminary Moral Act,
Annihilation of Self"), and "The Everlasting Yea" ("Love not pleasure, love
God"). Such an evolution leaves one prepared to "Pierce through the time
element, glance to the Eternal" (259) in order to see "That with God as it
is a universal HERE, so it is an everlasting NOW" (259). The speaker of "An
Old-World Thicket" has an inkling of that NOW, but has no way of identifying it as other than literal, as its own physical death. The speaker has not
passed through the stages necessary to interpret death as salvation, but
has simply gone around in a desperate circle:

> Rage to despair; and now despair had turned
>   Back to self-pity and mere weariness,
> With yearnings like a smouldering fire that burned,
>   And might grow more or less,
>   And might die out or wax to white excess.
>   (136–40)

"An Old-World Thicket" evokes the linear progress of *The Divine Comedy, Paradise Lost,* and *Sartor Resartus* only to emphasize more bleakly
the nature of its own *selva oscura,* its failure to achieve a way out. And it
uses a Coleridgean dream-form the better to stage a disruption that
propels the poem into its concluding vision of salvation.

At the very edge of the dream-vision, the speaker hears what can only
be described as the harmony of the spheres, when "Silence and sound
[are] in heavenly harmony." But immediately, "reality" breaks through as
the sound of a lamb: "At length a pattering fall / Of feet, a bell, and
bleatings, broke through all." "Then I looked up," says the speaker. What
the speaker sees upon looking up closely resembles the first extended—
harmonious—view of nature in the dream, with the critical addition of
the flock of sheep and its "patriarchal ram." That addition suggests salvation, and the speaker offers itself the pastoral scene as the explanation of
and *reward* for the trial that makes up the rest of the poem. But just as

---

37. Thomas Carlyle, *Sartor Resartus: The Life and Opinions of Herr Teufelsdröckh* (New
York: A. L. Burt, n.d.). Packer notes that Ford Madox Brown wrote the following in his diary:
"CR called; she is reading Carlyle with her mother." Packer quotes from Ford Maddox Ford's
Ford Madox Brown (1896), p. 131 (Packer, *Christina Rossetti,* 427).

the dream-vision is about to mitigate the speaker's suffering, it is inter-rupted, and there exists no adequate transition to the poem's outcome. Instead, there is just "Then I looked up," after which the "I" disappears from the poem, and, therefore, from the redemptive pastoral event. Furthermore, the exegetical path that would lead from a literal account of suffering to an anagogical interpretation of salvation is strewn with the fragments of the incomplete dream-vision, leaving that vision in danger of being merely a detailed, psychologically gruesome depiction of suffering, isolated in its "full meaning of terror" from its possible allegorical resolution.

Like "The Thread of Life," "An Old-World Thicket" works out the problem of describing the event of salvation, and the role of the re-deemed self in that event. Once again, a subjective perspective—the urgent demands of a particular self that is the speaking voice—obstructs progression, or a continuous path to the place of that event, this time not by recantation but by interruption. In this poem, the need for a certain meaning, that present suffering can be interpreted as future redemption, results in an abrupt shift from the internal, the "I's" state of suffering, and the subservience of the natural world to that suffering, to the external, a pastoral scene of harmony. An abrupt shift to a transcendent scene can-not enact transcendence, and the movement of the poem does not re-hearse *The Divine Comedy*'s upward spiral to Paradise. Unlike the *Paradiso*'s persona, the voice in "An Old-World Thicket" cannot fully reward itself in the "here and now" of the poem, and must exclude itself from its own redemptive vision. Or rather, it must exclude itself from the poetic *presentation* of that vision; its self-effacement is the prerequi-site of that presentation.

The most frustrating insight achieved by the speaker in *Fear and Trembling* about the indecipherability of Abraham, the paradigmatic "single individual" or "knight of faith," is the complete inaccessibility of that individual experience even to other knights of faith: ". . . the single individual is only the single individual" (69), and "The one knight of faith cannot help the other at all" (71). If the moment of salvation really arrives for a "single individual," at that moment the individual becomes incommunicado, its story removed from the realm of *publice juris,* like a "book under divine confiscation." In "An Old-World Thicket" two possi-bilities exist. Either the speaking "I" suffers such torment that in order to retain its faith it must interpret its sufferings anagogically, forcing, per-haps ineptly, an allegorical meaning of salvation onto the scene it surveys upon emerging from its torturous spell; or it really does experience redemption as a reward for its torment, but must then become unavailable to the poem, which offers the allegory as a substitute for its erstwhile speaker. The poem itself withholds any clues about which possibility is stronger; instead it lays out in detail the dilemma of subjective faith, the condition where anagogical meaning is always vexed either by doubt (is the meaning forced upon the experience?) or by indecipherability (where is the saved individual in the picture of salvation?).

"The single individual is only the single individual" and "I am who I am even I" evoke the same quality of isolation as Hopkins's "taste of myself." Both of them hint at the danger of tautological solipsism inherent in the state of subjective belief. The following poems by Hopkins, like Rossetti's "The Thread of Life" and "An Old-World Thicket," inquire into that danger; indeed, they actively court it for themselves. But such a diabolical courtship is necessary in the exploration of the doubt and indecipherability that plague a modern condition of belief. Not surprisingly, these poems also have salvation and the saved self as their poetic subjects.

In December of 1881, Hopkins wrote a long letter to Dixon that attended in detail to the Jesuit Order and his role in it. He begins with an eloquent apology for his Jesuit self *qua* poet:

> When a man *has given himself* to God's service, when he has *denied himself* and followed Christ, he has fitted himself to receive and *does receive from God a special guidance,* a more particular providence. This guidance is conveyed partly by the action of other men, as his appointed superiors, and *partly by direct lights and inspirations.* If I wait for such guidance, through whatever channel conveyed, about anything, about my poetry for instance, I do more wisely in every way than if I try to serve my own seeming interests in the matter. Now if you value what I write, if I do myself, much more does our Lord. And if he chooses to avail himself of what I leave at his disposal he can do so with a felicity and with a success which I could never command. And if he does not, then two things follow; one that the reward I shall nevertheless receive from him will be all the greater; the other that then I shall know how much a thing contrary to his will and even to my own best interests I should have done if I had taken things into my own hands and forced on publication. (My emphasis)[38]

---

38. *Correspondence of Gerard Manley Hopkins and Richard Watson Dixon,* ed. Claude Colleer Abbott (London: Oxford University Press, 1955), 93.

This passage follows the orthodox valuation of death-to-self as the means to union with God promoted by the *Imitatio Christi* (a work Hopkins knew well). A self-deprecatory claim for the poet-believer as God's amanuensis, merely the means to God's mysterious ends, this same passage nonetheless betrays its writer's self-interest and artistic ego, even in its avowal of paradigmatic Christian disinterestedness. As the characteristic act of a man in "God's service," self-denial elicits "special guidance" of that self. And in the case of Hopkins, that guidance yields poetry that either serves as raw material at God's disposal, which He can use as He likes (though with incomparable felicity and success) or, in its rejection by God, will itself yield a reward "all the greater." De la Mare's insight into Rossetti ("She asks, Am I saved? rather than Are you?") speaks also to this letter, in which Hopkins the cleric and poet explains to Dixon the cleric and poet the intricate relationship between priesthood and poetry. Hopkins's explanation does not, however, generate communal understanding, for the similarities between him and Dixon are implicitly preempted here by the greater difference between a Jesuit Catholic and a clerical Protestant. Instead, it offers Hopkins as a synecdoche for those who "follow Christ" (a member of "Christ's Company," a partly military, partly fraternal name the Jesuits used for themselves), and who are hierarchically placed, guided by "appointed superiors." The letter, however, simultaneously isolates that synecdoche in its privileged direct revelation from God ("partly by direct lights and inspirations"). The synecdoche soon breaches synecdochic propriety, and Hopkins unabashedly writes of *his* poetry, *his* relationship with God, in short, *his* "best interests."

Hopkins's letter does not present an overt agenda in order to protect a covert one with untoward implications; rather its surface reflects a single agenda, earning God's reward, impossible to describe as anything except "*my* own best interest," unless he were to absent himself, like the voice in "An Old-World Thicket." "This myself as king unto my King / I give, to Him who gave Himself up for me ... ," says a speaker in "The Thread of Life," and this extraordinarily self-possessed statement of dispossession as godly reciprocity (I give to God as He gave to me) is rehearsed by Hopkins in the path he forges from self-denial to self-promotion. At his most Simeon-esque in this passage, Hopkins manifests the same hyperbolic self-effacement or "artless egotism" as Rossetti's Esther, as Taciturnus's Quidem. Perhaps he most resembles Johannes's "present author," however, in his disingenuousness, about whom Johannes claims: "He is *poetice et eleganter* (in a poetic and refined way) a supplementary clerk who neither writes the system nor gives *promises*

of the system. . . . He writes because to him it is a luxury that is all the
more pleasant and apparent the fewer there are who buy and read what
he writes" (*Fear and Trembling,* 7). No one buys Hopkins's poetry
(since it is unpublished), and almost no one reads it, but this isolation,
which would make most poets miserable, becomes for Hopkins the sign
of special reward from God. Johannes dissimulates with his "supplementary clerk" long before Jacques Derrida bestows the status of primacy on
the supplement. *Fear and Trembling* may supplement the story of Abraham, but as supplement it more than just completes Abraham's incomplete story. Since Abraham is silent, the work of a "supplementary clerk"
tells the only available story. As he who leaves his work at God's "disposal," Hopkins also makes a disingenuous pitch for his own primacy;
this is his "artless egotism."

Like Rossetti's speakers, and like Johannes de Silentio, Hopkins is a
complex apologist for his own life, particularly his artistic life, and "artless ego" again tells only part of the story. Hopkins wrote this letter to
Dixon in response to Dixon's dismay at the thought that Hopkins had
destroyed poetry after he became a Jesuit. He wants Hopkins to understand that priestly and poetic careers can be combined, and points to the
Jesuitical tradition as evidence:

> So I will say nothing, but cling to the hope that you will find it
> consistent with all that you have undertaken to pursue poetry
> still, as occasion may serve: & that in so doing you may be sanc-
> tioned and encouraged by the great Society to which you belong,
> which has given so many ornaments to literature. Surely one
> vocation cannot destroy another: and such a Society as yours will
> not remain ignorant that you have such gifts as have seldom been
> given by God to man. (*Correspondence,* 90)

Hopkins begins his answer with the passage already quoted, and then he
lists Jesuit writers, depicting them as mediocre stylists even when profoundly intelligent or talented (i.e. Suárez and Molina, two of the most
important Jesuit thinkers), or deliberately ordinary (Ignatius), for "Brilliancy does not suit us" (95). "I quote these cases," writes Hopkins, "to
prove that show and brilliancy do not suit us, that we cultivate the
commonplace outwardly and wish the beauty of the king's daughter the
soul to be from within" (96). Dixon has innocently offended the Jesuit
sensibility that downplays worldly success; the Order would be dis-
mayed to find itself credited with the creation of "ornaments." And yet
Dixon also exposes, still innocently, the Jesuit two-step by which in fact

the Order *does* produce a disproportionate number of literary talents, Suárez and Molina notwithstanding. Roland Barthes, far less innocent than Canon Dixon, exuberantly stomps where the Canon softly treads, and posits the unholy trinity of Ignatius, the Marquis de Sade, and Charles Fourier as "logothetes," inventors of a language with which they indulge in the "happiness of writing" and classic Barthesian "pleasure of the text."[39]

One might argue that Barthes gives new meaning to Johnson's famous *discordia concors,* but he wants to "dissipate or elude the moral discourse that has been held on each of them" (9), and sees the estrangement of each from his regular context as the way to do this. He begins his section on Loyola with the choreographic key by which the Jesuit two-step can be danced. In response to the literary praise heaped upon Ignatius's *Spiritual Exercises,* one Jesuit protests, as Barthes quotes him, that "it is all labored, literarily impoverished." "Here," writes Barthes,

> we find once more the old modern myth according to which language is merely the docile and *insignificant* instrument for the serious things that occur in the spirit, the heart or the soul. This myth is not innocent; discrediting the form serves to exalt the importance of the content: to say: *I write badly* means: *I think well.* . . . thus it is that literature, whose function is a worldly one, is not compatible with spirituality; one is detour, ornament, veil, the other is immediation, nudity: this is why one cannot be both a saint and a writer. (39–40, Barthes's emphasis)

Like Hopkins's cultivated "commonplace" that both hides and *means* (can be interpreted as) "the beauty of the king's daughter the soul . . . within," Barthes's analysis relies on the conventions of rhetoric and expectations of hidden meaning to make his point. Hidden beneath, or better, pointed to by, "I write badly" is "I think well"; to expose Jesuitical dissimulation requires exposure of, and therefore acknowledgment of, an esoteric code that obscures the deictic path from the literal word to its "real" meaning. As Rossetti's "Old-World Thicket" illustrates, however, a movement from the literal (or the "real" or the material) to its "meaning," may be governed by the *need* for that meaning, because the literal would be intolerable without it, especially when the governor is the subjective "I." *I* write badly; therefore, *I* think well; if I am a Jesuit,

39. Roland Barthes, *Sade, Fourier, Loyola,* trans. Richard Miller (Berkeley and Los Angeles: University of California Press, 1989).

according to Barthes, I *need* this equation. *I* am experiencing mental and physical torment, therefore *I* will earn a place in the scene of salvation; if I am a believing Christian, I *need* to believe this. Rossetti's poem equated present suffering with future salvation, and the problems with and possibilities of that equation. Hopkins's poem "On the Portrait of Two Beautiful Young People" rehearses a different version of that equation: present beauty—a portrait—points out the human condition of mutability, and points to past corruption, for "corruption was the world's first woe" (*Gerard Manley Hopkins,* 176).

Hopkins called "On the Portrait of Two Beautiful Young People" "an elegy in Gray's metre" in letters to both Dixon (*Correspondence,* 150) and Bridges.[40] To Bridges, he further described the poem as "severe, no experiments." By "severe, no experiments," he no doubt distinguishes it from more prosodically innovative poems written around the same time such as "Spelt from Sibyl's Leaves." The poem is "severe" in its import as well, however, allowing no comfort or pleasure to be derived from a painting of a brother and sister that captures their youth, prosperity, and beauty. During the Christmas season of 1886, a happy interlude in his otherwise miserable time in Dublin, Hopkins began a poem inspired by a real portrait (of a boy and a girl from the neighborhood of his hosts [*Correspondence,* 150]). The story of its composition—and incompletion, for he never finished it—contributes a biographical analogy to another "complex song," this time a dirge, mourning in obsessive anticipation of a loss not yet incurred.

Hopkins's correspondence to Dixon indicates that he continued to work on "On the Portrait of Two Beautiful Young People" at least through July of 1888; its incompletion characterizes his work during this period. Leaving his convivial Christmas quarters in County Kildare for his dismal existence in Dublin seems to have sapped his creative energy immediately. In his first letter about the poem (January 27, 1887, from University College in Dublin) he tells Dixon, "I happened to see the portrait of two beautiful young persons, a brother and a sister, living in the neighborhood. It so much struck me that I began an elegy in Gray's metre, but being back here [in Dublin] I cannot go on with it" (*Correspondence,* 150). Earlier that same month, still in County Kildare, he wrote to Bridges about the poem, expressing some hope about his poetic powers: "I have had a bright light, and begun a poem in Gray's elegy metre, severe, no experiments" (*Letters,* 248). Between the hopeful

---

40. Gerard Manley Hopkins, *The Letters of Gerard Manley Hopkins to Robert Bridges,* ed. Claude Colleer Abbott (London: Oxford University Press, 1935), 248.

letter to Bridges and the less sanguine one to Dixon, Hopkins wrote the famous "eunuch" letter; the early months of 1887 were surely roller-coaster ones of inspiration and enervation. Seventeen months after beginning "On the Portrait of Two Beautiful Young People," Hopkins wrote to Dixon: "I have done some more of my elegy and hope to finish it" (*Correspondence,* 157). In April of 1889, he wrote to Bridges: "The river is the Barrow, which the old Irish poets call the dumb Barrow. I call it the burling Barrow Brown. Both descriptions are true. The country has nevertheless a charm. The two beautiful young people live within an easy drive" (*Letters,* 306). The "burling Barrow Brown" is from "On the Portrait . . . ," as are the beautiful young people; if he was not still working on his poem he was at least still thinking about it within two months of his own death from typhoid. Rossetti's line, "Mourning grows natural to us who mourn / In foresight of an end," could serve as an epitaph for this poem-fragment whose future completion was as doomed as its hold on Hopkins was strong.

As with "Pilate," no one can guess how Hopkins envisioned completing "On the Portrait of Two Beautiful Young People." It is futile to speculate about whether the extant version of the poem would have begun or ended the complete work, or whether its parts would even have been ultimately distributed throughout a work the length of "An Elegy Written in a Country Churchyard." But the fragment repays careful attention in the way, for instance, Coleridge's "Kubla Khan" does. It follows Gray's elegiac meter quite faithfully; nonetheless, the poem is a quirky elegy, in spite of Hopkins's claim of severity and "no experiments." It begins by evoking suitably ambivalent emotions for an elegy: "O I admire and sorrow! The heart's eye grieves / Discovering you, dark tramplers, tyrant years." The occasion for the elegy, however, is not a death, but the closest thing to immortalization that human culture has—the capture of a youthful hour in a portrait, a shore against "Time's winnowing": "The fine, the fingering beams / Their young delightful hour do feature down / That fleeted else like day-dissolved dreams / Or ringlet-race on burling Barrow brown."

Peter Sacks writes that in an elegy all mourners perform a substitutive "turning" (troping) act, turning from "the object of [their] love to a sign of [it]," and that "[c]onsolation thus depends on a trope that remains at an essential remove from what it replaces."[41] "On the Portrait . . ." "tropes" in the opposite direction, turning a "sign"—the portrait—into

41. Peter M. Sacks, *The English Elegy: Studies in the Genre from Spenser to Yeats* (Baltimore: The Johns Hopkins University Press, 1985), 6.

an apparent object of love, and ruthlessly deprives the poem's speaker of consolation by erasing the temporal distance between the "young delightful hour" and death. Hopkins himself intuits the intricacy of the process he has undertaken to complete. A full year after he began the poem he writes to Dixon: "I cannot get my Elegy finished, but I hope in a few days to see the hero and heroine of it, which may enable me (or quite the reverse; perhaps that: it is not well to come too near things)" (*Correspondence,* 154). The poem scrutinizes precisely such equivocation. In the poem, no one is dead; the boy and the girl of the portrait exude the qualities of "beautiful young people," and the speaker lives in his capacity as viewer of the portrait. What, therefore, is the true object of love and loss in a poem that has no dead body over which to mourn? Or, by what deictic path does a poem called "On the Portrait of Two Beautiful Young People" point to a meaning of loss and corruption?

One could say the speaker mourns for himself and for mankind's shared fate of death, or one could say that Hopkins mourns his own work (perhaps remembering the "slaughter of the innocents," the poems burned when he became a priest), using the portrait as a metonym for art, which would then include his poetry. This second understanding would make the poem about writing poetry, or about failing to write poetry, or about how writing a poem always means failing. A third alternative, explored here, takes the question, "What is the true object of love and loss," not as one answered by the object elegized, but as one that the poem, on its most literal level, finds posed for and imposed on itself by a speaker who constructs an unsparing meaning out of its contemplation of the beautiful portrait. That meaning satisfies the speaker, who desires to strip itself of aesthetic sensibility, the dangerous affinity for a beautiful portrait of beautiful people. This ironically results, however, in self-portraiture, one more assertion of the self in an attempt at self-curtailment.

After the speaker exclaims in the very first line of the poem "O I admire and sorrow," "I" never appears again until the last extant stanza, when it bursts onto the mise-en-scène it has just created, not so much to conclude or to resolve, but to interrupt:

> Enough: corruption was the world's first woe.
> What need I strain my heart beyond my ken?
> O but I bear my burning witness though
> Against the wild and wanton work of men.
>
> (33–36)

What happens between the first-person identifications of the speaker resembles the disappearance of the "I" in the salvation scene of "An Old-World Thicket," because only the "I," through whose eyes the scene can be viewed, controls both scenes. But "On the Portrait..." also differs significantly from "An Old-World Thicket" because its speaker creates a fictive situation in which it places itself within its own view, an accomplishment Rossetti denies her speaker. The fourth extant stanza, a verbal "portrait" of the portrait itself, begins the speaker's fiction:

> She leans on him with such contentment fond
> As well the sister sits, would well the wife;
> His looks, the soul's own letters, see beyond,
> Gaze on, and fall directly forth on life.
> (13–16)

The portrait acquires another spatial dimension, the space occupied by the "life" (the speaker viewing, and therefore standing within view of the portrait) on which the boy gazes. This inclusion in the now altered portrait emboldens the speaker to challenge the beauty and prosperity in which it now plays a part, and this challenge literally takes the form of a sermon, which begins with a rhetorical question:

> But ah, bright forelock, cluster that you are
> Of favoured make and mind and health and youth,
> Where lies your landmark, seamark, or soul's star?
> (17–19)

There follows an unequivocal moral answer, "There's none but truth can stead you. Christ is truth" (20), and finally a reiteration of the answer with biblical support:

> There's none but good can be good, both for you
> And what sways with you, maybe this sweet maid;
> None good but God—a warning waved to
> One once that was found wanting when Good weighed.
> (21–24)

The prosperity of the boy and girl so evident to the speaker elicits from him a harsh directive, for the "One once that was found wanting" is the man in Matthew 19, who asked Christ, "what good shall I do, that I may have eternal life?" Christ tests the man with his answer, demanding that he abandon all worldly goods and choose the unornamented life of the ascetic. The man fails, prompting one of Christ's most famous axioms: "It is easier for a camel to go through the eye of a needle, than for a rich man to enter the kingdom of God" (Matthew 19:24). Famous and infamous, for this axiom receives as much mitigating attention as Christ's order to hate one's family for his sake. In *Fear and Trembling*'s second Problemata, the speaker concludes by alluding to the passages from Luke and Matthew as soulmates in their severity: "Therefore, either there is an absolute duty to God . . . or else one must interpret the passage in Luke 14 as did that appealing exegete and explain the similar and corresponding passages in the same way" (81).[42] The speaker of "On the Portrait . . ." preaches the same lesson; "There's none but good can be good" provides a tight tautological defense against attempts at mitigation.[43]

The speaker's sermon is decidedly Jesuit, and the next extant stanza articulates the Ignatian principle of Election central to *The Spiritual Exercises:*

> Man lives that list, that leaning in the will
> No wisdom can forecast by gauge or guess,
> The selfless self of self, most strange, most still,
> Fast furled and all foredrawn to No or Yes.
>
> (25–28)

Exercise Five of the First Week of *The Spiritual Exercises,* inextricably and paradoxically binds election—choice—to *indifference* and to eschewal of "any inordinate attachment,"

> so that I am not more inclined or minded to take the thing proposed than to leave it, nor more to leave it than to take it; but that I hold myself as in the mean level of a balance to follow that

---

42. See the notes to this passage in *Fear and Trembling* for the allusions to Matthew and Luke (351).

43. An early draft in Gerard Manley Hopkins, *Poems of Gerard Manley Hopkins,* ed. Robert Bridges (London: Humphrey Milford, 1918), contains a stanza that refers to the Book of Matthew more overtly:

> Who yet was inward-lovely, bravèd well
> That world-breath's ransack nor wrestling nor stealth
> The least foil. How then? Rise he would not; fell
> Rather; he wore that millstone you wear, wealth.
>
> (381)

course which I feel to more to the glory and praise of God our
Lord and the salvation of my own soul.[44]

"The selfless self of self," a troublesome concept as we have already seen,
is bound up ("furled") in its "foredrawn" task, a choice to be made with
indifference ("No or Yes"), in order to praise God and simultaneously
save itself. The *Electio* dominates *The Spiritual Exercises,* and as the
Jesuit Walter Ong knows well, it is an act of immense solitude: "The
Exercises pivot on the *Electio* or the making of a decision, inevitably an
isolating and lonely act" (Ong, *Hopkins, the Self, and God,* 58).

The meter of "On the Portrait..." may be severe, but it softens in
comparison to the severity of the sermon that one part of the poem
embraces. The speaker "follows a course" from the beauty of the portrait
to the parable of the needle's eye to the prohibition on "inordinate
attachments," an ideal state of indifference. The poem turns the occasion
of aesthetic pleasure into an opportunity for, and gives it a meaning of,
ascetic self-discipline and denial. To do this, the full weight of death and
corruption must burden a literal portrayal of the full bloom of youth,
must prompt the question, "What worm was here... / To have havoc-
pocked so, see, the hung-heavenward boughs?" (31–32). The other part
of the story measures the loss and the gain. The speaker's ambivalent "O
I admire and sorrow!" cannot be permitted, for admiration implies pleasure, a dangerous detour on the "course" to ascetic indifference. Yet to
purge all admiration and to read the necessary dire message in the
painting seems to become intolerable; "Enough," says the speaker, "What
need I strain my heart beyond my ken?" But in the last two extant lines
the speaker reinforces the centrality of purgation as part of the revised
portrait created from the experience of the viewer. "O but I bear my
burning witness..." begins the penultimate line, and "witness" takes in
everything that has preceded it. The speaker has "witnessed" the portrait, its view being the single view available. In its sermon it has fur-
nished evidence for the portrait's meaning, the role of the witness, and
the etymological connection to "knowledge"; and "bearing witness"
strikes the right religious note for a now fully ascetic sensibility, purified
by the burning of its aesthetic contingency. The sentence continues to
the next line, "though / Against the wild and wanton work of men." The
speaker has set a course for itself, and perceives itself as hewing a path

44. Ignatius Loyola, *The Spiritual Exercises of St. Ignatius Loyola: Spanish and English
with a Continuous Commentary,* ed. Joseph Rickaby, S.J. (London: Burns, Oates, and
Washbourne, 1923), 153.

through a "selva oscura," the Wood of Error that is the "wild and wanton work of men"; at the same time, the speaker communicates its performative power in the vigor of this utterance. Such vigor also bears witness, however, to the tenacity of the self in the very act of self-denial. By the end of the extant "On the Portrait of Two Beautiful Young People," the two young people and the painting meant to immortalize them have vanished. The speaker leaves them behind (or burnt—another "slaughter of the innocents") on the course from "O I admire and sorrow"—an utterance that requires an object—to "O but I bear my burning witness"—one whose "I" provides its own object, "my burning witness," like the speaker's object of possession in Rossetti's sonnet, "ever my own," and like the special guidance from God to those who eschew self-interest, "in my best interest."

In the last two existing lines of "On the Portrait of Two Beautiful Young People," the speaker makes itself into a spectacle, or imagines itself that way, in its grand isolation from the "wild and wanton works of men." By first insinuating itself into the portrait, and then preempting it as the focus of the poem, it carves out a space for itself and the burning witness it bears. In doing so, however, it risks becoming the poem's new aesthetic object. In displacing and effacing the portrait, and by not effacing itself, it resembles Simeon, the ascetic protester as aesthetically interesting performance artist. Attempting to explain his individuality *as* believer, Hopkins takes this same risk, or gamble, a risk that must be taken, because there exists no other available way of expression in writing, even when the writing is for himself.

Ignatius's *Spiritual Exercises* begins: "Man was created to praise, do reverence to and serve God our Lord, and thereby to save his soul" (18). In 1880, Hopkins wrote a commentary on the *Exercises,* and though never finished, it contains his famous utterance:

> And this [the power that created human nature] is much more true when we consider the mind; when I consider my selfbeing, my consciousness and feeling of myself, that taste of myself, of *I* and *me* above and in all things, which is more distinctive than the taste of ale or alum, more distinctive than the smell of walnutleaf or camphor, and is incommunicable by any means to another man (as when I was a child I used to ask myself: What must it be to be someone else?).[45]

45. Gerard Manley Hopkins, *The Sermons and Devotional Writings of Gerard Manley Hopkins,* ed. Christopher Devlin, S.J. (London: Oxford University Press, 1959), 123.

In its implications of uniqueness and consequent isolation, "Taste of myself" contradicts his other famous coinages, "inscape" and "instress," both terms that forge connections between unique elements of nature, and specifically between a perceiver (a human being capable of imagination) and what it perceives. In its self-reflexivity, "taste of myself" obviously seems to preempt connection with externalities, but must be understood in its context, the explication of the *Exercises*'s First Principle and Foundation, whose beginning I quote above. Hopkins isolates his self to mount an argument for God as the undisputed First Cause, what Hopkins calls "some extrinsic power." In the midst of the profusion of nature, he asks himself: "And when I ask where does all this throng and stack of being, so rich, so distinctive, so important come from / nothing I see can answer me" (*Sermons,* 122). He hypothesizes three possible answers: chance, "myself, as selfexistent," or "some extrinsic power" (123). He eliminates the first two and therefore determines that "The third alternative then follows, that I am due to an extrinsic power" (*Sermons,* 128). "Taste of myself" leads to the most orthodox of resolutions and partakes of the time-honored Scholastic method of deriving through logic an answer that corresponds with a belief already held. But in fact this whole section is curious, not because of the isolating "taste of myself," but because of another isolation, a rhetorical one in his written reflections.

Hopkins had in mind a close reading of *The Spiritual Exercises,* perhaps in the mode of Augustine's attempt at a line-by-line exegesis of Genesis in his *Confessions.* Ignatius's first clause, as we have seen, is "Man was created to praise . . ." it is the same in the Spanish original ("El hombre es criad para alabar . . .") and in Latin ("Homo creatus est laudere . . ."). And yet, what Hopkins isolates for extended contemplation is not this first clause, but a fragment of it, "Homo creatus est." Man is created, the very first act, significantly *not* man's (his act is to praise), and the very first puzzle. Looking around at all that exists, even discovering the inscape in perceivable nature, simply does not suffice as an explanation of, or as evidence that "Homo creatus est," or at least it does not match the experience of the self: "I find myself with my pleasures and pains, my powers and my experiences, my deserts and guilt, my shame and sense of beauty, my dangers, hopes, fears, and all my fate, more important to myself than anything I *see*" (*Sermons,* 122, my emphasis). The self as perceiver (I see therefore I am) pales in comparison with this awesome roster of the individual's experience of *being* (I am therefore I am, or "But what I was I am I am even I"). In other words, the aesthetic self, all perception, does not adequately explain itself, but the ascetic self, focused inwardly on its multitudinousness, does. Hopkins emphasizes how stripped-down his self truly is: "And even those things with which I in some sort identify myself, as my country or family, and those things which I own and call mine, as my clothes and so on, all presuppose the stricter sense of *self* and *me* and *mine* and are from that derivative" (*Sermons,* 123).

This close look at Hopkins's own close reading prompts two possibly contradictory observations. First, "taste of myself" partakes of the shared language of the senses (taste), even as it declares itself "incommunicable by any means to another man." Second, the last quotation from Hopkins's writings echoes the harsh passages from Luke and Matthew that insist upon renunciation of family and possessions as the only means to salvation; if such renunciation is God's directive, it is also already the condition of the individual. These two observations in fact summarize the dilemma on which all of the poems in this chapter dwell. How can language communicate the "stricter sense of *self* and *me* and *mine*" as the proof for a power extrinsic to myself, to what is me and mine, when language is a medium of the senses? Both the immensity of the task and the inadequate means to its achievement define the subject of the poetry. The most poignant poetic manifesto of this dilemma is Hopkins's sonnet "To seem the stranger," for its speaker already inhabits a state of (involuntary) renunciation:

> . . . Father and mother dear,
> Brothers and sisters are in Christ not near
> And he my peace/my parting, sword and strife.
>   (2–4)

The sonnet ends with an appeal to the ear in order to declare itself and its speaker unheeded, that is, unheard: "This to hoard unheard, / Heard unheeded, leaves me a lonely began" (*Gerard Manley Hopkins,* 166). "A lonely began," a verbal noun characteristic of Hopkins's poetry, reverberates in the repeated attempts of "The Thread of Life," the circular path back to the self in "An Old-World Thicket," and the lonely vocation of the witness bearer in "On the Portrait of Two Beautiful Young People." A "lonely began" exploits the past tense to describe a process already tried and failed. That process tries to deflect away from the self only to return to its isolated beginning. "That Nature Is a Heraclitean Fire and of the Comfort of the Resurrection" plays the world of the senses against the "little world made cunningly" that defines the "I" of this poem in order to stage this doomed-to-fail process.

"That Nature Is a Heraclitean Fire . . . ," which Hopkins called a sonnet, begins and continues for the fourteen lines of the sonnet proper with tastes of literally everything but "myself." Nature is on parade: ". . . heaven-roysterers, in gay-gangs // they throng; they glitter in marches" (*Gerard Manley Hopkins,* 180, line 2). Even if the parade leads toward apocalypse, a massive bonfire, we cannot mistake the poem's own exuberant indulgence in visceral language, as if it were the last meal of a condemned linguistic gourmand, hungry for "ooze" and "parch" and "treadmire toil," as well as for the elegant "shivelights and shadowtackle." Parades and meals mix uneasily as similes, but "That Nature Is a Heraclitean Fire . . ." is a visual and tactile wanton, a challenge to look at and even more of a challenge to read aloud. Hopkins himself seems caught up in its sensory stimulation; in a letter to Bridges he compares it to liquor: "I *must* read something of Greek and Latin letters and lately I sent you a sonnet, on the Heraclitean Fire, in which a great deal of early Greek philosophical thought was distilled; but the liquor of the distillation did not taste very Greek, did it?" (*Letters,* 291).[46] In an earlier letter he calls the poem "a sonnet in sprung rhythm with two codas" (*Letters,* 279). As Bridges points out in his original annotations to the 1918 edition, however, there are really three, if we distinguish the codas from the sonnet-proper by counting off fourteen lines and then marking Hopkins's indentations (*Poems,* 381). Without making too much of the difference between the poem he writes about and the poem he writes, we can note this discrepancy as an indication of how he has packed to capacity, has stretched to its utmost formal limits the poem "That Nature Is a Heraclitean Fire . . ." Its sonnet form is barely discernible because of the lengthy lines, and a coda implies an unmanageable excess. This discrepancy directs our attention to the speaking "I," which does not emerge so much as it explodes into the poem in the third coda, individuated, self-celebrated, and most important, saved.

Norman MacKenzie describes the tone of "Heraclitean Fire" as elegiac up through line 16, a line interrupted by a full-stop and then "Enough! the Resurrection."[47] While the *tone* is anything but elegiac, the poem does eulogize, or better commemorate, all that becomes fuel for "nature's bonfire." Included in this commemoration is "Man," distinct on the one hand from clouds and elms and dried mud, but on the other hand, an

---

46. Etymologically "liquor" is related to "liquidity," a suggestive word in relation to Heraclitus, and a connection Hopkins the linguist and classicist certainly might have noticed.

47. Norman H. MacKenzie, *A Reader's Guide to Gerard Manley Hopkins* (Ithaca: Cornell University Press, 1981), 196.

undifferentiated mass, "Manshape," as transient as everything else in
nature, in spite of the intellect: "Man, how fast his firedint, // his mark on
mind, is gone!" (11). The commemoration ends abruptly with "Enough!"
(just as the sermon ends in "On the Portrait . . ."), and the poem's Resurrection purges a being who achieves individuation by first shedding its
"Manshape": ". . . Flesh fade, and mortal trash / Fall to the residuary
worm; // world's wildfire leave but ash" (19–20). This radical *askesis*
leaves the pure ash of the ascetic self. But the act of *askesis* occurs
simultaneously with an impossible act of appropriation and the strongest
assertion of self seen in all the poems dealt with in this chapter. The last
coda rebels against the constrictions of time, so necessary in an articulation of transience, in order to insinuate itself into Christ's exemplary act
of *askesis:*

> In a flash, at a trumpet crash,
> I am all at once what Christ is, // since he was what I am, and
> This Jack, joke, poor potsherd, // patch, matchwood, immortal diamond,
>   Is immortal diamond.
>
> (22–24)

This coda appropriates and asserts with abandon: "I am all at once what
Christ is . . ." The apocalypse of the poem still resonates in the coda's
"trumpet crash," while the Resurrection becomes the speaker's event in
its assumption of Christ's role. Destruction (apocalypse) and salvation
(Resurrection) become as indistinguishable as the ascetic self and the
self in the ultimate Hypostatic Union of man and God. Out of these
simultaneities, the speaking "I" adamantly projects itself, metamorphos-
ing from the indistinct "This Jack" into "immortal diamond," hard, fire-
proof, inimitable, and immutable. And finally unmodifiable, except by
the repetitious, tautological extension, "Is immortal diamond." This ending, ". . . immortal diamond, / Is immortal diamond," resonates with Rossetti's "ever mine own," and even more so with her line, "But what I was
I am, I am even I." And *that* line's recapitulation of God's self-
identification to Moses brings this chapter to a "lonely began." Simeon
sits atop his pillar, alone, stripped bare of all earthly goods, but a spectacle of self-assertion as he draws himself into the picture of sparkling stars
of the heavens.

If Abraham's "dirge" is like a "book under divine confiscation" in *Fear
and Trembling*'s Problemata II, in Problemata I Shakespeare's work is
presented as the best of available writing, and the speaker gives thanks

to a man who, to a person overwhelmed by life's sorrows, and left behind naked, reaches out the words, the leafage of language by which he can conceal his misery. Thanks to you, great Shakespeare, you who can say everything, everything, everything just as it is—and yet, why did you never articulate this torment? Did you perhaps reserve it for yourself, like the beloved's name that one cannot bear to have the world utter, for with his little secret that he cannot divulge the poet buys this power of the word to tell everybody else's dark secrets. (61)

By no accident, in Problemata III, Shakespeare's Richard the Third belongs in the category of the demonic, along with Faust; the demonic is the very closest analogy to Abraham inventable by language. The next line in this homage to Shakespeare anticipates the later use of Richard, and of Faust, and captures the quality shared by the lyric poems discussed in this chapter in a powerful aphorism: "A poet is not an apostle; he drives out devils only by the power of the devil." In Hopkins's commentary on *The Spiritual Exercises,* he describes from where that power comes: "This song of Lucifer's was a dwelling on his own beauty, an instressing of his own inscape, and like a performance on the organ and instrument of his own being, it was a sounding, as they say, of his own trumpet and a hymn in his own praise" (*Sermons,* 200–201). Lucifer *was* beautiful; that is what his name *means,* and, in Hopkins's rendering, his sin is self-reflexivity, the unwillingness to make his beauty stand humbly for something else external to him, thus signaling both the inadequacy and the contingency of that beauty.[48] But he is a maker of songs, and, as Hopkins tells it, Lucifer's story should warn the poet-believer against captivation by the beauty of his or her own song when that song should be singing "the sweet new song of the redeemed set free." Problemata I, on the other hand, insists that this warning must also be seen as a dare by the poet-believer, who belongs, impossibly, to two opposing leagues: the Apostles, who received from Christ the power to cast out Satan (Mark 3:15), and Satan himself. The poet "reaches out the words, the leafage of language," to "conceal" misery—specifically in all

---

48. See Harold Bloom, *The Anxiety of Influence: A Theory of Poetry* (New York: Oxford University Press, 1973). Early in his study he portrays Satan (or at least Milton's Satan) as the "authentic voice of the ruminative line, the poetry of loss, and the voice also of the strong poet accepting his task" (33). In his final chapter he addresses the very problem of ego that plagued Satan as an angel and enhanced him as a poet. "The mystery of poetic style," writes Bloom, "the exuberance that is beauty in every strong poet, is akin to the mature ego's delight in its own individuality, which reduces to the mystery of narcissism" (146).

of these poems the misery of self-reflexivity—but to conceal inadequately, and to let through the leafage some glimpse of a saved self that must also be a renounced self. In Problemata I's aphorism we see the triple-bind that defines the poet-believer's dilemma. The "leafage of language" performs only well enough to communicate the particular experience of the speaking "I," making self-reflexivity inescapable. Even a glimpse at the saved self implies knowledge of a "book under divine confiscation," and "special guidance" from the divine confiscator. Self-renunciation can only be communicated as *publice juris* by a symbolic effacement that inevitably performs literally as self-promotion, the problem of Simeon. The beauty of a poem about salvation must announce its contingency, but always draws attention to itself (away from the confiscated text upon which it is contingent) by virtue of its announcement.

The modern Mephistopheles here is Jacques Derrida, whose supplementary clerk always threatens to displace what it ostensibly means to supplement. The grammar of these poems always provides an "I" whose act of self-annihilation can only be an act of "sous rature," whereby in crossing itself out, it not only remains visible, but draws attention to itself as that with the line through it (or he who is atop the odd pillar, itself a kind of line).[49] But Derrida only provides a literary term for the ultimate act against which all of these poems measure themselves. Christ on the cross physically allows Himself to be "crossed out" because he is not only privy to, but part author of the confiscated text (or he is the Word that the text articulates), and his "cross" and his death always point to/mean Resurrection and eternal life. The believer has a mandate to imitate Christ; guides like the *Imitatio Christi* and *The Spiritual Exercises* indicate how to do so. When the poet (or writer, including à Kempis and Ignatius) wants to capture the nature of that imitation in writing, however, she or he always must at least intimate that she is privy to divine "spelling" and a perspective that transcends a particular subjectivity. And when "beyond the heavens" is reinterpreted as "beyond the self," the task becomes even more difficult and dangerous, because any attempt to go "beyond the self" always involves bringing that self along. In writing, self-renunciation can only be a symbolic gesture; "I, if I perish, perish" cannot rid itself of the strength of Esther's self in a performance of perishing.

---

49. Jacques Derrida, *Of Grammatology*, trans. Gayatri Spivak (Baltimore: The Johns Hopkins University Press, 1976), 60.

4

Wreck and Reprise:
Hopkins

They were nearly all Islanders in the Pequod, Isolatoes too, I call such, not acknowledging the common continent of men, but each Isolato living on a separate continent of his own.

And now, concentric circles seized the lone boat itself, and all its crew, and each floating oar, and every lance-pole, and spinning, animate and inanimate, all round and round in one vortex, carried the smallest chip of the Pequod out of sight.

—Herman Melville, *Moby-Dick*

The attempt at poetic expression seems always to jam the poet-believer between the rock of poetry and the hard place of faith. Abraham is an impossible model for the poet, inimitable in his silence, even to one who takes silence as his name. Christ, who is the Word in the orthodox Christian understanding of divine discourse, is the appropriate model for imitation sanctioned by Christian dogma and discipline, but any such imitation leads (inevitably) to the "place" of the crucifixion and the act of self-annihilation. The event on Golgotha is finally no more imitable in devout writing than the event on Mount Moriah. What always turns out to be in danger of sacrifice, at least in poetry, is not the writing, but the devotion. The poet-believer "drive[s] out the devils only by the power of the devil," and incurs the concomitant risk of such an action; nonetheless, an aesthetics of asceticism enables a negotiation between overt faith and the subver-

sive poetic apostasy that appears to plague expression of that faith. Hopkins's "The Wreck of the Deutschland" and "The Loss of the Eurydice"
seek just such a negotiation, and the path they forge is both formal and
philosophical, a path constructed by the poet's rhetorical investigation
of the idea of repetition.

In *Repetition: A Venture in Experimenting Psychology,* Kierkegaard
explores the making of a poet in terms of repetitional dynamics. *Repetition* offers Job as an exemplary model for the modern poet, and quite
aptly, since "[t]he poet of Job ... relates psychology to aesthetics in a
manner which strikingly answers the search of contemporary art."[1] Psychology and poetry together form *Repetition*'s "venture." In spite of its
reliance on Job, *Repetition* is the pseudonymous Kierkegaardian text
least concerned with overtly religious matters. Its supposed author, Constantin Constantius, identifies himself as a proto-psychologist, a professional "confidant" who knows what to do "in dealing with a depressed
person." He has "years of training" and "a case history" of the young man
who occupies his attention. Like a good analyst, he performs self-
analysis, using himself in an experiment on the phenomenon of repetition. Wedged between Constantin's "Report" and his "Concluding Letter" are dated letters from the young man who seeks Constantin's help.
Constantin tells us that this young man is a poet, and his letters attest at
least to poetic ambition and a naïve poetic sensibility. *Repetition* seems
at first an unlikely guide into the complexities of poetry dealing with
religious problems. But it anatomizes self-colloquy, a hallmark of modern
poetry, by dividing its writing persona into the Machiavellian Constantin
and the Jobean young man.

Repetition presents an anatomy of the written text, but it is itself a
written text, of course, and is therefore compelled to imitate its own
subject of inquiry and to reflect formally upon its philosophical reflections. Imitation alternates between the writer and his fictional persona in
a similar manner in Hopkins's repetitional elegies. Such destabilizing
exchanges—in which authority oscillates between "author" and "authored"—lie at the heart of *Repetition.* Constantin "recovers" the young
man by allowing him his epistolary autonomy, and yet that "autonomy"
may be just a repetition in writing of Constantin's own imagination.
These two versions of repetition, a work imitating its own subject of
inquiry, and a written "recovery" that is also an act of the authorial

---

1. As Samuel Terrien observes in *Job: Poet of Existence* (New York: Bobbs-Merrill, 1957),
19.

imagination, operate more subtly in Hopkins.[2] But *Repetition* clarifies the underlying paradoxes bequeathed both Hopkins and Rossetti by their interests in repetition and imitation.

These paradoxes emerge poetically on both a micro and a macro level.[3] Within a poem lines echo each other not only through rhyme, but through such rhetorical devices as anaphora, parallelism, even antithesis. Nonetheless, every line is necessarily different and distinguishable from what comes before and after it. Even identical lines differ in their unavoidably different contextualization: a refrain might appear again and again, and yet each repetition of it differs from every other at least by location within the poem. By its poetic and prosodic strategies, every text embraces a tradition. A poet writing in a formal mode always sets herself or himself a disciplinary task, a curtailment of unbridled creativity in order to resemble the selected mode, while at the same time she or he can and must unleash personal creativity enough for a wholly original performance. The dialectic of self-discipline (self-curtailment) and self-expression particularly matters for Hopkins and Rossetti, whose works (and lives) are driven by it to an unusually large degree. This repetitional dialectic results in poems like Hopkins's shipwreck elegies and Rossetti's sonnet sequences, all organized to set as well as transgress limits. It unfolds as a temporalizing event, since repetition in its most ordinary sense is something of a trick. An event of repetition poses as a projection into the future—something happens and then, *after that,* happens again. And yet we cannot identify a repetition except in hindsight, as an act in the past. And however unavoidable such hindsight is, backward glances can make Eurydice vanish.

Embedded in *Repetition* is the figure of Job, who has (and takes) the opportunity to speak on his own behalf, and yet remains subject to an invisible engine (invisible to Job, that is) that generates the Book of Job from its second chapter on. In *Repetition* the young man described as a poet invokes Job again and again, as if Job were the muse to his outbursts of pain. Job, who both contends with God and is subject to His will, also serves Hopkins as a muse for the poetic expression of loss. Because Hopkins must *re*create Job, borrowing him from a prior text, Job comes to figure the place or problem of writing as a repetitional endeavor. And

2. And in Rossetti. See Chapter 5 for a discussion of repetition in Rossetti's two sonnets of sonnets.

3. A distinction J. Hillis Miller usefully draws in his analysis of "The Wreck of the Deutschland." See note 5 for the history of Miller's engagement with Hopkins's poem.

because this place is a differential locus marked by both discontinuity and continuity, Job also figures the *promise* of writing as repetition. Despite contemporary emphases on the textual disjunction of language and meaning, and the implications of that disjunction for devotional writing, the figure of Job illustrates the mediatory power of figuration. Job marks the place where devotion and writing can be seen as not compatible, but not incompatible either, where they formally join in the uneasy cultural alliance between art and religion. Thus, as the previous chapters explored the threats to the firmament of belief always present in the act of writing, this chapter examines how that threat is managed by an aesthetics that refuses to reduce language to mere subversion—an aesthetics of asceticism. Recognizing the centrality of this aesthetics in both Hopkins and Rossetti, we must read them, especially their more ambitious works, from a perspective that itself refuses poststructuralist Unmeaning. This perspective will be mediatory, but also mediated: available only through mediators who remind us that reading is also a form of repetition, Crusoe-like tracing of footprints.

That our first mediator is Kierkegaard is both ironic—he battled against the notion of mediation in nearly all of his pseudonymous works—and appropriate, since mediatory negotiation requires indirection, discretion, even sometimes obscurity to be successful. Indirection, discretion, and obscurity characterize Kierkegaardian "indirect communication" and are qualities prominent in the poetry of Hopkins and Rossetti. That the other mediator is Job keeps on the negotiation table at all times the issue of religious belief, so often bargained away in poststructuralist separations of Logos and meaning.

The pseudonymous author of *Repetition* loses no time making a large claim for the importance of his central concept. "If God himself had not willed repetition," says Constantin Constantius, "the world would not have come into existence."[4] This claim matters for several reasons, as once again the subject of the book is inscribed in the name of the "author," the redundant "Constantin Constantius." "If Kierkegaard himself had not willed repetition," we might well say, "Constantin Constantius would not have come into existence." Furthermore, we might hypothesize that if a poet did not participate in some mode of repetition, there would be no poetry, or at least no formal poetry. "The dialectic of repetition is easy," explains Constantin, "for that which is repeated has been—otherwise it could not be repeated—but the very fact that it has

---

4. Søren Kierkegaard, *Fear/Trembling* and *Repetition,* trans. and ed. Howard V. Hong and Edna H. Hong (Princeton: Princeton University Press, 1983), 133.

been makes the repetition into something new" (149). Constantin captures the paradox and ambiguity of repetition, that mode by which there is similarity and proximity (between that which has been and that which repeats), while at the same time there is dissimilarity and distance (the "something new"). His optimism is deceptive, though, for the ambiguities can become highly unstable and problematic, not "easy" at all. "The Wreck of the Deutschland" illustrates these difficulties, and Hopkins's interest in ruination as an organizing metaphor for self, world, and language opens his elegy to poststructuralist reading at its most subversive.

We have an elegant if unremitting example of such reading in J. Hillis Miller's repeated considerations of "The Wreck of the Deutschland."[5] In the last version of his argument, Miller concludes that:

> There are indeed two texts in Hopkins, the overthought and the underthought. One text, the overthought, is a version (a particularly splendid version) of Western metaphysics in its Catholic Christian form. In this text the Word governs natural objects and selves. Like Father, like Son; and the sons, all the particular words, are a way back to the Father.... On the other hand, Hopkins's underthought is a thought about language itself. It recognizes that there is no word for the Word, that all words are metaphors. Each word leads to another word of which it is the displacement, in a movement without origin or end. (*The Linguistic Moment,* 263–64)

These two texts are not in "happy correspondence," but exist in a relationship of chiasmus:

> The theological thought depends on the notion of an initial unity that has been divided or fragmented and so could conceivably be reunified. The linguistic underthought depends on the notion of

5. "The Linguistic Moment in 'The Wreck of the Deutschland' " appeared in *The New Criticism and After,* ed. Thomas Daniel Young (Charlottesville: University Press of Virginia, 1976), 47–60. Described by Miller as an adaptation of a work in progress, it was followed a year later by "Nature and the Linguistic Moment," in *Nature and the Victorian Imagination,* ed. U. C. Knoepflmacher and G. B. Tennyson (Berkeley and Los Angeles: University of California Press, 1977), 440–51. Finally, in 1985 he included an expanded essay on Hopkins in the fully worked out version of his theory in *The Linguistic Moment: From Wordsworth to Stevens* (Princeton: Princeton University Press, 1985). By 1985, Miller's main point, that a poem always subverts its own meaning via its linguistic apparatus, had become a position commonly taken by deconstructionist critics of poetry.

an initial bifurcation that could not by any conceivable series of linguistic transformations . . . reach back to the primal word. There is no such word. (265)

From out of this wrestle of texts Miller borrows Hopkins's own term to state unequivocally: "Hopkins's linguistic underthought undoes his Christian overthought" (265).[6] This is a major undoing of the gravest implications, for the Christian overthought includes the Doctrine of Real Presence (the main reason for Hopkins's conversion); Christ as the Word, enabling the most disparate objects to harmonize as derived rhymes of that initial Word (the basis of Hopkins's theory of language and poetry); and the belief that one can move from the state of isolation commemorated by the famous "taste of myself" to some state of communion. For Miller, all of these things become undone.

Through the interrelated categories of linguistics, repetition, and theology, I argue that "The Wreck of the Deutschland" is *about* the very thing Miller claims is the poem's undoing in its attempt to make meaning—the failure of language as the means by which the language-user can communicate what he or she believes to be metaphysical or religious truth. To declare linguistics the winner over theology simply updates by reversal a reading of "The Wreck of the Deutschland" as theologically untroubled.[7] In other words, where Miller declares a win-

6. See *Further Letters of Gerard Manley Hopkins, Including His Correspondence with Coventry Patmore,* 2d ed., ed. Claude Colleer Abbott (London: Oxford University Press, 1956). Hopkins writes to his friend A.W.M. Baillie about his (never realized) plans to write a book on "Greek Lyric Art":

> My thought is that in any lyric passage of the tragic poets . . . there are—usually; I will not say always, it is not likely—two strains of thought running together and like counterpointed; the overthought that which everybody, editors, see . . . and which might for instance be abridged or paraphrased in square marginal blocks as in some books carefully written; the other, the underthought, conveyed chiefly in the choice of metaphors etc used and often only half realised by the poet himself, not necessarily having any connection with the subject in hand but usually having a connection and suggested by some circumstance of the scene or of the story. . . . Perhaps what I ought to say is that the underthought is commonly an echo or shadow of the overthought, something like canons and repetitions in music, treated in a different manner, but that sometimes it may be independent of it. (252–53)

Though "only half realised by the poet himself," the underthought of a lyric as Hopkins defines the term does not subvert the overthought. For Hopkins, moreover, counterpoint is a linguistic situation of tension, not contradiction. The subversive twist Miller gives the term is his own, not Hopkins's.

7. See, for instance, John Pick, *Gerard Manley Hopkins: Priest and Poet* (New York: Oxford University Press, 1942), and Margaret Ellsberg, *Created to Praise: The Language of Gerard Manley Hopkins* (New York: Oxford University Press, 1987).

ner in a wrestle between overt and subversive texts, I call a draw between competing but equally manifest impulses that drive the poem.

In *The Linguistic Moment,* Miller recalls his main structural point in *The Disappearance of God* to make an observation about repetition in Hopkins's use of rhyme: "Rhyme operates in 'The Wreck' both on the microscopic level of local poetical effect and on the macroscopic level of the large structural repetitions organizing the whole" (250). In this operation, however, "the underlying assumption is theological as well as technical," according to Miller:

> The fact that Christ is the Word, or Logos, of which all particular words are versions, variations, or metaphors, allows Hopkins even to accommodate into his poem words that are similar in sound though opposite in meaning. Christ underlies all words and thereby reconciles all oppositions in word sound and meaning: "Thou art lightning and love, I found it, a winter and warm" (line 70).
>
> The same assumptions ground the various forms of *repetition with difference* of word meaning in the poem. (251, my emphasis)

If it is true that "Hopkins's attempt to rescue himself from language through language begins with a linguistic assumption about the relation of individual words to the Logos—Christ the Word"(248), then he does sow the seeds of theological failure; Miller persuasively demonstrates that such reconciliation is a linguistic impossibility. If, however, Hopkins constructs a poetic scenario where irreconcilables such as winter/warm and lightning/love are permitted their consonantal repetition or similarity, only to accentuate their substantive opposition, then we have not a doomed attempt at accommodation (and therefore validation of God's arbitrariness), but an appeal to the imagination to entertain two mutually exclusive thoughts without exercising the urge to reconcile. "Repetition with difference" then becomes not endless digression from a bifurcated and therefore compromised origin, but an anti-dialectical process that disrupts reconciliation in order to insist on the eventual inevitability of decision. The poem presents an endless wrestle between texts, not a covert victor over an overt victim (linguistics over theology). By recourse to Kierkegaard and to Hopkins himself, we can separate warring but equally matched elements in "The Wreck," and define the nature of the conflict.

Though Miller does not define the theology of the poem any more specifically than "Western metaphysics in its Catholic Christian form," he informs his argument with the fundamental assumption that theology in "The Wreck of the Deutschland" is theodicy, a thoroughgoing attempt to "justify the ways of God to man," when those ways seem impossible to reconcile with an orthodox view of "the Father compassionate." This is a "theological mystery" incommunicable except "in a cascade of metaphors" that are really catachreses, that is to say, quite simply, wrong, though wrong in complex ways. This assumption resides in Miller's reading of Hopkins as trying to make all things, good and evil ("lightning and love," "winter and warm"), rhyme with each other as they rhyme with Christ the Word. Miller sees Hopkins's poetic project as desperately (because futilely) rehearsing the Catholic sacrament of Communion (different from Protestant Communion because of the Doctrine of Real Presence): "Poetry, if it is to have value, must repeat that magical assimilation of the dispersed into one. Like the words of the priest in the Communion, poetry must not describe things as they are *but make something happen*" (243–44). "The Wreck of the Deutschland," a poem about the cruel deaths of innocents and believers (the five nuns), wants to make these deaths and the ship's catastrophe into a convincing case for a merciful God—this is the pervasive "Christian metaphysics" that Miller leaves unstated but nonetheless radically destroyed by the poem's linguistic machinery. The thrust of my argument does not rescue theodicy for the poem, but instead challenges the assumption that theodicy drives the poem. All three claims—that linguistics wrestles with theology but does not win, that the strategy of repetition does not reconcile subversive differences, and that the poem is not a theodicy—stake their success on a reading of the poem that credits it with a Jobean consciousness: an awareness of gaps in human understanding that it notices but does not fill, regrets but does not compensate.

In the part of *Repetition* entitled "Report by Constantin Constantius," Constantin performs an experiment. He returns to Berlin and tries to reenact a previous trip in all details, from food and board to entertainment. As might be expected, he experiences nothing as he had on the first visit, and most of the scenes and events fall flat in reenactment. His conclusions about his endeavor describe ironically the trick of repetition: "The only repetition was the impossibility of a repetition" (170), and "My discovery was not significant, and yet it was curious, for I had discovered that there simply is no repetition and verified it by having it repeated in every possible way" (171). In the course of his report, busy mostly with proving this repetition of difference, Constantin pauses for several separate epiphanies, when he "reports" in the mode of poetry. He remembers from his first trip a moment of rapturous laughter at a farce in the Königstadter Theater, during which, he recalls, he apostrophized his "unforgettable nursemaid," the "fleeting nymph" that inhabited a brook near which he played in his childhood. The Heraclitean nymph who is his muse becomes a mnemonic for memory and therefore an impossible constant, retrieved once at a farce and then again in the memory of that farce, a symbol of inimitable serendipity relied upon to conjure up repeatedly the same remembrances.

Another poetic epiphany (it really occurs first in Constantin's report) also evokes a natural phenomenon, one that is even more capricious than a brook, but the evocation serves a parable with a different message, against a facile understanding of "the consistency and sureness of human freedom":

> In a mountain region where day in and day out one hears the wind relentlessly play the same invariable theme, one may be tempted for a moment to abstract from this imperfection and delight in this metaphor of the consistency and sureness of human freedom. One perhaps does not reflect that there was a time when the wind, which for many years had its dwelling among these mountains, came as a stranger to this area, plunged wildly, absurdly through the canyons, down into the mountain caves, produced now a shriek almost startling to itself, then a hollow roar from which it itself fled, then a moan, the source of which it itself did not know, then from the abyss of anxiety a sigh so deep that the wind itself grew frightened and momentarily doubted that it dared reside in this region, then a gay lyrical waltz—*until, having learned to know its instrument, it worked all of this into the melody it renders unaltered day after day.* Similarly, the individual's possibility wanders about in its own possibility, discovering now one possibility, now another. But the individual's possibility does not want only to be heard; it is not like the mere passing of the wind. It is also *gestaltende* [configuring] and therefore wants to be visible at the same time. *That is why each of its possibilities is an audible shadow.* (155, my emphasis)

From the hauntingly wild primevalism of its earliest noise to its present song, the wind's discipline enacts the repetition of both the player of music and the music played, since its instrument is nothing other than itself. As the apparent foil to the individual, it cautions against naïve belief in endless and absolutely diverse possibilities implied in notions of "human freedom" by turning each of those possibilities into "audible shadows" of all the others. Along with the impossibly constant serendipity signified by the nymph of the brook, it is this impossible notion of "audible shadow," both sound and form (*gestalt*), extracted from the parable of the wind, that can be put to work in understanding Hopkins's "Wreck."

There is an "audible shadow" of Constantin's "audible shadow" in the poetic discourse of Hopkins; it is his idiosyncratic use of the word "sake" in "The Wreck of the Deutschland" and later in "Henry Purcell," a use he defines very carefully in his correspondence to Bridges. Stanza 22 of "The Wreck" begins "Five! the finding and sake / And cipher of suffering Christ": "Five!" refers to the five doomed nuns and the five marks of the stigmata borne by St. Francis. In "Henry Purcell" the speaker forges a symbiotic relationship with the "fair fallen" Purcell, not through "mood in him nor meaning":

> It is the forged feature finds me; *its the rehearsal*
> *Of own,* of abrupt self there so thrusts on, so throngs the ear.
>
> Let him oh! with his air of angels then lift me, lay me! only I'll
> Have an eye to the *sakes* of him, quaint moonmarks, to his pelted
> plumage under
> Wings . . .[8]

In May of 1879 Hopkins glosses "Henry Purcell" for his friend, and includes this explanation of his affection for "sake":

> *Sake* is a word I find it convenient to use: I did not know when I did so first that it is common in German, in the form *sach*. It is the *sake* of 'for the sake of', *forsake, namesake, keepsake*. I mean by it the being a thing has outside itself, as a voice by its echo, a face by its reflection, a body by its shadow, a man by his name, fame, or memory, *and also* that in the thing by virtue of which especially it has this being abroad, and that is something distinctive, marked, specifically or individually speaking, as for a voice and echo clearness; for a reflected image light, brightness; for a shadow-casting body bulk; for a man genius, great achievements, amiability, and so on.[9]

8. Gerard Manley Hopkins, *Gerard Manley Hopkins,* ed. Catherine Phillips (New York: Oxford University Press, 1986), 143, lines 6–11.

9. Gerard Manley Hopkins, *The Letters of Gerard Manley Hopkins to Robert Bridges,* ed. Claude Colleer Abbott (London: Oxford University Press, 1935), 83.

Hopkins also records the weighty significance of the historical ship-wreck that becomes the watershed in a period of self-imposed poetic silence. In 1875 he asks his mother for any newspaper clippings about the tragic fate of the German ship that met disaster near the mouth of the Thames. In his letter he writes: "It made a deep impression on me, more than any other wreck or accident I ever read of" (*Further Letters*, 135). The fate of the Deutschland triggers another historical "event," at least in the world of literature, the event of Gerard Manley Hopkins's return to poetry. As an incentive to move Bridges to reread his poem, Hopkins promises him, even bribes him with, insight-producing veracity: "I may add for your greater interest and edification that what refers to myself in the poem is all strictly and literally true and did all occur, nothing is added for poetical padding" (*Letters*, 47).[10] This promise signals that the poem tells the story of a poet, and whether or not "strictly and literally" about Hopkins himself, the promise matters. One of the poem's themes is the possibility of a poet's own being, the record of becoming a poet.[11] Furthermore, an emphasis on the historical event that prompted the poem (the wreck), and the historical event that *was* the poem (Hop-kins's return to poetry), begins to counteract poststructuralist emphasis on the poem's linguistic subversion of the origin. For Miller, "The Wreck" conveys the tragic failure of language. My analysis also always answers questions of origin with "it is this but also that and therefore perhaps neither," but disputes readings that declare verbal powerlessness to be the main effect of "The Wreck of the Deutschland."

Whatever cannot be said in words about God, still, it can be said with authority that in December of 1875 a shipwreck off the Thames inspired a young man in Wales to resume a poetic career that had been inter-rupted for seven years by the vocation of priesthood. But "The Wreck of the Deutschland' both begins a new phase in Hopkins's life and returns him to an old one; while original, therefore, it repeats at least in genre what came before it. This compositional paradox bequeaths the text its stylistic and thematic challenge.

The first stanza of the poem accepts this challenge by commemorating a Paterian second flowering and explaining why such an event is strange. Apostrophizing God, the speaker recalls how He made him, and then "almost unmade" him. Now, at the moment of the poem, this crisis of

---

10. For a factual summary of the story of the *Deutschland,* see *Further Letters of Gerard Manley Hopkins,* 439–43.

11. In all versions of his theory, Miller proposes that "one theme of the poem is *its* own possibility of being" (*The Linguistic Moment,* 256; my emphasis).

near-destruction has passed, and the speaker ends the stanza by asking, "and dost thou touch me afresh? / Over again I feel thy finger and find thee" (7–8). This is a reference to rebirth, no doubt, and yet it is a strange rebirth—rather, it accentuates the strangeness that *is* rebirth— because it results from a previous dismantling imitated in earlier lines of the poem. "Thou hast bound bones and veins in me, fastened me flesh," says the speaker, "And after it almost unmade, what with dread, / Thy doing . . ." (5–7). In the very line where the work of God the "giver of breath and bread," is recognized as a consolation ("Thou hast bound"), the speaker presents himself as dissected into his parts: bones, veins, and flesh. The poem begins, in other words, with a taking apart and a putting back together, a return to or repetition of a prior state ("afresh" and "over again") that is nonetheless irrevocably different for the dismantling. To stress this difference, the stanza evokes Job, the exemplary undone and then redone man, who early in his story appeals to God in similar language: "Remember, I beseech thee, that thou hast made me as the clay; and wilt thou bring me into the dust again? Hast thou not poured me out as milk, and curdled me like cheese? Thou hast clothed me with skin and flesh, and hast fenced me with bones and sinew" (Job 10:9–11).

The second burden the first stanza bears is a formal one that results directly from the thematic burden of dismantling, because every stanza that follows imitates formally the process of dismantling and reassembling. Almost every stanza (and every stanza in Part the First) begins with a very short line, and then blossoms, though tentatively, over the course of eight lines into an eighth line that is very long. Hopkins controls this flowering both visually and aurally. One can see the gradual movement from short to long just by looking at, not reading, the poem. The aural control is in the pattern of stress, which Hopkins identifies in a piece he wrote in anticipation of its publication. Note also his instructions for the eye:

> Be pleased, reader, since the rhythm in which the following poem is written is new, strongly to mark the beats of the measure, according to the number belonging to each of the eight lines of the stanza, and the indentation guides the eye, namely two and three and four and three and five and five and four and six. (*Gerard Manley Hopkins,* 335)

Tentatively, the lines expand, from two stresses to three to four, and back for a line to three, and so on. Then, as a stanza proceeds from another, first the expansive result that is the last line of the previous stanza is undone, followed by yet another reproduction of that expansion; this pattern continues roughly, straight through to the last stanza. The first stanza is instantly undone by the second, and then restored as the the- matic and formal guide of the whole poem; it is undone and redone thirty-three more times. "The Wreck of the Deutschland" thus immedi- ately introduces the undone/redone man, who, we will see, is the model for the writer. And in its structural properties, it mimics the labor of the apprentice poet, practicing a poetic form (here eight lines of increasing stresses) over and over again. If we return now to the wreck that precipi- tated such a poem, we can see how that first event on the Thames and its reduplication in the poem might be seen either to follow or to have inspired the governing pattern of wreck and restoration. Again, *Repeti- tion* provides a framework within which to work out the important issue of artistic opportunity (or opportunism) necessary in the making of a poet.

Constantin Constantius, not a particularly sympathetic "author," is perhaps at his least attractive when he serves as the conduit through which we learn about a love relationship between the "young man" who has come to him for help and the young woman who has every reason to believe the young man is in love with her. In the delineation of this relationship, *Repetition* itself repeats a dilemma that plagues several of Kierkegaard's characters, that of choosing between romantic love and some "higher calling." In *Repetition* Constantin calls it the "poetic colli- sion" between erotic love and poetry (140).[12] Here the young man, according to Constantin, has the problem of extricating himself from a relationship that provided him the very inspiration that now gives him cause to escape. Constantin coolly assesses this predicament: "The young girl was not his beloved: she was the occasion that awakened the poetic in him and made him a poet" (138).

The second part of the book, which contains letters from the young man to Constantin, both challenges and corroborates this assessment and reveals Constantin to be diabolically manipulative as well as very perspicacious. But the most important part of the book is the "Conclud- ing Letter" from Constantin to the reader: "Although you are indeed fictional, you are by no means a plurality to me but only one, and

12. This is the dilemma Kierkegaard himself faced, of course, in his relationship with Regine Olsen. This piece of autobiography appears repeatedly, in *Repetition,* in Johannes Climacus's rejection of family life in *Fragments* (see Chapter 1), and in "Quidam's Diary" and the banquet scene (a *Symposium* imitation whose topic is woman) in *Stages on Life's Way.*

therefore we are just you and I" (225). And then he implicitly identifies the origin of the young man as he appears in the book: "The young man I have brought into being is a poet. I can do no more, for the most I can do is to imagine a poet and to produce him by my thought. I myself cannot become a poet, and in any case my interest lies elsewhere" (228). In other words, Constantin very nearly admits that the young man as he appears in the work is his own fictional creation, while he leaves unanswered, or makes irrelevant, questions about whether that fiction evolved *ex nihilo* (there never was any young man at all, and Constantin made the whole thing up) or as an interpretation (of some "real" young man with a convenient predicament). And this ambiguity lies at the heart of *Repetition,* for if the young man may (or must) be pure fiction, obviously so may the young woman, the ostensible point of origin. We can trace a pattern of repetitive opportunism: the love of the young woman provides the young man with a "higher calling"; the consequent predicament provides Constantin with the script for his story; and finally, the interrelationship of all these characters gives Kierkegaard the opportunity to compose *Repetition.* (The pattern is reversed in the "real" chronology of composition, beginning with Kierkegaard, and ending with the young woman.) And yet the origins also vanish. The young woman, banished from the story by the young man's rejection, also may or may not vanish into a mere shadow of Constantin's imagination. At the end of the book, Constantin calls himself "a vanishing person, just like a midwife in relation to the child she has delivered" (230). He differs from the young girl, however, for in the same paragraph he also calls himself a spokesman for the fledgling poet he has delivered, so to the extent that he really is a "vanishing person," he becomes the Cheshire Cat, his invisibility marked by a maniacally visible mouth, with that mouth as the substitute for the impossible, the voice of a poet not yet ready to speak.

On the cusp of a sustained poetic silence, Hopkins breaks that silence by inventing in his poem a speaker who plays both parts, the spokesman for the still-silent poet, and the silent poet herself (the tall nun). The expansion and retraction in the stanzaic pattern of "The Wreck of the Deutschland" is the formal equivalent of this interplay; the configuration of characters in the poem, its manifestation in theme. In "The Wreck of the Deutschland" an occasion is provided, and a persona to make of that occasion what he can in poetry; thus Hopkins delivers this poem about becoming a poet, the "first born" in his strange second flowering.

In his epigraphs Hopkins dedicates his poem "to the happy memory of five Franciscan nuns, exiled by the Falck Laws, drowned between midnight and morning of December 7" (*Gerard Manley Hopkins,* 110).

These nuns, the fact that they *were* nuns, the report of this heroism (they yielded safer spots on the ship to others), and their devout deaths, met in the act of prayer, surely stoked creative fires that burnt away his scruples about writing poetry. The dedication contains an ambiguity, moreover, that points to the nuns' fate as opportunity taken. Though "To the happy memory of five Franciscan nuns" belongs to the conventional "in memoriam" language of eulogy, and "happy" can be merely the right word from a believer about another believer's deliverance from the world and to God's kingdom, still the dedication can just as easily refer to Hopkins's own happy memory of learning about the wreck because of the efficacious effect it had on him. The double origin identified in the epigraphs corresponds to the dual nature of the poem as Hopkins sees it, "discourse" and "narrative," weighted in favor of "discourse" due to, or responsible for, its lyrical quality: "The Deutschland would be more generally interesting if there were more wreck and less discourse, I know, but still it is an ode and not primarily a narrative" (*Letters,* 49). Always, in all aspects of the poem, two things go on in "The Wreck of the Deutschland"; if we tally what we have so far, there is formal contraction and expansion, public history and personal memory, and a generic combination of "discourse" and "narrative." By the climactic stanza there will also be two voices, the speaker's and the tall nun's. The most important role played by Part the First, devoted exclusively to the speaker's personal experience, is the preparation undergone by the speaker to project the nun's voice, in the same relationship Constantin describes between him and the young man: "Every move I have made is merely to throw light on him; I have had him constantly *in mente* (in mind); every word of mine is either ventriloquism or is said in connection with him. . . . For that reason all the movements are purely lyrical, and what I say is to be understood as obscurely pertaining to him or as helping to understand him better" (*Repetition,* 228). Preparing to be a poet, however, is a self-absorbing process, and the ventriloquism to which the speaker aspires in order to "tell" the tall nun's tale is achieved by enumerating "autobiographical" details of the ventriloquist. The first of these details to be disclosed in an elaborate prologue (Part the First) is that the speaker is a convert.

Part the First of "The Wreck of the Deutschland" ends by doubling back on itself (though always with a difference) through recourse to an idiosyncratic biblical typology. Job, the Old Testament undone and redone man, reappears as the New Testament Paul in stanza 10, whose instant remake is itself rehearsed more slowly by Augustine's prolonged period of conversion. Stanza 10 spells out possible ways for God to achieve a conversion, Paul and Augustine being examples of two very different methods: "Whether at once, as once at a crash Paul, / Or as Austin, a lingering-out sweet skill..." (77–78). The difference in method (choice from an array of possibilities) matters as much as the similarity in result (conversion), making Paul and Augustine "audible shadows" of each other, and of Job. In the next two lines, the last of Part the First, the speaker allies himself with these shadows of the conversion experience: "Make mercy in *all of us,* out of us all / Mastery, but be adored, but be adored King" (79–80, my emphasis). Conversion itself depends upon the principle of repetition; just as Job, Paul, and Augustine reflect each other typologically, each of them converts into a new version of himself and becomes the same man with a difference. Stanza 7 suggests, if not insists, that a typological correspondence (in the Christian tradition, the very method of establishing simultaneous difference and similarity) should be drawn between the beginning and end of Part the First by interrupting with the story of Christ. "It dates from day / Of his going in Galilee..." begins the stanza, as it compresses Christ's story to its first and penultimate parts: "Warm-laid grave of a womb-life grey; / Manger, maiden's knee; / The dense and the driven Passion, and frightful sweat..." (51–53). Each stanza attains a full flowering of its eight lines; Old Testament becomes New Testament in conformity with the Christian principle of typology; and every convert becomes (newly) himself. And each convert becomes himself in great measure by becoming *articulate,* for the most significant trait Job, Paul, and Augustine share is their role as self-explicators, even as that role subordinates itself to "correct" articulation of the religious experience of being mastered. That the speaker experiences a conversion can be deduced in Part the First; that the conversion makes him a poet is implied by the company in which he places himself. *How* he is a poet, however, can be seen only retroactively, in the context of Part the Second, whose second stanza (stanza 12) begins the poem's poet's poem with the straightforward "On Saturday sailed from Bremen..."

Part the Second works through yet another series of duplications and refigurings. Almost every aspect of its twenty-five stanzas eventually finds, or is faced with either its double or its antithesis (a doubling in reverse). Though the tall nun will soon become the star of the second part, she is prefigured tellingly by the image of the man who dangles over the boat from the rope he tied to himself as he tried to save "the wild woman-kind below" (122). In death he is transformed on the one hand into an icon of death, on the other into a grotesque parody of a rosary, for "They could tell him for hours, dandled the to and fro /

Through the cobbled foam-fleece" (126–27). His appearance is no less dramatic than the tall nun's, and he is her avatar, as she, in the very next stanza, also emerges spectacularly from the panic-stricken "rabble": "Till a lioness arose breasting the babble, / A prophetess towered in the tumult, a virginal tongue told" (135–36). Where he is told—made out against the storm—she tells, "a sister calling / A master..." (145–46). Here, in the most literal sense, the nun is the "audible shadow" of the silent hero.

Stanza 19, where the nun calls her master, records the single-mindedness of the nun, but uses a word to describe this single-mindedness that slyly inscribes in itself the real "double-mindedness" of Part the Second. The nun "Has one fetch in her: she rears herself to divine / Ears..." (150–51). "Fetch" is generally glossed here in its nautical use as a way of tacking; it then becomes an event of a verbal noun, so characteristic of Hopkins's poetry. But in another, peculiarly British, archaic use of the word, "fetch" can be a noun meaning a doppelganger, an "apparition, double or wraith of a living person."[13] After its appearance, doublings proliferate. Germany divides into St. Gertrude and Luther to mean "O Deutschland, double a desperate name!" (155). St. Francis's stigmata, the five-point replication of Christ's passion, itself is replicated in the five nun's sufferings, just as they, and all Franciscans, duplicate St. Francis. (Just as Shakespeare's sonnets are not Shakespearean until they are imitated, Francis does not become a Franciscan until he is followed.) As the poem concludes, "The Christ of the Father compassionate" both fetches—gathers to Him or brutally kills his *Deutschland* disciples, depending on how you look at it—and is doubled, "fetched in the storm of his strides" (264). The doubling culminates in the penultimate stanza, where the most accurate description of God's name, chased after throughout the poem, is "Double-natured name" (266). The nun, however, has but "one fetch" in her, and it is not the silently dangling hero. So far my reading shores up the argument for initial bifurcation by locating a schism in the single-minded nun, later praised for her "single eye" (226). Before recasting the reason for such persistent and endless divi-

---

13. See Robertson Davies's *World of Wonders* (Toronto: Macmillan of Canada, 1975). An old Scotsman in the book needs to teach the protagonist how to be a perfect double—more than a double—for the vaudeville star for whom they both work (what we would call a stuntman for the aging star). To explain the nuances of being a double, and to give the protagonist a good stage name, he tells this story: "Well, in Scotland, when I was a boy, we had a name for such thing. If a man met a creature like himself in a lane, or in town, maybe, in the dark, it was a sure sign of ill luck or even death.... Now: such an uncanny creature was called a fetch" (209). The protagonist's stage name becomes "Fetch."

sion, however, one more element must be drawn into the analysis. Off in Wales, the speaker must now be brought into his own fiction, in an appropriately dual role as the nun's double and antithesis.

"Away in the loveable west / On a pastoral forehead of Wales" (185–86), the speaker sets the scene for poetic composition. He has already revealed that he is a convert; now he locates himself geographically, emphasizing the comfort of that locale: "I was under a roof here, I was at rest..." (187). "Loveable" [*sic*] and pastoral, this scene of writing could not be more different or more distant from the scene of the wreck, and yet the difference and distance between the two scenes improbably collapse as they appear contiguously in the same stanza. "I was under a roof here, I was at rest" is immediately followed by and grammatically implicated in "And they the prey of the gales... ," a clause that makes sense elliptically by sharing the first line's verb ("And they *were* the prey of the gales"). In this stanza the speaker breaks a pattern of omniscient narration (a break itself prefigured in the ambivalent interruption of stanza 18), and yet in his sentient and unignorable presence he "yields" the power of poetry to the nun, whose "virginal tongue" gets to speak "in tongues," the language of metaphor. "Yield" is in quotation marks, of course, because he does no such thing; as he imagines her, she is his fiction, helpless as the ventriloquist's dummy really to speak. He invents the following: The nun "Was calling 'O Christ, Christ, come quickly': / The cross to her she calls Christ to her, christens her wild-worst Best" (191–92). To christen one's "wild-worst" as "Best" is to rename metaphorically, to attach the peculiar signifier "Best" to what needs resignifying in order to make it consonant with a merciful God, the "wild-worst" experience of the tall nun. The nun speaks metaphorically through the poetic machination of her "fetch," the poet-in-Wales, who then promulgates his own fiction of the nun-as-poet by casting himself in the role of interpreter, as the next stanza begins: "The majesty! What did she mean?" And what did she mean? Or what does he have her mean? And how does he say poetically what he has her mean? He says it haltingly, incompletely, and insufficiently: that is the thrust of stanza 28, where the apprenticeship of the poet-in-Wales as the spokesman for the poet-nun in the wreck is put to the test. "But how shall I... make me room there: / Reach me a... Fancy, come faster—" (217–18).

For Miller, this stanza brings the poem to its linguistic climax, just as stanza 24, where "the tall nun saying the name of Christ and thereby being saved, transformed into Christ at the moment of her death" (*The Linguistic Moment,* 261), is the dramatic climax. The two climaxes represent the wrestle between theology and linguistics that, according to Miller, linguistics wins:

> Its dramatic climax is the tall nun's saying the name of Christ and thereby being saved, transformed into Christ at the moment of her death. The linguistic climax is the implicit recognition, in stanzas 22 and 28, that there is no way of speaking of this theological mystery except in a cascade of metaphors whose proliferation confesses to the fact that there is no literal word for the Word. Since these "metaphors" do not replace a literal term, they are, strictly speaking, not metaphors but catachreses, names thrown out toward the unnameable Word and more covering it in human noise than revealing it or speaking it out. (261)

Stanza 28 only demonstrates, however, that there is no way for the *poet-in-Wales,* the speaker in the poem, to speak of this theological mystery. From his strong, straightforward start ("On Saturday sailed from Bremen") he falters into incoherent ellipsis ("But how shall I . . . make me room there . . ."), into a proliferation of inadequate terms ("Master, *Ipse,* the only one, Christ, King, Head"), and then into an odd language of command: "Do, deal, lord it with living and dead; / Let him ride, her pride, in his triumph, despatch and have done with his doom there."[14] But as the notes to the fourth edition of Hopkins's poetry point out, the falter into ellipsis on the part of the speaker is communicated through a rhetorical trope, aposiopesis, a very deliberate strategy to create the effect of unwillingness or inability to finish a thought or sentence.[15] What we glimpse here is not a failure of language, but a fiction of the speaker, and we are reminded that he is "newly himself," a convert and a poet (or a convert to poetry), and therefore a novice with the enormous task of reconstituting the nun out of the wreck, turning her into a poet and her experience into poetry, and interpreting that poetry. "Do, deal, lord it with living and dead . . ." is a self-address, an expostulation to

---

14. In *The Lucid Veil: Poetic Truth in the Victorian Age* (Madison: University of Wisconsin Press, 1987), David Shaw unaccountably attributes this line to the nun, using it as an example of a nineteenth-century holistic theory of language. The result of his misinterpretation is a thoughtful insight, provocative though unusable for citation because of what seems to me to be an error. For Shaw, in her use of optatives (Do, deal . . . Let him) the tall nun resembles Job, in his "mysterious act of acknowledging that the God who has given has also taken away" (84).

15. Gerard Manley Hopkins, *The Poems of Gerard Manley Hopkins,* 4th ed., ed. W. H. Gardner and N. H. Mackenzie (London: Oxford University Press, 1967), 261.

persevere and succeed following a moment of artistic crisis. As such it imitates its "fiction," the tall nun's perseverance in renaming and therefore reinterpreting *her* crisis.

That the imitation is in the act of articulation, and of making metaphor, Miller points out as an example of "Hopkins's awareness of [the] tragic eccentricity of language" (*The Linguistic Moment,* 259). Miller notes that stanza 22 is made up of a list of words meaning the "act of stamping something with a sign, making it a representation or metaphor for something else," or in other words, an "act of wording": "Finding, sake, cipher, mark, word, score, stigma, signal, cinquefoil token, lettering" (259).[16] No "unmoving word . . . outside the play of differences" controls this series as far as Miller is concerned; but he can sustain this judgment only by ignoring the pun in the very center of the stanza: "And the word of it Sacrificed." There *is* a controlling word—"And the word of it" *is the word* "Sacrificed"—and there is not—because "the word of it" has been sacrificed. The words for the "act of wording," all "audible shadows" or "sakes" (or fetches) of each other and of the central "word of it" (though inadequate, being marks "of man's make") gather around but do not fill in the gap that *may* exist in the center of the stanza. Without even attending to the obvious paschal meaning of either that which is the word "sacrificed" (the "word of it Sacrificed" like Christ) or that "word" which has been "sacrificed" (Christ Himself), "Sacrificed" lies outside the linguistic series that dominates the stanza, having nothing to do with "Finding," "sake," "cipher," etc. As the stanza most concerned with the act of writing and therefore the role of the writer, it may be the best example of what Miller means by "human noise" (marks of "man's make") being thrown at the "unnameable Word." Its effect, however, is not obscurity, but emphasis on the gap between that noise and what it wants to articulate, even as it maintains its integrity as an attempt at articulating for the "sake" of what lies beyond the purview of human language. "Stigmata," for instance, will always invoke Christ's wounds, even as its sufferer always bears the stigmata "for the sake" of Christ, but similarity will never be replaced by identity. The poem will soon move into its climax with this stanza as its keynote, revealing nothing, but commemorating in advance the struggle of language to make meaning around a metalinguistic mystery.

"The Wreck of the Deutschland' therefore documents the poet's own possibility of being (not "the poem's own possibility of being"), and documents that it happens twice, to the nun as she is given authorship of a text

---

16. See Irving Massey's *Uncreating Word* (Bloomington: Indiana University Press, 1970) for a "pre-post-structuralist" critique of Hopkins that is very close to Miller's here (92–94).

("O Christ, Christ, come quickly . . ."), and to the speaker as he positions himself as both her ventriloquist and her reader ("what did she mean?"). We have thus located more than one text on the surface of the poem, and not as overthought and subversive underthought. This claim depends on repetition and *Repetition* in order to read the poem as populated on its surface with interacting texts and *words* that nonetheless remain separate, as separate as the demarcated parts of Constantin's story. Just as Constantin lodges between his "Report" and his "Concluding Letter" the letters of the young man, the poet-in-Wales inserts the tall nun's tale (by "virginal tongue told") between his preparatory Part the First and the concluding stanzas of Part the Second. The young man's letters elude Constantin's explanatory power, even though he claims them as his own fiction. So too does the nun's tale elude the poet-in-Wales, even as he bears the authorial burden of creating "her" (for the "real her" dies in the shipwreck), and of making "her" talk. But such a revision does not yet address the religious complexities of the poem, the theology Miller sees as undone by the poem's language. I will begin to address these complexities by renaming "contentio" what Miller has called "catachresis." This substitution replaces the explaining away of troubling events (the suffering of innocents and believers) that catachresis accomplishes with the more pugnacious linguistic art of antithesis, always based on the existence of two equal and oppositional concepts.

In "Hopkins Revisited," Geoffrey Hartman characterizes the poet's style as the style of *contentio,* and supplies the two ways in which he means such a characterization:

> In a stray comment Hopkins once urged what he names "*contentio,* or strain of address." No phrase can better describe his own strain of style. *Contentio* is a term from rhetoric designating an antithetical or pointed repetition of words. But in Hopkins's mind the term has somehow fused with the Jobean contentio, with a raising of the voice to God, with a like insistence of address. . . . Language is shown to be *contentio* in essence—there is nothing disinterested or general about it; its end as its origin is to move, persuade, possess. Hopkins leads us back to an aural situation (or its simulacrum) where meaning and invocation coincide.[17]

17. Geoffrey Hartman, "Hopkins Revisited," in his *Beyond Formalism: Literary Essays 1958–1970* (New Haven: Yale University Press, 1970), 238–39. Miller dismisses Hartman's thesis in one long sentence: "If Hopkins' basic poetic strategy, as Geoffrey Hartman has noted, is a differentiation of language that attempts to say the Word by dividing the word, these divisions are controlled by no central word that could be enunciated in any language" (*The Linguistic*

Contentio enables an understanding of the poem as using, exploring, and imaginatively rendering "initial bifurcation" (Miller's phrase) not to elide the gaps between the dualities, dichotomies, and chasms present in the poem, but to announce their existence, an announcement already made by stanza 22. Hartman contributes the dual definition of *contentio* as Hopkins employs it, and draws Job into this discussion of "The Wreck" as it begins its final task of proving why the poem is not a theodicy, and why that matters. Michael Sprinker's reading of stanza 22 reinforces the notion of endless wrestle (vs. a clear call of victory and defeat) that resides in the use of *contentio:*

> The general semiotic project disclosed in the twenty-second stanza of "The Wreck of the Deutschland" is identical with the *central theological question* that haunts the entire poem: the difficulty of understanding the meaning of sacrifice, in the immediate instance the death of the five Franciscan nuns, but more generally the necessity for suffering in the world. (My emphasis)[18]

Sprinker's comparison of Derridean *écriture* and Hopkins's poetry enables a reading of "The Wreck" as endlessly dynamic and unresolving (and unresolvable). By positing a "central theological question," rather than a "theology" or a "metaphysics," and by implicating that question in the semiotics of the poem, he precludes a judgment of theological defeat and participates in the more fruitful exploration of the symbiotic relationship (marked nonetheless by tension) between theology and linguistics, or, more accurately, between theology and poetry. One cannot question the existence of suffering and simultaneously reconcile suffering with a "Father compassionate"; the two cognitive acts (questioning and reconciling) can at best alternate, but they cannot coexist. The first act defies a heteronomous order (and theodicy assumes such an order), while the second act reinforces a reigning heteronomy. Such is the lesson taught to Job and taught by Job.[19]

Moment, 259). But Miller ignores the impact of *contentio* on the discourse of "The Wreck" to the detriment of his thesis, because in fact it supports his insistence upon an initial bifurcation at the event of the origin of language—*contentio,* after all, always means "two," the minimum number in any bifurcation.

18. Michael Sprinker, *A Counterpoint of Dissonance: The Aesthetics and Poetry of Gerard Manley Hopkins* (Baltimore: The Johns Hopkins University Press, 1980), 106.

19. See Kenneth Seskin's "Job and the Problem of Evil," *Philosophy and Literature* 2, no. 2 (October 1987): 226–41, for a treatment of theodicy, the limits of human knowledge, and suffering as they are attended to in the Book of Job, an example for Seskin of Biblical "protest literature."

One more return to *Repetition,* this time to the letters of the young man, helps establish "The Wreck of the Deutschland" as Jobean and contentious enough to stave off subtle charges of theodicy. Though the young man in *Repetition* writes no poetry for the reader to see, in his letters he refers to himself as a poet in the bleakest of ways. "In our time," he writes to Job (in his letter to Constantin), "it is thought that genuine expressions of grief . . . must be assigned to the poets . . ." (197–98), and he asks rhetorically (for he gives Constantin no return address and no hint as to where he is), "Or is becoming a poet my compensation?" (202). The young man in his plaintive letters would be hardly more sympathetic than Constantin (since, after all, the manipulative Constantin invented him), if it were not for his strong appeal to Job ("Job! Job! Job!" begins his first letter, and he refers to him throughout) and his equally strong appeal to be seen as like Job. But his *question,* "Or is becoming a poet my compensation?" reverberates with the Book of Job, which unfolds as the vexatious compensation for an "initial bifurcation" between God and Satan and the consequent "wreck" of Job's happy life. And the same question resonates *in* "The Wreck of the Deutschland." Becoming a poet, the record of which is the poem, means inventing metaphors for a Pascalian unavailable God as the compensatory act for "past all Grasp God's" absence from the realm of human language. Such compensation, self-consciously ensconced in a never-fully-answered question, makes poetry the consolation prize for the limits of human knowledge and understanding. But it also lends integrity to that knowledge and understanding. An answer to the "Why" of human suffering remains as hidden as the God who ordains it. The fact that the question can be asked, however ("is the shipwrack then a harvest, does tempest carry the grain for thee?" the poet-in-Wales queries God), permits the proliferation of human language in its most sublime form, as the "audible shadow" of what cannot be seen or heard, for the sake of God, certainly, but also for the sake of the "Five Franciscan Nuns exiled by the Falck Laws" and the poet in whose "happy memory" they are recovered and reconstituted as (that is, converted into) poetry.

When Hopkins sent "The Wreck of the Deutschland" and "The Loss of the Eurydice" to Canon Dixon, he included reading instructions: "It is best to read the Eurydice first, which is in plain sprung rhythm and will possess you with the run of it. The Deutschland, earlier written, has more variety but less mastery of the rhythm."[20] References in his correspondence to the two poems, such as "the two ship-wreck pieces,"

---

20. Gerard Manley Hopkins, *The Correspondence of Gerard Manley Hopkins and Richard Watson Dixon,* ed. Claude Colleer Abbott (London: Oxford University Press, 1955), 26.

suggest strongly that they were a pair in Hopkins's mind, and their shared fate of rejection by the Jesuit periodical, *The Month,* cemented the relationship between "my two wrecks." Their similarities are obvious: both commemorate shipwrecks, exemplify Hopkins's "sprung rhythm," have regular stanzaic patterns, and, significantly at this point, are long poems that have been completed. Hopkins himself identifies their differences by identifying the flaws in "The Wreck of the Deutschland." When he allows to Bridges that "The Wreck" includes more narrative and less discourse, his letter continues: "This poem on the Eurydice is hitherto almost all narrative however" (*Letters,* 49). In 1881 he apparently responds to commentary by Bridges: "I agree that the Eurydice shews more mastery in art, still I think the best lines in the Deutschland are better than the best in the other. One may be biassed in favor of one's firstborn though" (119). In fact, throughout his correspondence to both Bridges and Dixon, Hopkins persistently defends the newness and innovation of "The Wreck of the Deutschland," while implicitly acknowledging the difficulty in such newness through his instructions to Dixon to read it after "The Loss of the Eurydice," and to Bridges, somewhat bullyingly, simply to read it again. "I must tell you I am sorry you never read the Deutschland again," he laments in a letter where he explains in no uncertain terms just why he is sorry:

> When a new thing, such as my ventures in the Deutschland are, is presented us our first criticisms are not our truest, best, most homefelt, or most lasting but what comes easiest on the instant. They are barbarous and like what the ignorant and the ruck say. This was so with you. The Deutschland on her first run worked very much and unsettled you, thickening and clouding your mind with vulgar mudbottom and common sewage.... I did not heed them [Bridges's criticisms] therefore, perceiving they were a first drawing-off. (50–51)

If Bridges resisted returning to "The Wreck" (though of course eventually he did, as editor), no less sensitive a reader than Coventry Patmore articulates in a letter to Hopkins why such a return seems useless: "But I do not think that I could ever become sufficiently accustomed to your favorite poem, 'The Wreck of the Deutschland' to reconcile me to its strangeness" (*Further Letters,* 353).

In the view of his three readers, Hopkins travels to the beat of a different drum in his "ventures in the Deutschland," but the drum, at least in Hopkins's mind, beats a strict rhythm, even if only he recognizes it. He thus defends himself to Bridges: " . . . with all my licenses, or rather laws, I am stricter than you and I might say than anybody I know" (*Letters,* 44).[21] But what is the dynamic between "my two wrecks," and how does understanding it penetrate the obscurity of which "The Wreck of the Deutschland" has been accused, to reveal the strict logic Hopkins claims for it? The fact that he tried to have both poems published (he never tried to publish again, and protested against friends' efforts to do so for him) and that he devoted a proportionately large amount of letter-writing over a three-year period to explaining them, argues for a poet who wants to be understood as a poet, albeit on his own terms.

In 1878, living in a place inhospitable to his muse (as often was the case in Hopkins's last ten years), he writes Bridges: "My muse turned utterly sullen in the Sheffield smoke-ridden air and I had not written a line till the foundering of the Eurydice the other day and that worked on me and I am making a poem—in my own rhythm but in a measure something like Tennyson's *Violet*" (48). For a second time a shipwreck galvanizes Hopkins, and perhaps because it *is* the second, it hints of opportunism. Though the Eurydice's fate repeats the effect on Hopkins that the Deutschland had had on him, the two events are unconnected, and objectively they share few characteristics except in their nature as seagoing tragedies. They are two of many "wreck[s] or accident[s]." As unplanned and uncoordinated testimonies to the capriciousness of Constantin's brook-nymph's powerful sibling (and origin, or conversely, destination), they are yoked together and singled out from other wrecks and accidents by Hopkins's own imagination. Such a yoking may suggest a Freudian repetition-compulsion, reminiscent, for example, of Freud's seemingly innocent return again and again to a red-light district in the effort to take a walk and not get lost.[22] But that suggestion places false emphasis on Hopkins's complicity in the wrecks, and underplays Hopkins's real roles, which are, first, the agent of appropriation of what would be called in insurance language "acts of God," and second, the agent of repetition as he reenacts each event in his poetry. Unlike the case of Constantin, Berlin comes to Hopkins, but like the parable of the wind, his acts of appropriation and repetition retroactively configure similar events; by virtue of his poems, one wreck becomes an "audible

21. See W. H. Gardner's introduction to the fourth edition of Hopkins's poems. Gardner says that Hopkins's prosody gave him a "maximum of rhythmic flexibility within a fixed stanzaic form" (xxiii).
22. Sigmund Freud, "The Uncanny," in *Collected Papers,* vol. 4, trans. Joan Riviere (London: The Hogarth Press, 1949), 389–90.

shadow" of the other. Hopkins's poetic activities, furthermore, epitomize repetition's tricky maneuvering of difference and similarity; the two historical events will always remain separate and different from each other, or no more like each other than like any other shipwreck. But the poetic events that are the wrecks of the *Deutschland* and the *Eurydice* impose and then commemorate proximity and similarity; the poems begin, then, as "audible shadows" of the historical events as well as of each other. In other words more specifically directed to "The Loss of the Eurydice," this second shipwreck poem is written for the sake of, or as a keepsake of "The Wreck of the Deutschland."

Once attention is drawn to Hopkins's own pairing of his "two wrecks," the title of the second poem announces its alliance to what has come before it. What is lost is Eurydice, the dead wife of Orpheus, and the exemplar of the silenced, vanquished woman, lost not once but twice. Experiencing both losses is Orpheus, model of the song-maker, or poet, and eventually subject to brutal dismantling and consequent refiguring (head here, limbs there). The Orphic motif of loss permeates literature, as does the Jobean, and indeed, Job and Orpheus configure each other especially as makers of poetry, with one major difference. Job loses all and regains all (the young man says Job "has received everything double—This is called repetition" [212]); Orpheus loses all (Eurydice, without whom he has nothing) and then loses all again. And it is this "repetition with difference" of a loss motif that "The Loss of the Eurydice" enacts in its companionship with "The Wreck of the Deutschland." As a companion, therefore, it exposes the fragility of the dismantling/ restoration process dominating "The Wreck." Where "The Wreck" left exposed the gaps in human understanding surrounded by compensatory attempts to narrow them, "The Loss of the Eurydice" severely curtails such attempts and does not just expose the gaps, but widens them.

In *The Anxiety of Influence,* Harold Bloom calls Orphic poets "the poets of askesis," linking askesis to sublimation in the making of poetry: "sublimation of aggressive instincts is central to writing and reading poetry.... Poetic sublimation is an *askesis,* a way of purgation intending a state of solitude as its proximate goal."[23] Violence begets violence: it is this axiom that is tamed in a Jobean response to what looks like divine violence; begotten instead is a sublimation of the fiercer instinct, the poem itself. "The Loss of the Eurydice" displays greater effort than "The Wreck of the Deutschland" at containing an aggressive instinct, but only

---

23. Harold Bloom, *The Anxiety of Influence: A Theory of Poetry* (New York: Oxford University Press, 1973), 115–16.

because the instinct is stronger and less containable. Hopkins himself recognizes the aggression at the heart of his poem. He tells Bridges about reading it again after a time lapse: "I opened and read some lines, reading, as one commonly reads whether prose or verse, with the eyes, so to say, only, it struck me aghast with a kind of raw nakedness and unmitigated violence I was unprepared for: but take breath and read it with the ears, as I always wish to be read, and my verse becomes all right" (*Letters*, 79).[24] The curtailment of voice implied in the Orphic label characterizes the speaker in "The Loss of the Eurydice," who assumes the role of poet, no longer in a Jobean mode but in an Orphic one, no longer allowed expansive "discourse," but self-limited to "narrative." This self-limitation has as its goal an Orphic spirit of isolation at the poem's conclusion. As Sprinker concludes his chapter on "The Wreck," he projects forward to Hopkins's sonnets as the disciplined reaction to what he calls the "attainment of the Sublime":

> Poetry always remained for Hopkins perilously close to the song of Lucifer . . . as the poetry after "The Wreck of the Deutschland" shows, his response to the attainment of the Sublime was an immediate curtailment of his imaginative energy, a willful restriction of his poetic powers within the most demanding and disciplined of English verse forms, the sonnet. (119)

One need not go to the sonnets for this reaction. Hopkins responds poetically with "curtailment" and "willful restriction" in "The Loss of the Eurydice" to his wild and wondrous "first born," "The Wreck of the Deutschland." The speaker of the "Eurydice" gets right to his contentious point, gets right to the magnitude of the violence: "The Eurydice— it concerned thee, O Lord: / Three hundred souls, O alas! on board . . ." (1–2). Almost exactly half the length of "The Wreck" (its stanzas are exactly half the length of the stanzas of "The Wreck"), the "Eurydice" strips down a shipwreck-inspired product to the wreck itself, one survivor, one dead man, and a speaker left radically unconsoled (uncompensated) by his poetic act.

The first fourteen stanzas record the collusion of nature's deceit ("And you were a liar, O blue March day" [21]) and human error born from pride ("Too proud, too proud, what a press she bore!" [33]), and the

---

24. While Hopkins reads away the "raw nakedness and unmitigated violence" by reading it aloud, remembering his advice to Bridges about rereading "The Wreck," one suspects that simply reading it a second time domesticates his poem for him as much as reading it out loud does.

panicked attempts at self-rescue that ensue. In stanza 15 Sydney Fletcher, the wreck's sole survivor, emerges from the "messes of mortals" in what at first seems a reprise of the tall nun's "breasting" of "the babble." But where we might expect the nun's "audible shadow," we get only an inaudible one; after two stanzas of his harrowing experience, the young man is saved, but as a member of the poem, he is doomed to inexpressibility: "And he boards here in Oh! such joy / He has lost count what came next, poor boy—" (71–72). He disappears from the poem silently, making nothing of his experience into poetry. The story of a "sea-corpse cold" immediately follows him, a second-hand story ("They say who saw") about one of the dead sailors. Like the dangling man in "The Wreck" this dead man is an icon of death, representing the "leagues of seamanship" who "Slumber in theses forsaken / Bones, this sinew, and will not waken" (82–84). But by reversing the order of appearance of the dangling man and the nun, Sydney Fletcher followed by the rigid corpse (the first silent, the second, silence), commemorate only loss and compensate with nothing, as the beautiful tar disintegrates into anonymity: "He was but one like thousands more" (85).

Un-"fetched" by the figures he evokes, the speaker then tries for compensating resignation and achieves only angry poetic digression. "I might let bygones be—our curse..." continues the poem. But the speaker interrupts this one conscious attempt at resignation, and in a stanza that begins a rant against the Reformation oppressors of English Catholics, the poem leaps, or digresses from remembering the loss of humanity of the Eurydice to a sectarian lament: "Deeply surely I need to deplore it, / Wondering why my master bore it, / The riving off that race..." (97–99). Gone, with the men on the Eurydice, are the "English souls" of "rare-dear Britain" on whose behalf the speaker appeals to the tall nun ("Dame, at our door / Drowned") as "The Wreck of the Deutschland" ends. Left is the speaker who cannot let bygones be bygones. Allowing a digression hardly seems like strict self-curtailment, but the aposiopesis in "I might let bygones be—our curse" signals self-censure and the refusal to allow Fletcher's silence and the tar's death a consoling meaning. Perhaps Hopkins's most *politically* Catholic poem, "The Loss of the Eurydice" revises "The Wreck's" strategy of proceeding from (and therefore moving away from) a political disaster for Catholics (the Falck Laws) by interrupting itself with a similar disaster, the Reformation, and therefore privileging it and the rift it causes. Moreover, denouncing "the riving off that race" and questioning God's composure at such an event ("Deeply surely. I need to deplore it, / Wondering why my master bore it...") replicates in the politico-religious sphere the rift between human understanding and divinely ordained catastrophe.

Finally, the speaker turns the whole enterprise over to mother, wife, and sweetheart, not poets but pray-ers, not empowered to remake the meaning of disaster, but only able to plead—retroactively—for "Grace that day grace was wanted" (116). These are figures marginal to the action because separated in time and space from it, whose "grief yield them [their dead sons, husbands, lovers, and themselves] no good" (107). The theological worry here is that the dead men did not receive Last Rites, and are therefore condemned to Hell, at least until the Second Coming. The "words put into the mouth of a mother, wife, or sweetheart who has lost a son, husband, lover" (*Letters,* 78) are addressed not to a "winter and a warm" Lord, but to "Christ lord of thunder," boding ill for the efficacy of the prayer composed for them (111–16). The last stanza fully capitulates to the state of human unknowing by articulating a theological contradiction: "Not that hell knows redeeming, / But for souls sunk in seeming / Fresh, till doomfire burn all, / Prayer shall fetch pity eternal" (117–20). Hell knows no redeeming, but prayer fetches eternal pity: logically both cannot be. And so the poem ends.

Sprinker's comment above about Hopkins's reactionary self-curtailment reminds us of the danger in poetry by invoking the other model for the poet. The case of Lucifer, seduced by his own beautiful sound, warns the wary of their own vulnerability, particularly if they produce works that "drive out the devil . . . by the power of the devil." Hopkins was quite taken with his first "wreck" and promoted its poetic cause vigorously; a human catastrophe rewarded him with regained poetic speech after a long silence. When the opportunity came to repeat what he clearly thought was a success, he reined himself in, purging his new product of all but the most dire implications of "The Wreck of the Deutschland" and its sophisticated linguistic strategies. Where "The Wreck of the Deutschland" left unanswered the Why? of human suffering but permitted the proliferation of human language as the "audible shadow" of the divine, "The Loss of the Eurydice" only leaves unanswered the Why? of human suffering. As the "audible shadow" of "The Wreck of the Deutschland," it repeats with difference by curtailing the proliferation of human language both in its stripped-down structure and its lack of an "autonomous" speaking figure (a tall nun, a young man) invented by the narrator. Its last stanza offers only a conundrum-like jingle that defies decipherability.[25] "The Loss of the Eurydice," Hopkins's second opportunity to make poetic sense of a contemporary human catastrophe, reconstitutes all of the major aspects of "The Wreck of the

25. "Not that hell knows redeeming / But for souls sunk in seeming" has the same clever effect as "Men don't make passes / At girls who wear glasses."

Deutschland" only to demolish them and restrict further the scope of human understanding. It is a severe, contentious poem disciplined not to mitigate the violence it takes upon itself to narrate with verisimilitude. Hopkins glimpsed the truth about his "second-born" in that quick, unprepared-for reading he gave it, and could subdue its "raw nakedness and unmitigated violence" only by retreating to its sound. But the poem even sounds austere, stripped of the lyrical quality "The Wreck" has with its many linguistic flourishes.

In defending himself against anticipated charges that his approach to Hopkins's poetry appears too harsh, Sprinker "can only respond by say-ing that harshness and sterility, and even a certain dogmatism, are the very themes in Hopkins that strike me as important" (3). Sprinker's response begins to get at the real issue in understanding Hopkins's "two wrecks." Far from being rationalizations in the tradition of theodicy, the poems reveal the harshness of Hopkins's Christian theological vision at the center of his writings. The "book under divine confiscation" that would explain the "ways of God to man" remains confiscated. In a pas-sage from what was intended to be a sermon but was evidently never delivered, Hopkins articulates *not* a way of understanding "providence," but a way of receiving its actions; this passage speaks directly to the import of the "two wrecks" taken as a pair:

> And when we do not see the providence it may still be there and working in some secret way. Hope for it then and pray for it and yet fear and tremble, *work out your salvation in fear and trem-bling. For I must end as I began* [my emphasis]. One of God's providences is by warnings—the deaths of others, sermons, dan-gers, sicknesses, a sudden thought: beware, beware of neglecting a warning. This very discourse of mine, this meditation, is a warn-ing. A warning leaves a man better or worse, does him good or harm; *never leaves him as it finds him* [my emphasis].[26]

Miller condemns Hopkins to ending "where he was in the beginning, imprisoned within a self-taste that can be communicated by no means to another man" (*The Linguistic Moment,* 265). Hopkins beats him to this condemnation and also nullifies it. Beginning where he ends, and yet effecting a sea change—a conversion: that will remain the pattern in Hopkins's poetry in his poetic "second flowering." Constantin's young

---

26. Gerard Manley Hopkins, *The Sermons and Devotional Writings of Gerard Manley Hopkins,* ed. Christopher Devlin, S. J. (London: Oxford University Press, 1959), 252.

man answers the obvious question about Job, "Was he right to contend with God?" with one last "repetition with difference" in this section on Hopkins's "wrecks": "Yes, eternally, by being proved to be wrong *before God*" (*Repetition,* 212, editors' italics). The young man revises the definition of "right" to mean, impossibly, its opposite, just like the tall nun's "wild-worst Best." In both cases, the contradiction is simply left to stand, unsolved, unsolvable, unsolving, and unabsolving. "Hopkins's poetic problem," argues Miller, "was to find a way to communicate the incommunicable." One last revision is necessary. Hopkins's costly poetic success was that he found a way to communicate the incommunicability of the incommunicable.

5

Wreck and Reprise:
Rossetti

Nuns fret not at their convent's narrow room.
—William Wordsworth

In the preface to the posthumously published *New Poems of Christina Rossetti,* William Rossetti characterizes his sister's "habits of composing" as "eminently of the spontaneous kind":

> I question her having ever once deliberated with herself whether or not she would write something or other, and then, after thinking out a subject, having proceeded to treat it in regular spells of work. Instead of this, something impelled her feelings, or "came into her head," and her hand obeyed the dictation. I suppose she scribbled the lines off rapidly enough, and afterwards took whatever amount of pains she deemed requisite for keeping them right in form and expression . . . (strange as it seems to say so of a sister who, up to the year 1876, was almost constantly in the same house with me) I cannot remember her in the act of composition.[1]

In the Memoir accompanying *The Poetical Works,* he reiterates this characterization, adding: "It came to her (I take it) very easily, without her meditating a possible subject. . . . If the thing did not present itself

---

1. Christina Rossetti, *New Poems of Christina Rossetti: Hitherto Unpublished or Uncollected,* ed. William Rossetti (New York: Macmillan, 1896), xii.

before her, as something craving a vesture of verse at her hands, she did not write at all."[2] William's characterization of Rossetti as a spontaneous poet is a damaging one because it implies a lack of seriousness, as if she were a scribbling versifier; it is also a peculiar one for the person who had the first long view of Rossetti's complete works. For with this long view a reader can see that Rossetti's poems are not spontaneous, but obsessive, that they meditate repeatedly and intensively on a handful of subjects that the poetry makes its own in a wholly original way. After all, she earned her reputation for morbidness by repeated attention to deprivation and death, for the stubborn insistence on pairing hope with fear, in short for the very matters that obsess a mind preoccupied with a humanly incomprehensible God. A poet's obsession for an obsession—is such an idea tenable? It is if we remember, first, that obsession yields repetition, infinite returns to an original idea, and infinite expressions of that idea; Rossetti's oeuvre can be described as enacting precisely this process of repetition: "[S]he is a repetitious poet, in her themes, in her words, phrases, rhymes, sounds."[3] Second, those expressions ironically proceed by indirect means, making each return original even as it is repetitive; such indirection and renewal are hallmarks of original poetry, which declares its allegiance to a prior form (even if it departs radically from that form) and at the same time, makes the form new in its service to a unique poetic vision. With recourse to the letters of Constantin's young man in *Repetition,* we can first examine how her double sonnet of sonnets, *Later Life,* exploits the sonnet form to choreograph a highly sophisticated movement through the complexities of religious belief. Second, in *Monna Innominata: A Sonnet of Sonnets,* we can explore the believing persona embedded in the highly allusive psuedo-medievalism that constitutes this poem's fiction.

Long before literary theorists saw the rise and fall of dominant literary genres to be a system of "defamiliarization," Christina Rossetti used the

---

2. Christina Rossetti, *The Poetical Works of Christina Georgina Rossetti, with Memoir and Notes by William Michael Rossetti* (London: Macmillan and Co., 1914), lxviii–lxvix. Antony Harrison disproves the allegation of spontaneity by examining the careful revisions of "Maud Clare," which has "not an unusual textual history" for a Rossetti poem (*Christina Rossetti in Context* [Chapel Hill: University of North Carolina Press, 1988], 3–8). Crump's variorum edition by itself stands as proof of the massive number of revisions Rossetti undertook over the course of her career.

3. Kathleen Blake, *Love and the Woman Question in Victorian Literature: The Art of Self-Postponement* (Totowa, N.J.: Barnes and Noble, 1983), 14.

sonnet of sonnets to examine and remark upon the conventional sonnet
and its claims to unity and coherence. It is as if she holds the sonnet form
under a microscope. Where the naked eye sees a tightly bound sequence
of continguous lines, the microscopic view shows fourteen distinct
units, demarcated and isolated by white space. Each sonnet in a sonnet
of sonnets testifies to the usually unseen effort in recording a single line
of poetry, by expanding that single line into fourteen. The trick a sonnet
of sonnets plays with time blocks easy understanding of meaning; reading a short-form-turned-long upsets the easy process of cumulative sense
from "line" to "line." Elongating a sonnet into a sonnet of sonnets differs
importantly from merely stringing sonnets together into a sequence, a
generic maneuver practiced by many of Rossetti's peers, including her
brother Dante. It estranges the form from the conventional ways of
understanding it and plays havoc with a genre that usually pays homage
to the brilliant succinctness of Petrarch and Shakespeare. For instance,
when reading *Monna Innominata: A Sonnet of Sonnets* and *Later Life: A
Double Sonnet of Sonnets,* one is faced with inevitable temptations: To
look for an "octave," eight "lines" connected and unified thematically; for
a "volta," an identifiable turning point, at "line" eight or nine. To ask of
Later Life whether all these elements are doubled somehow, either as
fourteen pairs of two or two pairs of fourteen. To play anagram games,
gathering the first line of each sonnet into a "real" sonnet. Yielding to any
of these will turn reading the poem into an accountant's tabulation, to no
avail. Rossetti's sonnets of sonnets reenact the sonnet form, and yet they
are not sonnets, but poetic explorations of the sonnet. And in large
measure, they explore how a poem is managed—or not managed—by
its structure, by the imposition of temporal and spatial constraints that
give a poem shape.

   Later Life and its more popular generic companion, *Monna Innominata,* undertake such exploration, and its implications for the religious
mind Rossetti obsessively examines. The most significant characteristic
of the sonnet of sonnets is that it brings together its diverse parts as
much to emphasize fissures and disjunctions as to establish continuity;
this characteristic rehearses structurally the fissures and disjunctions in
a mind grappling with what cannot be grasped. Resolution is not the aim
of the sonnet of sonnets, but its target. And if resolution is the target,
proliferation of intepretations forestalls closure, keeping all questions of
religious belief unanswered and therefore vital.

   A preliminary way of understanding the two sonnets of sonnets is as
the interplay between isolation (the white space) and writing. And yet
the repetitive exercise of rendering estrangement and isolation does

culminate in one long poem, not many short ones. "When one reads the sonnet as a whole in a sequence," argues Barbara Hardy, referring to Shakespeare's sonnets, "there emerges a shadowy story, with characters and events, so that the individual lyrics are both intense expressions of moments of feeling, and also imply a buried narrative. It is a submerged and suggested story whose action and relationships are often dark."[4] *Monna Innominata* has a story, but it does not seem to be submerged or suggested, though it is dark. *Later Life,* on the other hand, has not a hint of story, and few if any connected actions and relationships. Nonetheless, something like a "shadowy story," what she calls "connections," is what Rossetti herself had in mind when she defended her works against abridged publication. Tempered by her experience with *Goblin Market,* Rossetti anticipated attempts to publish excerpts from her long works by establishing a firm policy: "I now make a point of refusing extracts, even in the case of my Sonnet of Sonnets some of which would fairly stand alone."[5] In a letter to an American editor interested in including some poems in an anthology she writes:

> I do not mind what piece you select, subject only to your taking any piece in question *in its entirety;* and my wish includes your *not* choosing an independent poem which forms part of a series or group,—not (for instance) one no. of "Passing Away" . . . or one Sonnet of "Monna Innominata." Such compound work has a connection (very often) which is of interest to the author and which <the reader> an editor gains nothing by discarding. (*Rossetti-Macmillan Letters,* 154–55, Rossetti's emphasis)[6]

Monna Innominata would seem to need authorial protection far less than does *Later Life.* It has a coherent and intriguing prose prologue that supplies a fictional framework, quotations from Dante and Petrarch for each sonnet's epigraph, and all the weight of the Provençal love-poem tradition behind it. *Later Life* has no trappings, no notable literary allu-

---

4. Barbara Hardy, *The Advantage of Lyric: Essays on Feeling in Poetry* (London: Athlone Press, 1977), 3.

5. Lona Mosk Packer, ed., *The Rossetti-Macmillan Letters* (Berkeley and Los Angeles: University of California Press, 1963), 154.

6. The marks around "reader" indicate that the word was scratched out and substituted with "editor." I would note here that in the one published selection of Rossetti's poetry available right now, C. H. Sisson, its editor and selector, violates Rossetti's wishes and does indeed select "independent poem[s] which form part of a series or group." Since there is no ancillary material in this collection, that this is being done is never explained.

sions, nothing but its demanding subtitle and its motley crew of twenty-eight sonnets. Dorothy Margaret Stuart quaintly describes the difference between the two sequences: "The mentality of the poet is the one connecting thread [in *Later Life*], and on that thread are strung beads of unequal sizes and incongruous colours. It is otherwise with *Monna Innominata*, which has the effect of a chaplet of perfectly matched pearls."[7] Stuart's bead analogy is apt, though its implication is not—that perfectly matched pearls are better than strung beads of unequal sizes and incongruous colors.

In "The Nature of the Gothic," Ruskin's defense of Gothic architecture gives him the opportunity to lash out at standards of perfection he associates with the diminishment of art: "But accurately speaking, no good work whatever can be perfect, and *the demand for perfection is always a sign of a misunderstanding of the ends of art*" (editor's emphasis).[8] And in his final defense of "Savageness" (the first criterion for the Gothic), Ruskin makes a characteristic generalization about where art went wrong:

> Accept this then for a universal law that neither architecture nor any other noble work of man can be good unless it be imperfect.... [T]he first cause of the fall of the arts of Europe was a relentless requirement of perfection, *incapable alike either of being silenced by veneration for greatness, or softened into forgiveness of simplicity. (Art Criticism,* 101, my emphasis)[9]

Though ironically Ruskin himself failed to appreciate Rossetti's poetry because it was not polished enough, his sensitivity to the power of the imperfect form of the Gothic can be appropriated for Rossetti. First, her poetic power could be silenced by veneration for the greatness of the divine. Second, her poetry is deceptively simple, her diction a model of

---

7. Dorothy Margaret Stuart, *Christina Rossetti* (London: Macmillan and Co., 1930), 123–24.

8. John Ruskin, "The Nature of the Gothic," in *The Art Criticism of John Ruskin*, ed. Robert L. Herbert (Gloucester, Mass.: Peter Smith, 1969), 100.

9. In "Health and Decay in the Arts," Hopkins says something very similar (supporting Allison Sulloway's view that he borrowed much from Ruskin): "This will perhaps throw light on the history of the *renaissance:* right or wrong it was inevitable. It looks like an abjuration of nationality, but in fact Art had worked laboriously, and Perfection presented itself with irresistible attraction to men's minds" (*The Journals and Papers of Gerard Manley Hopkins*, ed. Humphrey House, completed by Graham Storey [London: Oxford University Press, 1959], 9). Also see Hopkins's "On the Origin of Beauty," where asymmetry is promoted as more beautiful than symmetry (86–114).

clarity, making her uninteresting to early twentieth-century critics hungry for ambiguity, for complex, well-wrought verbal puzzles. Third, and most important, Rossetti innovated, never more so than in her composition of *Later Life,* and innovation risks imperfection. As early as 1911 and as late as 1988, critics have seen her on the cutting edge of a new kind of poetry, her proper place no less than Hopkins's.[10] And yet Diane D'Amico subtitles her 1980 article on *Later Life* "The Neglected Sonnet Sequence," and as late as 1985 Edna Kotin Charles notes that *Later Life* is "the least reviewed of her sonnet sequences."[11] The imperfections that seem to plague the structural integrity of *Later Life* account for some of the neglect. Its apparently incoherent obsession with religious concerns probably accounts for the rest.

In establishing a protective publishing policy, Rossetti displays all the confidence of a seasoned artist trying to secure her own vision against misinterpretations by the public (these letters were written in 1886 and 1883 respectively, several years after *A Pageant and Other Poems* was published). This confidence includes great certainty about how—in what order and in what format—she wanted her poems to appear in their parent edition. Again, because so much of her poetic composition cannot be dated, including all parts of both sonnets of sonnets, her published arrangement of her work is the one reliable register of how she meant her poetry to be received. She published both *Monna Innominata* and *Later Life* in *A Pageant and Other Poems. Monna Innominata* appears very early in the collection, *Later Life* toward its end.[12] They fall on either side of the division between secular and reli-

10. See Ford Madox Ford, *Memories and Impressions: A Study in Atmospheres by Ford Madox Hueffer* (New York: Harper and Brothers, 1911), and Antony H. Harrison, *Christina Rossetti in Context* (Chapel Hill: University of North Carolina Press, 1988). Also see Blake, *Love and the Woman Question.* Blake points out that given Rossetti's unique poetic diction, "[i]t is no wonder that [she] found admirers not only in the mellifluous Swinburne but also in the more unorthodox and wrenching Gerard Manley Hopkins. Her lines could be very meaningfully sprung" (18). Blake sees an affinity between Rossetti's terseness and Hopkins's more systematically plotted sprung rhythm.

11. Diane D'Amico, "Christian Rossetti's *Later Life:* The Neglected Sonnet Sequence," *Victorian Institute Journal* 9 (1980–81): 21–28; Edna Kotin Charles, *Christina Rossetti: Critical Perspectives, 1862–1982* (Selinsgrove, Pa.: Susquehanna University Press, 1985), 121.

12. If one looks at the titles William Rossetti assembles under the rubric of "The Longer Poems" in *The Poetical Works of Christina Rossetti, Later Life* stands out as literally the only one that has no character, no "plot" element, no narrative control, or any other strategy for moving a lengthy poem along (i.e., the months of the year in "The Months: A Pageant," or the procession of the ecological train in "All Thy Works Praise Thee, O Lord: A Processional of Creation"). And though many of these other longer works have discernible religious subtexts, none except "All Thy Works Praise Thee" is overtly religious to the extent *Later Life* is. *Goblin*

gious poetry described in Chapter 3 as being formed by "The Thread of Life" and "An Old-World Thicket." Both sonnets of sonnets are probably compilations, at least in part, of sonnets composed individually. If Alexander Pope kept couplets around, in pockets and drawers, to dip into as he meticulously crafted his poetry, Rossetti may have had a comparable arsenal of sonnets. More to the point, especially in *Later Life,* randomness has its place in the otherwise strictly curtailed sonnet of sonnets. In brief, *Later Life* eschews the means available to give a long poem coherence in order to meditate on the mind in turbulence—this is the shadowy story, submerged, suggested, and indeed dark most of the time.

The title, *Later Life,* suggests the poem begins in medias res, at some later period in some life. It promises to anchor what follows in a temporal location—later, not earlier—and then not only reneges on the promise, but holds up such promises of secure temporality for scrutiny. It also depends upon repetition for its meaning, yet another promised anchor; a later life repeats some earlier life, only with a difference, the difference of time passed. As a complete work, the poem stretches the boundaries of its structural source, the sonnet so well contained in time and space, to its utmost limit, and in doing so, becomes like Ruskin's Gothic— imperfect, discontinuous.[13] But these imperfections and gaps belong to the surface texture of the poem; they are, in fact, its most important attribute, and, like the flaws in raw silk, give it its distinction and its integrity. The religious fabric of *Later Life* resists all attempts to hide its seams, and to understand how best to talk about the poem without

---

Market might be considered the Rossetti oddity because of its phantasmagoria, its highly wrought sexuality, and its fairytale quality (though one need only read her children's poems to see how markedly "Rossetti-esque" *Goblin Market* really is). But at least with regard to formal concerns, *Later Life* is the far more peculiar poem.

13. Ironically, Ruskin failed to appreciate this in Rossetti's poetry, since he held her accountable for not following to perfection the rules of meter, a practice he calls "the calamity of modern poetry." In a letter to Dante Rossetti, his standards for poetry, at least for the purposes of judging *Goblin Market,* differ sharply from his peaen to imperfection quoted above. Rossetti's poems "are full of beauty and power," writes Ruskin,

[b]ut no publisher—I am deeply grieved to know this—would take them, so full are they of quaintnesses and other offenses. Irregular measure . . . is the calamity of modern poetry. *The Iliad,* the *Divina Commedia,* the *Aeneid,* the whole of Spenser, Milton, Keats, are written without taking a single license or violating the common ear for metre; your sister should exercise herself in the severest commonplace of metre until she can write as the public likes. Then if she puts in her observation and passion all will become precious. But she must have the Form first. (Quoted in Packer, *Rossetti-Macmillan Letters,* 5–6)

solving it, one more return to *Repetition* is in order, this time directly to the young man's letters.

The letters from the young man, which comprise the middle section of *Repetition,* are carefully dated from August 15 to February 17 before they are interrupted by Constantin. This preciseness apparently gives the letters the task of marking time, and yet they supply no year, no location, and still no identification of the young man, leaving them ungrounded in time and space despite their ostensible concern with documenting time's passage. In fact, they record no "real" time, but record instead the more abstract state of *temporariness,* measured against not a particular August-February period, but against the young man's reading of the Book of Job. That is the temporal event of which the young man writes, and the letters' record of temporariness uses the language of the calendar to reiterate his particular reading of Job. According to the young man, Job undergoes an "ordeal" (*Prøvelse*), "a temporary category . . . defined in relation to time and therefore . . . annulled in time."[14] His "significance" is that "*the disputes at the boundaries of faith are fought out in him,* that the colossal revolt of the wild and aggressive powers of passion is presented here. For this reason Job does not bring composure as does a hero of faith [e.g., Abraham], *but he does give temporary alleviation*" (210, my emphasis). Job's ordeal is temporary, and so is the alleviation his story brings; the former situation offers hope, the second, a warning that such an ordeal will be repeated. "August 15 through February 17" will happen again.

What the young man finds at stake in his reading of Job, and what fascinates him—this is the sign that he is a poet—is Job's interpretation of his ordeal. This interpretation makes him right in his wrong before God: "Job's greatness is that freedom's passion in him is not smothered or quieted by a wrong expression" (207). The "right" expression does not equal the passive "The Lord gave and the Lord took away; blessed be the name of the Lord"; these words are coopted by "professional comforters, like formal masters of ceremonies" (197). Instead, the young man apostrophizes Job: "[Y]ou became the voice of the suffering, the cry of the grief-stricken, the shriek of the terrified, and a relief to all who bore their torment in silence, a faithful witness to all the affliction and laceration there can be in a heart, an unfailing spokesman who dared to lament 'in bitterness of soul' and to strive with God" (197). Thus obsessed with

14. Søren Kierkegaard, *Fear and Trembling / Repetition,* trans. and ed., Howard V. Hong and Edna H. Hong (Princeton: Princeton University Press, 1983), 209–10.

Job's interpretation of his sufferings, the young man applies his own interpretation to this interpretation. And in the context of *Repetition,* this epistolary interpretation belongs to Constantin (and ultimately to Kierkegaard), making it the center of a text that fans out in both directions (beginning and end—Constantin's Report and his Concluding Letters) in an effort to manage the Jobean "expression" it creates. Dating the letters is part of this management, and so is restricting them in time and in space (the middle section of a larger work). If *Repetition* is an anatomy of a written text, it instructs most usefully in this demonstration of how textual parts are ordered. But it also documents a slippage, as the young man's interpretation eludes Constantin's control. Between the penultimate and final letters from the young man is inserted a section called "Incidental Observations by Constantin Constantius." Here Constantin attempts to explain away the young man's letters: "It is easy to see that he [the young man] is caught in a total misunderstanding" (216). And about the young man's obsession with Job, who has usurped Constantin as the real addressee of the letters, he says dismissively: "It is his own business if he would want to give a religious expression to his expectancy if it is fulfilled—I have no objection to that" (216). But his explanation comes too early, for there is one last letter, dated May 31, and in it the young man slips from his maker's grasp:

> Three cheers for the flight of thought, three cheers for the perils of life in service to the idea, three cheers for the hardships of battle, three cheers for the festive jubilation of victory, three cheers for the dance in the vortex of the infinite, three cheers for the cresting waves that hide me in the abyss, three cheers for the cresting waves that fling me above the stars! (222)

Constantin's concluding letter, whose date includes a year (1843), proceeds to relegate all that came before to the realm of Constantin's imagination; nonetheless, the young man's poetic expression resists such relegation because of his collusion with Job: "Job is stationed at the confines of poetry. In the same breath: he stands at the limits of faith."[15] Thus *Repetition* anatomizes the complex relationship between a work and its author: the management of the text's fictions by the structure that holds them in time and space, and their simultaneous freedom from that structure.

Order and slippage: these two play off each other endlessly in *Later*

---

15. Louis Mackey, *Points of View: Readings of Kierkegaard* (Tallahassee: Florida State University Press, 1986), 87.

Life, as it attends to its business of "religious expression." Its strict sonnet form corrals into decorum a group of subjective perspectives that none-theless demand autonomy and prevail chaotically. *Later Life*'s first son-net immediately invokes Genesis: its fourteenth sonnet has Adam and Eve leave Paradise; its fifteenth sonnet backtracks to the *reason* they leave; its twenty-eighth sonnet celebrates "the dead." The boundaries of existence (and of the poem) seem set at the widest possible margins, for what phenomena can possibly exceed the distance between creation and death? And yet, formally the poem cannot exceed or fall short by even one line; to do so would make it something other than a sonnet of sonnets. As expansive as the universe and as tightly wound as a watch, *Later Life* progresses through its sonnets obsessed with time—past, pres-ent, sped up, slowed down, internal, and external—and with spatial configurations, as enormous as mountains (sonnet 22), and as small as a sonnet. Above all, *Later Life* advertises its own temporariness, for what-ever happens in the course of its repetitive unfolding, it must end at sonnet 28. But what does happen, and what has it to do with Job, or at least the young man's Job?

What happens is the erection of what Paul Ricoeur calls a "prescrip-tive and descriptive symbolic order."[16] Such an order, says Ricoeur, "can conjoin *cosmos* (the sphere of the world) and *ethos* (the sphere of human action) because it produces the *pathos* of actively assumed suffer-ing" (86), the *pathos* in the story of Job. The first sonnet of *Later Life* produces exactly this *pathos,* as it reproduces what the young man calls "the disputes at the boundaries of faith," while at the same time enforc-ing those boundaries. The dispute is a familiar one by now in the work of Rossetti, and in the work of Hopkins: how can a loving God allow unjust suffering? First, the sonnet offers the conventional theological answer that suffering is always merited: "And this God is our God, even while His rod / Of *righteous* wrath falls on us smiting sore."[17] But the sestet pro-gresses through an anaphoric repetition that keeps the dispute alive even in the midst of piety: "For *tho' He slay us* we will trust in Him; / We will flock home to Him by divers ways: / Yea, *tho' He slay us* we will vaunt His praise . . ." (1:9–11, my emphases). "Though He . . . we will" is the theological grammar that generates compliance in a believer who

16. Paul Ricoeur, "Toward a Hermeneutic of the Idea of Revelation," in *Essays on Biblical Interpretation,* ed. Lewis S. Mudge (Philadelphia: Fortress Press, 1980), 86.

17. Christina Rossetti, *The Complete Poems of Christina Rossetti, A Variorum Edition,* 3 vols., ed. R. W. Crump (Baton Rouge: Louisiana State University Press, 1979–90), II, 138, sonnet 1, lines 5–6. Further references to *Later Life* in the text will cite the sonnet and the lines.

suffers, and yet it also memorializes the fundamental contradiction: though He torments us, we will respond as if He loves us. Repeating the "Though He . . . we will" paradigm emphasizes both compliance and contradiction, introducing the double sonnet of sonnets with an exhortation to comply with the same contradiction Job encounters, while acknowledging that it *is* a contradiction.

Sonnets 14 and 15, the work's midpoint, jump to the end of the story of Genesis, and focus on human volition as a factor in suffering: "When Adam and when Eve left Paradise / Did they love on and cling together still, / Forgiving one another all that ill / *The twain had wrought* on such a different wise?" (14:1–4, my emphasis). The relationship between sonnets 14 and 15 comes as close to chronology as *Later Life* gets. Sonnet 14 shows Adam and Eve leaving Paradise; sonnet 15 flashes back to Eve's temptation by Satan, and stymies attempts to cast Rossetti as an incipient or covert feminist. "Let woman fear to teach and bear to learn, / Remembering the first woman's mistake" (15:1–2), it begins, burdening Eve with the sin sonnet 14 distributes evenly between her and Adam ("all that ill / The twain had wrought"). But the sonnet does something intriguing with the prevailing belief in the moral weakness of woman. "Eve had for pupil the inquiring snake, / Whose doubts she answered on a great concern . . ." (15:3–4). Satan as Eve's student is a peculiar conceit since he is usually cast in the role of seductive instructor, but he must have studied her before launching his seditious attack on Paradise. The reversal of role types in the octave sets up a relationship between Adam and Eve that enacts the "Though He . . . we will" paradigm in the human sphere. The octave ends with an act of fatal interpretation by Adam, his rationalization for eating the forbidden fruit: "Til man deemed poison sweet for her sweet sake / And fired a train by which the world must burn" (15:7–8). "Did Adam love his Eve from first to last?" begins the sestet, and continues, "I think so; as we love who works us ill, / And wounds us to the quick, yet loves us still" (15:9–11). "Though she slays me I will love her," Adam might be understood to say. The love relationship of Adam to Eve rehearses the relationship of human beings to God, with woman obliquely in the godly role. The last two lines of the poem discontinue this correspondence: "Love in a dominant embrace holds fast / His frailer self, and saves without her will" (15:13–14), and the "proper" role of the frail female is reestablished. But Eve as Satan's teacher and Adam's god exploits this "proper" role by turning "woman" into a trope for Christian. The discussion of *Monna Innominata* will draw upon Kathleen Blake's thesis that the female figure reiterates for Rossetti the paradigmatic Christian, but here in *Later Life,* that reiteration has a special twist. It draws a comparison *not* between the female and Christian as properly passive and humble (Blake's point), but between female renegade and Christian rebel against divine authority.[18]

Like Eve in sonnet 15, sonnet 28 also bears a burden, the burden of closure and completion. The sonnet rejects this burden out of hand. Invoking the faraway dead, it comments on the poetic discourse it concludes by positing another discourse not yet (and therefore perhaps never) available to human auditors. For the "absent friend's" death is defined as specifically beyond the reach of "words we say," and only "our" death can "lead him back in reach of words we say." For now, "He only cannot utter yea or nay / In any voice accustomed to our ear . . ." (28:5–6). The sonnet ends by alluding to an excess of language that cannot be contained in the here and now of the sonnet of sonnets, and to a store of knowledge beyond the purview of poetic work. The dead watch "us," the speakers of the "words we say," with "unslumbering eyes and heart; / Brimful of words which cannot yet be said, / Brimful of knowledge they may not impart, / Brimful of love for you and love for me" (28:11–14). At the very moment when the language of *Later Life* should end, linguistic possibility overflows its "man-made" container.

The "Though He . . . we will" paradigm, the reminder of humanity's complicity in its fallenness, and the commentary on the inefficacy of human language pervade Rossetti's oeuvre, and constitute the obsessions in her poetry. All three have mattered in understanding poems already analyzed in this work. In setting its formal and thematic margins, this double sonnet of sonnets tells the story of religious poetry, what it must contend with (a cruel, loving God, the believer's own fallenness and ultimate inadequacy) and how it cannot fully do so. But what falls within these margins, and what do they contribute to this story? Between sonnets 1, 14, 15, and 28 are sonnets that present subjective perspectives completely unmoored from their anchoring margins.

Because of this unmooring, generalities by way of an overview are hard to come by, and of questionable use. For instance, noticeably missing from this discussion so far (because so central in most of the preceding chapters) is any attention to the general question of voice in *Later Life,* an omission not so much deliberate as unavoidable. There simply is no way to categorize or characterize the proliferation of voice; randomness of perspective prevails from one sonnet to the next. Most sonnets in the first half are obsessed with time in some way, but time becomes not

---

18. Blake says: "A parallel may be drawn between Christ-like and feminine longsuffering" (*Love and the Woman Question,* 5).

the measurement of experience, but measured by experience, and therefore unique to each sonnet. In sonnet 2, for instance, time flies, because the sonnet deals with atonement, for which there is never enough time. Sonnet 3, a very private lament of spiritual ennui, remembers enervation as its past and projects it into its future. Memories abound, but are affixed to no consistent present. Sometimes a global first-person plural guides the sonnet; other times the singular first person asserts itself. As the first "octave" draws to a close, sonnet 8 rues the disjunctive perspectives that precede it: "We feel and see with different hearts and eyes:— / Ah Christ, if all our hearts could meet in Thee / How well it were for them and well for me ..." (8:1–3). But sonnet 9 institutionalizes such disjunction. The most well known sonnet of *Later Life*, it turns to astronomy to allegorize separateness and isolation: "Star Sirius and the Pole Star dwell afar / Beyond the drawings each of other's strength ..." (9:1–2). The moving star and the stationary star are irreconcilable in their respective milieux, and "They own no drawings each of other's strength, / Nor vibrate in a visible sympathy ..." (9:9–10). The sestet ends with a poignant hope that sympathy is achievable anyway, across the chasm of a difference troped as linguistic difference: "Mayhaps they talk together without speech."

The second half of *Later Life* differs from the first as much as the sonnets differ among themselves. Sonnet 16 posits the possibility of an exception to a universal rule, while also gathering together some of the issues that come before it. One and one make two; that is what teachers teach. One and one make one; that is what "Love rules": "The narrower total seems to suit the few, / The wider total suits the common run; / Each obvious in its sphere like moon or sun ..." (16:5–7), or like Star Sirius and the Pole Star. It ends with time-slowed-down: "And how about these long still-lengthening days?" But sonnet 17 shifts to an entirely new conceit: the connection between memory and place. "This foggy day" elicits a memory of a specific locale, "Past certain cliffs, along one certain beach ..." (17:4). The kind of ennui apparent in sonnet 4 reappears, but is communicated idiosyncratically, as a dissatisfaction with location: "I am sick of where I am and where I am not, / I am sick of foresight and of memory, / I am sick of all I have and all I see, / I am sick of self, and there is nothing new ..." (17:9–12). The sonnet ends with a quirk and some humor after so much disgust, as if it were a letter: "Thus with myself: how fares it, Friends, with you?"

The next four sonnets pass in a by now peculiarly reasonable fashion by passing through the seasons: sonnet 18 through autumn; 19, winter; 20, spring; 21, summer. But why? No discernible reason, and sonnets 22 and

23 interrupt the calendar to meditate on the "mountains in their over-whelming might" (22:1) and "beyond the seas we know" (23:1). Sonnets 24 and 25 focus on "life," and sonnet 26 begins with "life" ("full of numbness and of balk, / Of haltingness and baffled short-coming...") to end with death: "Unveil thy face, O Death who are not Death." Short-circuiting any notion of death as ease from life, sonnet 27 describes physical death in its visceral reality, "ghastly and uncouth" (27:3). Its graphic description also preempts a logical connection between sonnet 26's hopeful "O Death who are not Death" and the "absent friend" longed for in the concluding sonnet. In *The Modern Poetic Sequence: The Genius of Modern Poetry,* M. L. Rosenthal and Sally M. Gall define a "liberated lyrical structure" as that whose *"object is neither to resolve a problem nor to conclude an action but to achieve the keenest, most open realization possible"* (authors' emphasis).[19] In their study they claim this liberation for twentieth-century poetry (anticipated by Dickinson and Whitman) that "discard[s] superficial methods of organization" (vii) such as the sonnet. Not only is *Later Life* an example of a "liberated lyrical structure," it stands as a strong challenge to a theory of "modern" poetry such as Rosenthal and Gall's. It achieves the "most open realization possible" while remaining tightly structured, playing these two aspects of itself off each other to "produce the *pathos* of actively assumed suffering" with little sustained attempt to assuage that suffering. Rosenthal and Gall claim that "[t]he modern sequence goes many-sidedly into who and where we are *subjectively* (3, authors' emphasis). *Later Life* does precisely this, and though it must conclude at the boundary it sets (sonnet 28), it refuses to resolve the questions it raises about God, the "human condition," and language. This refusal marks *Later Life*'s modernity because it acknowledges the inadequacy of orthodox religious explanations (for instance, "The Lord gave and the Lord took away") without surrendering its lyrical religiosity. For Rosenthal and Gall, the modern poetic sequence "is a response to the lyrical possibilities of language opened up by those pressures in times of cultural and psychological crisis, when all past certainties have many times been thrown chaotically into question" (3). *Later Life* takes this chaos and makes it its point, while resisting final chaos through its curtailing form.

The most radical, if not blasphemous, commentary by the young man on the story of Job implicates poetry as the language of compromise. Since no one dare argue with God,

19. M. L. Rosenthal and Sally M. Gall, *The Modern Poetic Sequence: The Genius of Modern Poetry* (New York: Oxford University Press, 1983), 11.

In our time it is thought that genuine expressions of grief, the despairing language of passion, must be assigned to the poets, who then like attorneys in a lower court plead the cause of the suffering before the tribunal of human compassion. No one dares to go further than that. Speak up, then, unforgettable Job, repeat everything you said, you powerful spokesman who, fearless as a roaring lion, appears before the tribunal of the Most High! Your speech is pithy, and in your heart is the fear of God even when you bring complaints. . . . I need you, a man who knows how to complain so loudly that he is heard in heaven, where God confers with Satan on drawing up plans against man. (*Repetition*, 198)[20]

The story of Job proceeds not on the energy of his abject obedience, but on the energy of his imaginative contention, which is, nonetheless, always restrained by the boundaries of belief, the fear of God in his heart.[21] *Later Life*, a poem that rejects the option of coherent argument available to poets who resemble an "attorney in a lower court," recapitulates this combination of imaginative contention and self-limitation, and resides with Job at the outside boundary of poetry (filling the sonnet almost but not quite beyond its capacity) and the outside boundary of faith (presenting acute spiritual suffering with no easy rationale for it). Such positioning makes reading *Later Life* no easy task for its audience, and therefore susceptible to charges of incoherence and incongruity. But at the end of his essay on revelation, Ricoeur asks a question we might pose on behalf of *Later Life:* "If to understand oneself is to understand oneself in front of the text [perhaps the only means now available], must we not say that the reader's understanding is suspended, derealized, made potential just as the world itself is metamorphosized by the poem?" (*Toward a Hermeneutic*, 117). The texts to which he refers here are books of the Bible, including the Book of Job. The textual opportunity of self-understanding is precisely the experience of Constantin's young man in his letter-writing. It also describes *Later Life*, which transforms temporal

20. Remember from Chapter 2 Vigilius Haufniensis's scorn of "notorized facts" in his defense of psychological-poetical authority (*The Concept of Anxiety*, 54). These "facts" sound very much like what "attorneys in a lower court" summon as evidence. "No one dares go further than that," except, of course, one who wields psychological-poetical authority.

21. In "Toward a Hermeneutic of the Idea of Revelation," Ricoeur promotes imagination over obedience as the proper response to Biblical revelation: "For what are the poem of Exodus and the poem of the resurrection . . . addressed to if not to our imagination rather than our obedience? And what is the historical testimony that our reflection would like to internalize addressed to if not to our imagination?" (117).

and spatial configurations of "the world," or the *cosmos* (as Ricoeur defines it), into a proliferation of subjective interpretations. The sonnet-of-sonnets form reins in this proliferation, but never finally controls it, nor does it need to.

"The sequence is an experiment in aesthetic and psychological explora-tion," says Antony Harrison, "that also tests the boundaries of literary and religious traditions, especially as these appear to conflict and to intersect with each other" (*Christina Rossetti in Context*, 154). Harrison refers here not to *Later Life*, but to *Monna Innominata: A Sonnet of Sonnets.* Published in the same edition, linked incrementally by their subtitles ("A Sonnet of Sonnets" and "A *Double* Sonnet of Sonnets"), asymmetrical halves in their separation by the split between secular and religious poetry, these two poems are "audible shadows" of one another. Where *Later Life* tells the story of religious poetry, *Monna Innominata* tells the story of its storyteller. *Monna Innominata* has received its fair share of criticism; thus my discussion will be an eccentric one, concentrating as much on the parts of the sequence that are *not* the sonnets, e.g., the prologue, the epigraphs, and the spaces between the sonnets, as on the sonnets themselves. As Miller states in the first sentence of *The Linguis-tic Moment,* "The odd status of prefaces, as of titles, epigraphs, dedica-tions, and footnotes, has frequently been observed of late."[22] As in the discussion on the "two wrecks," the purpose here is to explore poetry that participates in a religious discourse, or to tell the story of religious poetry. As we have already seen in *Later Life,* that story thematizes and "structuralizes" the kinds of fissures and disjunctions in understanding that, for Miller, take the poem unawares.

In his preface, Miller argues that the "linguistic moment" is that mo-ment "of suspension within the texts of poems . . . when they reflect or comment on their own medium," and that moment is a parabasis, an uncontrolled digression that "break[s] the illusion that language is a transparent medium of meaning" (xiv). According to this definition,

22. J. Hillis Miller, *The Linguistic Moment: From Wordsworth to Stevens* (Princeton: Prince-ton University Press, 1985), xiii. In order to understand how Miller focuses on such things as epigraphs and translation problems, see his chapter on Browning in *The Linguistic Moment.* He gives a stunning reading of "An Englishman in Italy" and then undoes that reading by exposing the problems of translation the poem avoids explaining. "An Englishman in Italy" also has an Italian epigraph, and purports to be a monologue addressed to a young Italian girl. What language they speak is an unanswerable question, and this makes the poem "a verbal notation of failure," the failure of the Englishman to possess his Italian environment without doing linguis-tic violence to the indigenous language of that environment.

Later Life is all suspension, as it remains ever self-conscious about its medium—the sonnet of sonnets—and that medium's deliberately tenuous grip on its "meaning." Its parts also "digress" from any one narrative angle, allowing the proliferation of interpretations that make up the poem. Though at its most obvious *Monna Innominata* has a more seamless narrative surface, it also shatters illusions of transparent meaning, because in its prose prologue it self-consciously announces itself as a fiction, an indulgence in "what if" speculation that takes for its mode of expression the courtly love sonnet. In the poem's fiction, spelled out in the prologue, one lady plucked from "a bevy of unnamed ladies, 'donne innominate' sung by a school of less conspicuous poets" [than Dante and Petrarch] (*Complete Poems,* II, 86), "writes" for herself. "The portrait left us might have appeared more tender, if less dignified, than any drawn even by a devoted friend," states the prologue. *Monna Innominata* usefully complicates this discussion, because it presents a case of avowedly earthly love (of a woman for a man), but nonetheless rehearses an earlier tradition that always implicated religion (Christianity) in human love (the courtly tradition), and vice versa. In the prologue both the Albigenses, heretical ascetics, and the Troubadours, the first singers of the aesthetically elegant courtly love song, are invoked to set the scene. On the other hand, Elizabeth Barrett Browning, "the great Poetess of our own day and nation," appears in the prologue as the appropriate author of such a work, if only she "had been unhappy instead of happy."

Fourteenth-century and nineteenth-century poetic traditions thus conspire to silence the unnamed lady, too male-oriented in the first, too happy in the second. Moreover, sustaining the fiction of the fourteenth-century Provençal poetess is not really what *Monna Innominata* is about. The prologue establishes the fiction and establishes that it is fiction. The white space between each sonnet bears the burden of suggesting a fiction correspondent to the one manifest in the sonnets themselves. The sonnets are written to a lover in the periods between his visits, and the visits occur in the space between the sonnets. Sonnet 6, for instance, begins "Trust me, I have not earned your dear rebuke"; somewhere between sonnets 5 and 6, the lover has lodged a complaint. Progression of time must be gleaned from the gaps between writing.

Untranslated epigraphs from Dante and Petrarch introduce each sonnet, reinforcing the poem's fictional status by reminding us that if it were "real" it would have been written in Italian, or would be presented as a translation. The prologue has already eliminated the possibility of these epigraphs' availability to the anonymous "donna innominata":

These heroines [Beatrice and Laura] of world-wide fame *were preceded* by a bevy of unnamed ladies "donne innominat" sung by a school of less conspicuous poets: and in that land and that period which gave simultaneous birth to Catholics, to Albigenses, and to Troubadours, one can imagine many a lady as sharing her lover's poetic aptitude, while the barrier between them might be one held sacred by both, yet not such as to render mutual love incompatible with mutual honour. (*Complete Poems,* II, 86, my emphasis)

Monna Innominata exposes itself to an enthusiast of the "linguistic moment" in the way it plays with these epigraphs, for they are actually as inappropriate as they seem appropriate. The woman to whom *Monna Innominata* gives poetic voice (and for whom it imagines "poetic attitude") precedes Beatrice and Laura, and therefore logically precedes Dante and Petrarch. The sonnet of sonnets reveals itself as a construct composed of parts that could not come together except in the fictional use of language. By allying itself not with Dante and Petrarch, but with their predecessors, *Monna Innominata* claims both to follow the masters (by quoting them) and to precede them; it plays fast and loose as an act of imitation (and an act of homage). In a poem that wants to give voice to a heretofore silent woman, the ventriloquist's lips are moving, and the "unnamed" Provençal poetess remains unrecovered, because she never existed in the first place, except in the realm of literary speculation. Exposure of *Monna Innominata* in this particular way has intriguing implications for a feminist reading of the poem, because just as Hopkins, according to Miller, cannot force language to serve theology, Rossetti cannot force language to restore the voice of silenced women. Margaret Homans sees *Monna Innominata* as failing in just this way, with the failure already signaled in the prologue. "[T]he passage ends," argues Homans, referring to the prologue, "by turning the speaking woman back into the stone from which Rossetti would wish to redeem her, when it places her in a 'niche beside Beatrice and Laura.' The literary tradition privileging Laura's and Beatrice's 'charms' for male viewers over their unattractiveness for the woman poet reasserts itself against Rossetti's overt intentions."[23] Homans's use of "privilege" as a verbal gerund and "against Rossetti's overt intentions" signals her decon-

---

23. Margaret Homans, " 'Syllables of Velvet': Dickinson, Rossetti, and the Rhetorics of Sexuality," *Feminist Studies* 11, no. 3 (Fall 1985): 575.

structive approach in a feminist analysis; she finds that Rossetti's poem undermines Rossetti's poetic intention just as Miller finds "The Wreck of the Deutschland" undermines Hopkins's. Like Stuart's bead analogy, her unredeemed "monna innominata" is apt, the conclusion she draws, misguided: "but in the end tradition writes her perhaps as much as she rewrites tradition" (575). First, Homans's criticism is based on the assumption that *Monna Innominata wants* to redeem the speaking woman. Second, though the Provençal woman be shelved, this still leaves unexplained the agent that fashions the chronologically hybrid sonnet of sonnets, which is an aggressive rewriting of tradition. In other words, if the ventriloquist's lips are moving in *Monna Innominata,* that simply reminds us to heed the ventriloquist, to examine the sonnets themselves, the lines supposedly penned by the Provençal poetess.

I have said that Rossetti belongs in the Orphic line of poets of loss that Bloom describes; like "The Wreck of the Deutschland" and *Repetition, Monna Innominata* presents itself as an exercise in writing by a writer whose opportunity comes at the moment of acute loss. As has been seen in the relationship between Hopkins's "two wrecks," such opportunity taken also involves a reactionary curtailment, and it is this dynamic of opportunity and curtailment that drives *Monna Innominata.* In sonnet 1, which establishes the absence of the lover, the speaker begs him to return and yet not to return:

> Come back to me, who wait and watch for you: —
> *Or come not yet, for it is over then,*
> And long it is before you come again,
> So far between my pleasures are and few.
> (1:1–4, my emphasis)

The agony of his absence is also the joy of anticipation; his arrival interrupts the joy as much as the agony. Furthermore, her anticipation in his absence becomes something else as well: "While, when you come not, what I do I do . . ." What she does is write, but since she only exists as the putative author of the sonnets, she only "exists" when he comes not. Her life as a writer commences only in his absence, and since this is the only "life" she has, that absence and the productive suspense it creates for her is literally her lifeline. "Or come not yet, for it is over then" obviously refers to his arrival, which always signifies for her his inevitable departure. But it can also refer to that period of her writing presence, which is over as soon as he comes: "Or come not yet, for it [my writing] is over then." This explanation of her lover's coming and not coming of course exposes (or creates) any sexual innuendo in the first sonnet, and though the poem sounds sexier in its explanation than in a reading of it, the comparison to sexual anticipation and fulfillment is apt. Blake criticizes Gilbert and Gubar's *Madwoman in the Attic* for "valoriz[ing] eroticism," which "contrasts with [Blake's] proposition that literature may find its material and even creative basis in love's deferral as well as its consummation."[24] Literature in the courtly love tradition in fact thrives on such deferral. *Monna Innominata* simply replays the dynamic between deferral of sexual consummation and creativity with a twist, the substitution of a woman for a man. But with such a twist it subtly transforms the tradition.

Fourteen times the absence of the lover is repeated, each repetition an opportunity taken by a woman to combine Dante, Petrarch, and a well-wrought sonnet into a readable sign of the gap that precedes it. As markers of loss, however, the sonnets ostensibly mark the lover's absence, but also mark his arrival and the consequent loss of the woman's voice, the next blank space. The second sonnet emphasizes the inverse relationship between the lover's absence and the woman's loss of voice by mourning the lack of a written record of their first meeting, and therefore the lack of accurate memory. Writing and meeting are mutually exclusive activities:

> I wish I could remember that first day,
>   First hour, first moment of your meeting me,
>   If bright or dim the season, it might be
> Summer or Winter for aught I can say;
> So unrecorded did it slip away,
>   So blind was I to see and to foresee,
>   So dull to mark the budding of my tree.
>   (2:1–7)

This second sonnet, which rues her lack of a record, becomes a record of that rue. Several more losses are commemorated in *Monna Innominata*. Lost is the tradition that anoints distance and separation in romantic love as the proper state of things, allowing earthly love to imitate the love of a

---

24. Blake, *Love and the Woman Question*, xiii. Sandra M. Gilbert and Susan Gubar, *Madwoman in the Attic: The Woman Writer and the Nineteenth–Century Literary Imagination* (New Haven: Yale University Press, 1979). See their discussion of *Goblin Market*, for instance, where they find the "honey-sweet fruit of art . . . analogous to (or identical with) the luscious fruit of self-gratifying sensual pleasure" (570). They see Rossetti and her "surrogate selves," the personae in her poetry, as "reject[ing] the goblin fruit of art" (571).

distant God. Sonnet 6, the response to her lover's complaint, mounts the argument that she must love God more, in order to love him, the lover, in appropriate imitation of that religious love. The sestet reflects her introspection as she works out the proper relationship between earthly and divine love:

> Yet while I love my God the most, I deem
>   That I can never love you overmuch;
>   I love Him more, so let me love you too;
> Yea, as I apprehend it, love is such
> I cannot love you if I love not him,
>   I cannot love him if I love not you.
>   (6:9–14)

And finally, time lost is painstakingly measured, sonnet by sonnet. Sonnet 10's staccato rhythm reinforces its topic, the fast passage of time: "Time flies, hope flags, life plies a wearied wing . . ." (10:1). The last sonnet approximates this rhythm as it begins with a complex lament: "Youth gone, and beauty gone . . ." And even before the last sonnet ends, voice is gone. In the octave she capitulates to old age, the bane of a beautiful woman: "I will not bind fresh roses in my hair, / To shame a cheek at best but little fair . . ." (14:4–5).

The sestet of sonnet 14 needs to be looked at very carefully as the conclusion of *Monna Innominata*. In it the speaker silences herself even before the sonnet ends:

> Youth gone and beauty gone, what doth remain?
>   The longing of a heart pent up forlorn,
>   A silent heart whose silence loves and longs;
>   The silence of a heart which sang its songs
>   While youth and beauty made a summer morn,
> Silence of love that cannot sing again.
>   (14:9–14)

This sestet is a "corrective" companion to the end of *Later Life,* because where *Later Life* ends by spilling over the boundaries of the stretched sonnet form, *Monna Innominata* retreats from those boundaries, as the woman disciplines herself into the "silence of love" before she needs to do so, that is, before the sonnet ends and is therefore necessarily silent. The demands of a sonnet of sonnets insist nonetheless that poetry continue through the fourteenth line of the fourteenth sonnet. The last four lines repeat some version of "silent" three times in order to communicate self-censure, while meeting its most basic structural criterion (fourteen lines). The self-portrait of a fourteenth-century Provençal woman inscribes in itself a censuring silence, the punishment for growing old and unbeautiful, but also the curtailment of the writerly urge. Homans correctly sees the Provençal poetess as installed or imprisoned in the "niche beside Beatrice and Laura." The movement of the sonnet sequence toward premature, curtailing silence, however, suggests that such imprisonment is self-imposed as an integral part of the poem's fiction. The poem emphatically does not mean to redeem the speaking woman, because the act of writing must not usurp the male lover as the appropriate redeemer. Any effort at self-redemption through writing must be curtailed. The importance of such curtailment in understanding *Monna Innominata* and its relationship to *Later Life* can be discovered by attending to what are the by now familiar concepts of imitation and compensation. Rossetti's poetry connects these two in the literary nature of "female" as it displays itself in *Monna Innominata.*

The Kierkegaardian notion of "a book under divine confiscation," never available as *publice juris,* describes the impossibility of ever capturing in language the man of faith (Abraham). And yet Silentio and the speakers in Hopkins's and Rossetti's poetry continue to try imitating this confiscated text. Such an imitation always involves the risk of another, sinful imitation, the imitation of Satan, possessed by the beauty of his own song. Imitation always verges on usurpation, and is therefore an act that must be closely monitored. In the dynamic between ambition and curtailment, *Monna Innominata* rehearses the careful balancing act required in an imitation, which is also always a repetition. In *Monna Innominata,* a woman imitates a man and therefore displaces him as the sonneteer. Such displacement vexes the ostensible purpose of her imitation, which is to express her sorrow over his absence ("My hope hangs waning, waxing, like a moon / Between the heavenly days on which we meet..." [1:11–12]). She therefore imposes limits and exposes weaknesses in order not to cross over the line that divides imitation from usurpation, or permanent displacement. Until the last sonnet, the speaker continues to expect the return of her lover; even in sonnet 12, where she sounds like Chaucer's Patient Griselda ("If there be any one can take my place... / I do commend you to that nobler grace" [12:1–4]), she rationalizes a union with him even were he to leave her for another: "And you companioned I am not alone" (12:14). Furthermore, all but two of the fourteen sonnets apostrophize the male lover, a strategy that places him in the foreground and her in the background. This gesture of self-effacement belongs firmly in the courtly love song tradition, but as we have seen, a gesture of self-effacement in poetry is always compromised by the necessary presence of a self-effacer. One way of managing the danger of usurpation is to cast the process of writing as a compensatory act, and inadequate compensation at that. The modesty of "While, when you come not, what I do I do" counteracts the radical import of a woman writing, and a gesture of self-silencing (sonnet 14) implies that the compensatory act committed in the lover's absence is not effective enough to ward off despair, nor can the act be sustained.

If the Provençal poetess gives up on writing before *Monna Innominata* ends, and if she cannot possibly have written the prologue or the epigraphs, then what agent takes these experiences of loss as opportunities for composition, and manipulates historical chronology to compose the sonnet of sonnets? From the prologue emerges the profile of this agent as a nineteenth-century, British, unhappy, female poet. Clearly such a profile matches Rossetti's own (though "unhappy" is debatable as biography). Her brother William annotates a letter in which she discusses *Monna Innominata* and its reference to Elizabeth Barrett Browning: "It is indisputable that the real veritable speaker in those sonnets is Christina herself, giving expression to her love for Charles Cayley: but the prose heading would surely lead any reader to suppose that the *ostensible* speaker is one of those ladies, to whom it adverts, in the days of the troubadours."[25] Of course, nothing is really indisputable when it comes to reading a person's life into her work, especially Rossetti's love life, and Lona Mosk Packer finds an ulterior motive in William's candor, as she builds her case that Rossetti was secretly in love with William Bell Scott.[26] Cayley, the translator of Dante, or Scott, the married man (for Packer, the perfect unavailable love in a courtly song)? Both theories prove more about the dangers of "psychologizing reduction" than about Christina Rossetti.[27] Like the poet-in-Wales and like Constantin Constantius (and Kierkegaard's other pseudonyms), the conceit of a nineteenth-century, British, unhappy, female poet encourages and then inhibits biographical speculation in deciphering a text by being coexistent with but not identical to the "historical" author, though of course it

25. William Michael Rossetti, ed., *The Family Letters of Christina Georgina Rossetti* (New York: Charles Scribner's Sons, 1908), 97.

26. Lona Mosk Packer, *Christina Rossetti* (Berkeley and Los Angeles: University of California Press, 1963), 225 and passim.

27. Miller's phrase in *The Linguistic Moment*, where he warns against "the making of literature into no more than a reflection or representation of something psychic which precedes it and which could exist without it" (60).

is a historically determined conceit. The prologue is part of the fictional construction *Monna Innominata* (and therefore itself a fiction), and not part of it (as its explanation). It protects the poem proper from efforts to read Rossetti's biography into it by positing the Provençal poetess, while it diminishes the authority of that "poet" to model a work after masters whom she precedes.[28]

What is the nineteenth-century, British, female, unhappy poet, as distinct from who is Christina Rossetti? A nineteenth-century British, unhappy, female poet is a tropological compilation of the elements that imbue Rossetti's poetry, each element part of a trope for the agent who could create such works. If *Later Life* inscribes in its boundaries the pervasive thematics of Rossetti's poetry (an oblique God, human fallenness, and the inadequacy of language), *Monna Innominata* inscribes in its introduction the profile of the purveyor of these thematics. "Nineteenth-century" and "British" situate the poetry at the receiving end of influences such as Keats and Coleridge on the one hand (in Rossetti ballads and lyrics), and John Keble and Isaac Williams on the other (in "Feasts and Fasts," for instance, a Keble-like record of the "Christian year"). In particular, *Monna Innominata* is Pre-Raphaelite in its medievalism, Victorian in its intertextual reference to Barrett Browning and her *Sonnets from the Portuguese.* "Unhappy" and "female," the more provocative elements of the authorial trope, warrant careful attention, because it is around them that most current crticial attention to Rossetti's work resolves, and because for Rossetti's poetry they are inextricably bound to religiosity, even in a secular poem like *Monna Innominata.*

Blake notices that in her poetry Rossetti "returns again and again to the experience of one who loves but cannot act on that love, and which constitutes the woman's relationship to the man, in her view, and the soul's to God" (5). Blake wants to accord the ascetic impulse its due in any consideration of nineteenth-century female literature, and the figure of female becomes a trope for the figure of the Christian in her reading of Rossetti's works: "Outweighing hedonism in importance, the ascetic aspect of Victorian feminism is only beginning to be well understood" (ix). In *Monna Innominata,* the relationship between woman and Christian can be pushed further; the figure of woman becomes the reigning rhetorical trope for the figure of the writer, in particular, the religious writer. "While when you come not what I do I do" captures the voice of

---

28. Though not with complete success, given the zealousness of critics, particularly biographers, to ransack the sonnet sequence for clues about Rossetti's love life.

the believer, heard in the poetry discussed throughout this work. This voice does what it does, writes into the space left by an absent loved one—an earthly male lover or a God—in an attempt at decorous imitation. But that imitation also threatens to imitate the blasphemy of Satan enjoying the beauty of his music for its own sake. This threat can be managed by reducing poetry to the inadequate compensation of a self-abnegating poetic voice ("Or is becoming a poet my compensation?" asks Constantin's young man), but self-abnegation, like imitation, is only a compromised possibility at best in the act of writing. In *Monna Innominata* the rigors of the form may permit a self-silencing gesture, but it disallows premature silence. Self-abnegation and self-expression wrestle with each other as impulses both in the female as she is conventionally figured, and in the religious writer; both want to deflect attention away from themselves in decorous acts of homage, the first toward a male lover, the second toward God. And yet, a gesture can only be effective when noticed by some public, and that notice cannot but draw attention to the gesturer.

In *Memories and Impressions,* Ford Madox Ford understands well the complex mixture of gender, religion, and profession that manifests itself in Rossetti's work: " . . . it has always seemed to me to be a condemnation of Christianity that it should have let such a fate harass such a woman, just as perhaps it is one of the greatest testimonies to the power of discipline of Christianity that it should have trained up such a woman to such a life of abnegation, of splendid literary expression, and of meticulous attention to duty" (67–68). Caught up in what should be both condemned and praised, "such a woman" writes the experience of self-abnegation; but writing that experience is also a strong self-assertion. Such is the dilemma of a decorous woman writing, and of a writer with a religious mandate. As Ford knew, Rossetti is both; such is the "fate that harassed her."

A reading of *Monna Innominata* as a secular analogy to the predicament of the religious writer depends upon an understanding of failure as written into the surface of the poem. And from a certain angle (Miller's), *Monna Innominata* does fail. If one assumes that a Provençal poetess is the controlling agent in the poem, and that she takes up the pen of her absent lover in an act of appropriation and therefore subversion of the traditional male voice in the courtly tradition, then the prologue and epigraphs are unaccounted for. If instead, one reads the sonnets as parts of a more complicated whole, then the Provençal poetess can be understood as a device of the poem's real agent, the storyteller embedded in the prologue. Her use in telling the problematic story of writing as imitative homage and compensation must be understood in order to see the importance of failure and contradiction in such a story.[29]

Failure and contradiction: order and slippage; these elements operate in both of Rossetti's sonnets of sonnets. The term "sonnet of sonnets" is no less redundant than the name "Constantin Constantius," and the comparison of the two returns us to Constantin the controller—the "spokesman" who is also the "vanishing person." In his tightly controlled experiment of return (to Berlin) he proves that there is *no* return through the repetition of failed attempts (the room, the food, the theater), and thus illustrates— or even lives—the paradox of repetition. Immediately before the letters from the young man begin, Constantin concedes the power of this paradox, and the lack of real control he can wield: "... repetition is too transcendent for me. I can circumnavigate myself, but I cannot rise above myself. I cannot find the Archimedean point" (*Repetition*, 186).

In the shifting sands of nineteenth-century religious belief, there is no place to stand—or write—firmly, although the desire for such a place still remains in a writer such as Rossetti. Trying to "rise above" oneself, or acquire transcendence, is quixotic at best. *Later Life* captures this tension by allowing (but for no longer than twenty-eight sonnets) chaotic escape. *Monna Innominata*, with its apparatus of preface and epigraphs, allows a glimpse of the Cheshire Cat's smile, the historically specific tropological profile that drives the putative medieval vehicle of the "unnamed lady." Neither sonnet of sonnets offers an "Archimedean point." Rather, both document its lack, one through an imitation (a repetition) of the anarchic state of a religious mind in turmoil, the other through a deliberately ill-concealed failure to return to and revise an earlier tradition. As poems concerned with religious belief and the poetical expression of such belief, not only do they offer no theological system, they query the possibility of such systems, and do so systematically, sonnet after sonnet. In this querying, Rossetti's sonnets of sonnets are like the young man's Job, who "does not posture on a rostrum and make reassuring gestures to vouch for the truth of his propositions, but sits on the hearth and scrapes himself with a potsherd and without interrupting this activity casually drops clues and comments" (*Repetition*, 186).

---

29. See Mackey, *Points of View*. He says that for Kierkegaard, "[f]ailure is all the success there is: the oblique purpose of the Kierkegaardian text is to take itself out of the way and thereby facilitate its displacement and replacement by the discourse of the Other" (xxii). My argument throughout is that such a process of failure can itself never fully succeed, because there can be no full displacement, or there can never be a fully "self-consuming artifact."

6

Choice and the Cloister

He chose what he had to become.
—William Barrett on Kierkegaard

I n 1862 Rossetti published a poem entitled "The Convent Threshold" as part of her first collection, *Goblin Market and Other Poems.* In it a young woman apparently rebuffs the lover with whom she has committed "pleasant sin," exhorting him to repent also. In 1864 Hopkins began work on a poem tentatively entitled "A Voice from the World." Never to be finished, it took the form of a reply to "The Convent Threshold," having as its speaker the spurned lover.[1] Revisiting that one moment of poetic intersection between Rossetti and Hopkins, I argue that "The Convent Threshold" and "A Voice from the World" create and therefore converge around a Kierkegaardian chasm by becoming two mutually exclusive choices that are resistant to mediation. Either you are in the convent or you are out; between in and out of the convent is a no-man's/no-woman's land of present impossibility, though filled with some endlessly deferred future hope. My final chapter, a meditation on choice as a literary issue, bears the responsibil-

---

1. Its subtitle is "An answer to Miss Rossetti's 'Convent Threshold.' " Although critics of both poets generally take note of this exchange, in general little is made of it. Paul Mariani, in *A Commentary on the Complete Poems of Gerard Manley Hopkins* (Ithaca: Cornell University Press, 1970), mentions it to claim that Rossetti's influence on early Hopkins poetry was unfortunate (2), and that Hopkins grew tired of the response (39). Jerome Bump and G. B. Tennyson have regarded the two poets together, but without focusing particularly on these two poems. See Bump, "Hopkins, Christina Rossetti, and Pre-Raphaelitism," *The Victorian Newsletter* 57 (1980): 1–6; a version of this article also appears in *Gerard Manley Hopkins* (Boston: Twayne Publishers, 1982). See also Tennyson, *Victorian Devotional Poetry: The Tractarian Mode* (Cambridge: Harvard University Press, 1981).

ity of closure, a responsibility I both fulfill and eschew. In that I examine closely the two poems that were the germ of the whole study and therefore draw to an intersection what until now I have presented as parallel, I pull together structural loose ends. But in this chapter I fan out from that intersection to address explicitly what has implicitly informed all of the chapters so far: the isolated state of the believer when, as Ford Madox Ford says, "in outside things we can perceive no design, but only the fortuitous materialism of a bewildering world."[2] I will end by suggesting in which direction this book would go were it endless: toward an argument for the peculiar modernity of Kierkegaard, Hopkins, and Rossetti, not in spite of the religiosity of their work, but because of it.

In using *Either/Or* to study the dynamic between Rossetti's poem and Hopkins's poetic response, I will emphasize the structure of Kierkegaard's work as much as its content. It must be remembered that the two poems do not constitute an exchange; Rossetti could not have anticipated Hopkins's response nor even have known about it since it was not published in her lifetime.[3] An appropriate framework for a relationship between the two poems, therefore, must take into account the independence of Rossetti's poem, and the *de*pendence of Hopkins's. It also must account for the fact that Hopkins's poem is a fragment (albeit a long one), incomplete, whose "meaning" is vexed by its gaps.

Structurally, *Either/Or* builds itself on the freewheeling autonomy of Volume I and the measured though passionate response of Volume II. Its fiction is that neither volume has been "edited" to smooth transitions or bridge gaps (although each does have titles for its different sections) so that whatever transitional gaps the "authors" leave remain standing. On the other hand, the papers in Volume I require arrangement, so loosely gathered are they upon their discovery. Substantively, *Either/Or* takes a walk through the sensual world of the aesthete even as it mounts its own resistance to such a world. "The Diary of a Seducer," for instance (part of

2. Ford Madox Ford, *Memories and Impressions: A Study in Atmospheres by Ford Madox Hueffer* (New York: Harper and Brothers, 1911), 68. Ford is explaining here the attractions of medievalism for nineteenth-century artists.

3. Though Hopkins and Rossetti did meet. See *Further Letters of Gerard Manley Hopkins, Including His Correspondence with Coventry Patmore,* 2d ed., ed. Claude Colleer Abbott (London: Oxford University Press, 1956), 118–19. He sends his "kind remembrance" to Maria Rossetti through his mother, and praises Christina's poetry as superior to her brother's "thrown in the shade by him" though she may be. Also see Lona Mosk Packer, *Christina Rossetti* (Berkeley and Los Angeles: University of California Press, 1963), 185: "During this summer [1864] she met Gerard Manley Hopkins at the house of the Reverend Gurney, vicar of St. Barnabas, Pimlico."

Volume I), is itself no less seductive for eliciting the rebuke of Volume II than if it were excerpted and published alone.[4] Like "Habit of Perfection" and "Goblin Market," *Either/Or* goes among that which it purports to reject. Kierkegaard's own late reflections upon his first major work in turn reflect the contradictory literary events that are *Either/Or* and the paired "Convent Threshold" and "A Voice from the World."

In *The Point of View for My Life as an Author,* Kierkegaard declares that "strictly speaking, *Either/Or* was written in a monastery." About the impetus for writing the book he says:

> When I began *Either/Or* I was potentially as deeply under the influence of religion as ever I have been. I was so deeply shaken that I understood perfectly well that I could not possibly succeed in striking the comforting and secure *via media* in which most people pass their lives: I had either to cast myself into perdition and sensuality, or to choose the religious absolutely as the only thing—either the world in a measure that would be dreadful, or the cloister. That it was the second I would and must choose was at bottom already determined: the eccentricity of the first movement was merely the expression for the intensity of the second; it expressed the fact that I had become thoroughly aware how impossible it would be for me to be religious only up to a certain point. Here is the place of *Either/Or.* It was a poetical catharsis.[5]

As "poetical catharsis," *Either/Or* embraces both the "perdition and sensuality" it nonetheless rejects and the absolute "religious" it chooses. This study of Rossetti and Hopkins ends by grappling with how the act of choosing *is expressed* in an aesthetics of asceticism. Such expression must allow room for the corollary act, the act of rejecting (rejecting "glad fellowship," for instance). Choosing the cloister, metaphorically what all three writers do to practice their craft, means not choosing "the world," and yet both the cloister and "the world" receive equal weight in a literary expression of "either/or." In other words, by definition to

---

4. See, for instance, *A Kierkegaardian Anthology,* ed. Robert Bretall (New York: Modern Library, 1946). Its selections from *Either/Or* include "Diary of the Seducer." While the anthology also includes "The Aesthetic Validity of Marriage," the "Diary of a Seducer," stands as a very different text when removed from the context of *Either/Or* in its entirety.

5. Søren Kirekegaard, *The Point of View for My Life as an Author / A Report to History and Related Writings,* trans. Walter Lowrie, ed. Benjamin Nelson (New York: Harper and Row, 1962), 18.

choose is also to exclude, but exclusion becomes inclusion in an artistic rendering of that choice.

Christopher Norris points out that in reading *Either/Or* "Kierkegaard's reader is constantly on trial."[6] The single greatest cause for this trial is the particular strategy of pseudonymity employed in *Either/Or.* Like all of Kierkegaard's pseudonyms, *Either/Or's* "Victor Eremitas" puns to make a statement about the character of this fictional author. "Victor Eremitas" etymologically interpreted is a conquering "one of the desert," a victorious recluse with both religious connotations (a medieval hermit) and implications of closedness (a hermetic seal or, more loosely, a cloister). Readers of *Either/Or* learn almost nothing about Eremitas and the nature or cause of his solitude; and yet the meaning of his name matters, for he introduces the text in the role of discoverer and editor. After he launches the two volumes he retreats from his discovery, never making another appearance after the short preface. When we expect to see him again, helping us move from Volume I to Volume II, he simply does not appear. Instead, the two volumes converge upon his silence. Ironically, even perversely reclusive in the face of an editor's duty, Victor is victorious in leaving the reader alone with two texts that unite as a single work only to demonstrate how acute their mutual exclusiveness is without some mediating authorial presence.[7] The preface does at least reveal how the papers were discovered, and it suggests that they are the first of Kierkegaard's "rosewood boxes." The "rosewood box" is first an old desk with a hidden drawer and then a mahogany box. He accidentally discovers the papers in the old desk (which he bought after he yielded to the compelling urge to own what he found himself drawn to look at in a shop every day for two years).[8] Then he secures them in the mahogany box that holds his pistols; the act of reading, which takes place in a "romantic spot in the forest," is interpreted by his innkeeper as shooting practice (*Either/Or,* I, 6). Camouflage replaces camouflage until he presents the papers to the public, and then possible exposure replaces camouflage. Victor, like Frater Taciturnus, nominally worries that

6. Christopher Norris, *The Deconstructive Turn: Essays in the Rhetoric of Philosophy* (New York: Methuen, 1983), 89.

7. For a contemporary story that uses a similar strategy of editorial reticence, see Cynthia Ozick's "From a Refugee's Notebook," in *Levitation* (New York: E. P. Dutton, 1983). The fiction is that a "Redactor" finds fragments of two studies called "Freud's Room" and "The Sewing Harems." They appear as unrelated as possible, and the redactor makes no effort to explain; he or she just presents.

8. *Either/Or,* trans. and ed. Howard V. Hong and Edna H. Hong (Princeton: Princeton University Press, 1987), 4–5.

the identities of "A" and "B" (the two "writers" whose real names he does not know, though he can deduce an identity for B) will be discernible and possibly incriminating. He recommends silence to the authors should they be alive and reading because "nothing would result from the publication, provided that the authors themselves remained silent, for, in the most rigorous sense, these papers, as is ordinarily said of all printed matter, are silent" (*Either/Or,* I, 12).

Silent though the papers may be, they announce themselves as the interpretative project of Victor Eremitas, through whose reticence the either/or paradigm results. As the result of Victor's editing decisions, *Either/Or* is a text of literal description, or better, a demonstration of a necessity for radical choice. Choose A's exaltation of Mozart's *Don Juan* or choose B's aesthetic validation of marriage. Choose A's offering of "The Diary of a Seducer," purloined from "Johannes," or choose a sermon by the minister friend of B. Do not look to Victor for a way to reconcile and therefore choose both. *Either/Or,* in its length and generic diversity, provides the quintessential opportunity for radical choice, an act of the free will that nonetheless invokes a necessity of consequence because there can be no mitigating or moderating influence from the "other side." Either A or B: never a synthesizing C.

The mode of "editing" employed by Victor becomes the pattern within the text of *Either/Or* itself. What Victor Eremitas discovers are the papers, in fragments, of two writers. The first, whom he calls "A," is the prototypical aesthete with an affinity for *Don Juan* and a penchant for grief and sorrow as "interesting" concepts. "A" then also becomes something of an editor, rehearsing Eremitas's act of discovery by purloining the diary of a known Lothario, his friend "Johannes." "B," or Judge Wilhelm, writes two long epistles to A, praising marriage as the best life for a man and rebutting A's extended encomium on an aesthetic way of life by extolling the characteristics and virtues of the ethical. Finally, like Victor and A, he too delivers someone else's text, a sermon by his minister friend. A fictional persona presents a fictional persona, that fiction residing within the larger fiction of Eremitas's accidental discovery.[9] All of these parts come together by arrangement around the divisive slash in "either/or," making Victor's project one of unification through separation; and this is his interpretative accomplishment.

It is this slash of the "either/or" paradigm that best represents the no-man's land between Rossetti's and Hopkins's poems. In *Either/Or,* the

---

9. And outside of *that* fiction is the one whereby Kierkegaard should be identifiable and repulsive to Regine, his spurned fiancée, as either a committed loner, a cad, or a bore.

grammatical construct "either/or" derives its very power to mean from what it excludes—the possibility of mediation—and what it demands instead—an act of radical choice. Between the Either and the Or lies an unnegotiable space demarcated by a grammatical convention that usually denotes ad hoc unity. But in this case, the slash joins only to emphasize disjunction. The Either, aesthetic fragments by the "writer" called "A," and the Or, an ethical rebuttal by the "writer" "B," clearly come together to make up the single text, *Either/Or:* they share a "publisher/ editor," who found their papers hidden together. A and B know each other. Their texts are even Volumes I and II respectively, with "B's" part, a defense of marriage and of the ethical view of life, occasioned by "A's" multigeneric paean to an aesthetics of seduction. But though they come together, the Either and the Or emphatically do not meet. Instead an incomplete rapprochement results in a lacuna, its location marked by the slash, which, by signaling the presence of a gap obviously signals an absence as well, here the absence of an editorial presence.

Discussed in the context of *Either/Or,* the word "threshold" in "The Convent Threshold" seems antithetical to a notion of choice—if anything, evocative more of neither/nor or both/and than of either/or. A threshold, after all, is neither in nor out, but rather a place defined by the two things it is not and crafted out of a tension between two equally compelling possibilites. How then does a discussion of "The Convent Threshold" follow and benefit from one on *Either/Or?* And how does it change, if it does, as part of a duet with Hopkins's poem?

Rossetti's poem combines generic characteristics of dramatic monologue, epistle, and lyric in its creation of a speaking—or rather writing— persona whose choice of the cloistered religious life apparently does not mitigate a constitutional erotic passion nor eradicate from her consciousness, though it does sublimate, her memories of lust and "pleasant sin." Like several Rossetti personae, she reveals her passionate nature at the very moment of earthly renunciation.[10] But I want to argue against a reading of "The Convent Threshold" as testimony to the strength of covert desire in the face of overt renunciation, and explore how the poem presents itself as the description, like *Either/Or,* of the necessity of choice, incorporating into itself and therefore (almost) controlling all expression of erotic desire.

Crossing the poem's "threshold" into the poem itself immediately results in a challenge to the implications of suspension, of neither/nor, in

10. See especially her other poems featuring cloistered women: "Three Nuns," "Soeur de la Misericorde," and "An 'Immurata' Sister."

the title. The first three lines describe an unnegotiable barrier between the speaker and her ex-lover: "There's blood between us, love, my love, / There's father's blood, there's brother's blood."[11] Though these lines tantalize in their ambiguity concerning the *kind* of blood between them (parricidal? incestuous?), they do not equivocate in the prohibition they invoke: "And blood's a bar I cannot pass" (3). In contradistinction to the ambivalent title, they open the poem forcefully and forthrightly. Decision-making constitutes the action of the very next line of the poem: "I choose the stairs that mount above, / Stair after golden skyward stair" (4–5). "I choose," a strongly performative speech act, only performs, it must be emphasized, following the proclamation of the bar that *she* cannot pass; the willfulness of "I choose the stairs" then retroactively invests "cannot" with the sense of ethical decision ("I cannot in good conscience commit such an act") and diminishes the sense of inability ("I want to but cannot"). Following directly upon and from her choice comes a series of temporal and spatial reenactments of irreconcilability. On her way to "city and to sea of glass" where she anticipates purification, she appeals to him: "Mount with me, mount the kindled stair" (16). Instantly she sees the inefficacy of her appeal—to her lover she observes, "Your eyes look earthward, mine look up" (17). Dolores Rosenblum argues that "Through the woman's traditional role as mediatrix, then, she becomes the dominant figure; she leads, he follows."[12] But if the speaker dominates, it is because she *eschews* the option of mediation, and any traditional role a woman might play in such a process. In all respects she continues upward, her eyes on "the far-off city grand," her feet never retreating down the stairs to meet him "half way." Stairs only go one way for her: "Lo, stairs are meant to lift us higher" (15). As the poem gets under way, the speaker allows little hope of a negotiated *detente* between her and her lover.

After describing in some detail the different view each has in her or his position of choice, the speaker moves on to the irreconcilable temporal realities of each. Admonishing her lover, she reminds him of the swiftness of the hour, the little time he has left to repent and be saved. "You linger, yet the time is short" (38), she warns him and tries to create a mood of urgency: "Today while it is called today / Kneel, wrestle, knock, do violence, pray; / Today is short, tomorrow nigh: / Why will you die?

11. Christina Rossetti, *The Complete Poems of Christina Rossetti, A Variorum Edition*, 3 vols., ed. R. W. Crump (Baton Rouge: Louisiana State University Press, 1979), I, 61, lines 1–2.
12. Dolores Rosenblum, *Christina Rossetti: The Poetry of Endurance* (Carbondale: Southern Illinois University Press, 1986), 191.

why will you die?" (47–50). But she evokes an entirely different mood for herself. Her existence in time in no way resembles his; time passes as slowly for her as it does quickly for him. "How long until my sleep begin," she asks, "How long shall stretch these nights and days?" (56– 57). And then hyperbolically, "How long must stretch these years and years?" (60). Just as there is no place for them to see together as they look and move in diametrically opposed directions, there is no moment in which to meet, in her description of their respective temporal states.

One more enactment of the necessity of choice occurs in the poem through the use of rhetorical anaphora. The speaker says, "I tell you what I dreamed last night" (85) and proceeds to describe the travails of the man who searches for knowledge only to learn finally that "knowledge is strong, but love is sweet" (106), and that "love is all in all" (109). Immediately after this dream, she repeats herself exactly ("I tell you what I dreamed last night" [110]) and describes a nightmare in a no-place/no-time of horror ("It was not dark, it was not light" [111]) about her acute loss of erotic desire ("My heart was dust that used to leap / To you" [115]) and the dread with which this loss and her death smites him. The effect of anaphora here is the impression of non-sequence, anti-progression; instead of first one dream and then the other, "what I dreamed"$_1$ and "what I dreamed"$_2$ compete with each other for status as her dream.

The competition goes on all night: "For all night long I dreamed of you," she tells him (126). With these words she draws almost to the end of her address, and the poem begins its penultimate and climactic stanza. Climactic not because after so long a dream sequence she describes her waking self, but because in a long, detailed address to her lover she now records her experience of the unwriteable, the incommunicable: "I cannot write the words I said" (130). "The words [she] said" were only inept prolegomena ("My words were slow") to a truly unsayable, unnegotiable, loud silence: "But thro' the dark my silence spoke / Like thunder" (132–33). The whole poem moves toward and arranges itself around this one marker of silence, for what emerges on the other side of that marker is a persona grotesquely altered, even perhaps dead: "When this morning broke, / My face was pinched, my hair was gray, / And frozen blood was on the sill / Where stifling in my struggle I lay" (133– 35). The metamorphosed speaker, if not dead, resembles a frightening image of the "living dead," and she realizes she could only repulse her lover were he to see her thus: "If now you saw me you would say: / Where is the face I used to love?" (137–38). Such an appearance precludes once and for all any possibility of reunion in the present (present meaning their time on earth). Instead, the most the speaker offers is reunion deferred to a paradisal future where the lovers will meet again and "love with old familiar love" (148).

If a Kierkegaardian act of radical choice identifies itself and distinguishes itself from other less dramatic acts of decision by the necessity of its consequences, "The Convent Threshold" describes such an act in its resolutely anti-dialectical movement toward a thundering silence and a virtual sea change on the silence's other side. Spatial, temporal, and rhetorical descriptions based on the "either/or" paradigm of radical choice march the writer-speaker (and her reader-lover) toward this climactically silent moment, a moment of anti-writing ironically commemorated *by* writing ("I cannot write the words I said," she writes). "The Convent Threshold," then, describes the movement from a threshold, a place of tense indeterminacy, to the poem's climactic gap—what cannot be written—through a series of unnegotiable opposites: either up or down; time flees or it lingers; either love is all in all or love is defeatable. From the other side of the gap neither retreat to the threshold nor any present mitigating circumstances are possible. But there is a place in the poem where the speaker falters.

"How should I rest in Paradise, / Or sit on steps of heaven alone?" (69–70) the speaker asks plaintively before telling her dreams. She appeals to her lover on his terms, abandoning hers: "Should I not turn with yearning eyes, / Turn earthwards with a pitiful pang?" (75–76). In a heretical, not to mention unseemly fantasy for a novitiate, she foresees trouble in paradise without him. In her paradisal misery, she imagines, she will compromise her commitment to keeping her eyes fixed on the "far-off city grand" and yield to the temptation to look "earthwards," hoping for a glimpse of him among the "[y]oung men and women [who] come and go" (37). In "A Voice from the World," Hopkins invents the cause of this irresolution; in doing so he seeks to eradicate it.

The fiction created by these two poems is worth rehearsing at this stage. Rossetti invents her erstwhile passionate, presumably young, female persona who has cloistered herself in a convent after engaging in a love affair. She has her write her remarkable letter, *almost* a perfect rejection, though erotic even as it rejects eroticism. ("Cold dews had drenched my plenteous hair" [112], for instance, can only remind the young man of his love's hair, even as he gets her point.) Hopkins participates in Rossetti's fiction, inventing a worldly male persona who, helpless and confused by his love's action, desperately tries and fails (at least in fragments we have) to find the impossible—new common ground that is neither in the convent (where he cannot go), nor out (where she is not).

Hopkins creates the ideal recipient for the letter from the convent, in the same way that the aesthete, A, is the ideal opposite of the ethicist, B (or vice versa). Where Rossetti's speaker moves toward her critical moment of silence, Hopkins's speaker finds himself inappropriately and harmfully garrulous ("I plead: familiarness endears / My evil words thorny with pain . . ." and "I know I mar my cause with words: / So be it; I must maim and mar").[13] He does have his own moment of silence as we will see, but in its cowardliness it only throws into brilliant relief the strength of hers. Where she at least expresses the desire to forget their joint memories ("Woe's me the lore I must unlearn!"), he, after several lines indicating his willingness to repent with her help ("Teach me the paces you went" [124]), still does not desire forgetfulness and cannot entertain the idea of breaking with his (and her) past: "But grant my penitence begun: / I need not, love, I need not break / Remember'd sweetness" (137–39). He sees himself as very small and petty, comparing himself to Gehazi, the servant who traded nefariously on his master's miraculous recovery from leprosy. Nonetheless, he has a "counterpart" dream to hers, precisely about an act of radical choice (as radical as possible) in which he plays not the villain but the coward, and has his moment of silence.

The earthbound lover dreams of the final judgment, and of the arrival of an angel who tells him and his love, "The judgement done, / Mercy is left enough for one: / Choose, one for hell and one for heaven!" (104–6). Immediately she says salvation should be given to him ("Give him the gift" [111]), an enormous act of generosity, though based not on a willingness to go to hell, but on some confidence that she can make it to heaven on her merits, not needing mercy as he does. His role in his dream-choice is less clear but clearly less admirable: "I cannot tell / But all the while it seem'd to me / I reason'd the futility. / Or this, or else I do not love, / I *inly* said; but could not move / My fast-lodged tongue. ['To her the gift] / I yield' I *would have* cried" (111–17, my emphasis). Would have but did not, and in his dream he swoons, mitigating the consequences of his weak non-choice. The fragment's revisionary allusion to Rossetti's thundering silence, both here and in his earlier garrulity, iterates the speaker's moral ineptness and the gulf that results between him

13. Gerard Manley Hopkins, *Gerard Manley Hopkins,* ed. Catherine Phillips (New York: Oxford University Press, 1986), 42, lines 26–27 and 30–31.

and her. As B says to A in *Either/Or*, "it is important to choose and to choose in time" (II, 165). Not only does Hopkins's speaker not choose in time, his time and her time are so different that he *cannot* choose in time, or at least not in her time.[14] What Hopkins does is propose the antithesis to Rossetti's thesis, and the works come together—almost—in this ironic relationship of irreconcilability. As Hopkins participates in Rossetti's fiction, he invents a persona who imagines he has some hope of finding that common ground mentioned earlier. "At last I hear the voice well known," he says at the beginning of probably the first fragment, and finds some reason to feel encouraged to respond. To what does he owe this encouragement? Certainly not to her dreams, nor to her exhortations, nor especially to her description of her metamorphosed self upon waking. But there is a chink in her rhetorical armor, that very stanza where she worries about compromising herself in heaven. For a young lover reading an otherwise hopeless letter, this stanza extends a hint of compromise. In other words, the vexatious stanza really is weak, deliberately so, the place in the poem where the speaker falters. Reading "A Voice from the World" helps us see this weakness by its fiction of the responsive lover who attempts to establish reconnection, to dismantle the "convent wicket" separating them, and to reestablish their love relationship's equilibrium (or synthesis) on new territory.

Such an attempt must fail, and that is the point of "A Voice from the World"; it provides the Or to Rossetti's Either in a literary act of homage to the ethos of choice worked out in "A Convent Threshold." One can speculate that Hopkins found the attempt to write a "verbal notation of failure" inordinately difficult and finally impossible.[15] Hopkins himself, however, made a radical decision in 1866 in his conversion to Catholicism. Furthermore, after his own extended "moment" of artistic silence he emerged on the other side a poet who, in his use of paradox and ambiguity, refused to accommodate his poetry to standards of the day, courting charges of obscurity in the artistic decisions he made.[16] As we

14. In the introductory essay to *Kierkegaard and Literature: Irony, Repetition, and Criticism* (Norman: University of Oklahoma Press, 1984), Schleifer and Markley make the following comment, useful for connecting poetry and criticism: "Above all, Kierkegaard's insistence on choice is timely, and that timeliness defines the essential discursiveness of criticism" (10).

15. To borrow and somewhat alter the sense of a phrase J. Hillis Miller uses to describe Robert Browning's "An Englishman in Italy" (*The Linguistic Moment: From Wordsworth to Stevens* [Princeton: Princeton University Press, 1985], 228).

16. The "moment" lasted seven years. In writing to Bridges about "The Wreck of the Deutschland," Hopkins offers a defense of poetical obscurity (*The Letters of Gerard Manley*

have seen, conversion figures as a dominant theme in the poem with which Hopkins emerges out of his seven years of poetic silence. "The Convent Threshold" calls attention to the chasm between the "before" and "after" of a profound conversion, and Hopkins's dedication to it draws attention to the stronger similarity between Hopkins (as convert and poet) and Rossetti's persona than between Hopkins and his own. Though he abandons his "verbal notation of failure" in that he does not finish it, in a more profound way he *does* finish it—lives it out—in his period of silence and the radically new poetry he writes upon breaking it.

Rossetti made no dramatic decision equivalent to Hopkins's conversion and ordination, and there is no silent period similar to Hopkins's seven-year hiatus. In the same metaphorical sense that *Either/Or* was "written in a monastery," however, Rossetti worked in a self-fashioned cloister from whence she sent out poetical communications. But in the disrupted relationship between "The Convent Threshold" and "A Voice from the World" we do better to see not biography but allegory. For the interpretative linkage of these two poems spun out here allegorizes the fundamental thesis of this study: that the pseudonymous works of Kierkegaard and the poetry of Rossetti and Hopkins explore the disruption between the material and the divine worlds, and the isolation of the individual believer such a disruption engenders. In one sense, the cloister (or monastery) must be chosen in some form, from within which to write about such disruption. In another, starker sense, there is no choice but the cloister because each individual is always already sequestered within a self that is like no other self. The young nun's choice and her suitor's failure to dissuade her together constitute the inevitability of isolation insisted upon by all three authors' works. The "something dark and hard, like a kernel," that is the religion Woolf sees in Rossetti's work and which also resides in Kierkegaard's and Hopkins's, grows into an agon upon which the individual's relationship with God becomes a struggle with incomprehensibility. Yet

---

Hopkins to Robert Bridges, ed. Claude Colleer Abbott [London: Oxford University Press, 1935]):

> Granted that it needs study and is obscure, for indeed I was not over-desirous that the meaning of all should be quite clear, at least unmistakable, you might, without the effort that to make it all out would seem to have required, have nevertheless read it so that lines and stanzas should be left in the memory and superficial impressions deepened, and have liked some without exhausting all. I am sure I have read and enjoyed pages of poetry that way. Why, sometimes one enjoys and admires the very lines one cannot understand. (50)

out of that struggle comes the artistic product, not as a monument to the battle, but as the rare sign of communion, however tentative or conditional, with fellow *isolados.* If the chink in the young nun's armor raises false hopes in the heart of the young suitor, it does at least raise hopes and spawns a reply that may never have been completed, but remains as a readable fragment nonetheless.

In his preface, Victor addresses his reader: "Perhaps you yourself have concealed a secret that in its joy or in its pain you felt was too intimate to share with others. Perhaps your life has put you in touch with people about whom you suspected that something of this nature was the case, although neither by force nor by inveiglement were you able to bring out into the open that which was hidden" (*Either/Or,* I, 3). In his unfinished commentary Hopkins responds to *The Spiritual Exercises,* the most significant text in his life:

> The universal mind being identified not only with me but also with all other minds cannot be the means of communicating what is individual in me to them nor in them to me. I have and every other has . . . my own knowledge and powers, pleasures, pains, merit, guilt, shame, dangers, fortunes, fates: we are not chargeable for one another. But these things and above all my shame, my guilt, my fate are the very things in feeling, in tasting, which I most taste that selftaste which nothing in the world can match.[17]

In "Memory," Rossetti writes:

> I shut the door to face the naked truth,
>   I stood alone—I faced the truth alone,
> Stripped bare of self-regard or forms or ruth
>   Till first and last were shown.
>
> I took the perfect balances and weighed;
>   No shaking of my hand disturbed the poise;
> Weighed, found it wanting: not a word I said,
>   But silent made my choice.
>   (*Complete Poems,* I, 148, lines 5–12)

17. Gerard Manley Hopkins, *The Sermons and Devotional Writings of Gerard Manley Hopkins,* ed. Christopher Devlin, S.J. (London: Oxford University Press, 1959), 125.

All three passages refer to that most profoundly personal experience ironically shared by all and supremely un-shareable. All three are notes sent from behind the cloister of self, or from behind Pater's "thick wall of personality." They are notes to be taken seriously by a modern audience, and the fact that for these three writers the wall is built in large part with the materials of subjective religious belief only makes their message more relevant, if less easily decipherable, in the late twentieth century. The works of Kierkegaard, Rossetti, and Hopkins do not avoid the paradoxes in and tensions between writing and religious experience, or those in or between writing and personal experience in general. They do actively oppose solving or, especially, relieving them, which makes all three of these nineteenth-century religious writers the bearers of stark but starkly relevant messages for those who would read them now.

Works Cited

Augustine of Hippo. *The Confessions of St. Augustine.* Trans. Rex Warner. New York: New American Library, 1963.

Austin, J. L. *How to Do Things with Words.* Cambridge: Harvard University Press, 1975.

Ball, Patricia. *The Central Self: A Study in Romantic and Victorian Imagination.* London: Athlone Press, 1968.

Barthes, Roland. *Sade, Fourier, Loyola.* Trans. Richard Miller. Berkeley and Los Angeles: University of California Press, 1989.

Bataille, Georges. *Inner Experience.* Trans. Leslie Ann Boldt. Albany: State University of New York Press, 1988.

Battiscombe, Georgina. *Christina Rossetti: A Divided Life.* New York: Holt, Rinehart, and Winston, 1981.

Bentley, D.M.R. "The Meretricious and the Meritorious in *Goblin Market:* A Conjecture and an Analysis." In *The Achievement of Christina Rossetti,* ed. David A. Kent. Ithaca: Cornell University Press, 1987.

Blake, Kathleen. *Love and the Woman Question in Victorian Literature: The Art of Self-Postponement.* Totowa, N.J.: Barnes and Noble, 1983.

Bloom, Harold. *The Anxiety of Influence: A Theory of Poetry.* New York: Oxford University Press, 1973.

Bové, Paul. "The Penitentiary of Reflection: Søren Kierkegaard and Critical Activity." In Schleifer and Markley, *Kierkegaard and Literature,* 25–57.

Bump, Jerome. *Gerard Manley Hopkins.* Boston: Twayne Publishers, 1982.

———. "Hopkins, Christina Rossetti, and Pre-Raphaelitism." *The Victorian Newsletter* 57 (1980): 1–6.

Carlyle, Thomas. *Sartor Resartus: The Life and Opinions of Herr Teufelsdröckh.* New York: A. L. Burt, n.d.

Charles, Edna Cotin. *Christina Rossetti: Critical Perspectives, 1862–1982.* Selinsgove, Pa.: Susquehanna University Press, 1985.

Christ, Carol. *The Finer Optic: The Aesthetics of Particularity.* New Haven: Yale University Press, 1975.

Cole, J. Preston. *The Problematic Self in Kierkegaard and Freud.* New Haven: Yale University Press, 1971.

Coleridge, Samuel T. *The Portable Coleridge.* Ed. I. A. Richards. New York: The Viking Press, 1978.

Culler, Jonathan. *The Pursuit of Signs: Semiotics, Literature, Deconstruction.* Ithaca: Cornell University Press, 1981.

D'Amico, Diane. "Christina Rossetti's *Later Life:* The Neglected Sonnet Sequence." *Victorian Institute Journal* 9 (1980–81): 21–28.

Dante Alighieri. *The Inferno.* Trans. John Ciardi. New York: New American Library, 1954.

Davies, Robertson. *World of Wonders.* Toronto: Macmillan of Canada, 1975.

de Man, Paul. *Allegories of Reading.* New Haven: Yale University Press, 1979.

———. *Resistance to Theory.* Theory and History of Literature, vol. 33. Minneapolis: University of Minnesota Press, 1986.

———. "Shelley Disfigured." In *Deconstruction and Criticism,* ed. Harold Bloom et al. New York: The Seabury Press, 1979.

Derrida, Jacques. *Of Grammatology.* Trans. Gayatri Spivak. Baltimore: The Johns Hopkins University Press, 1976.

Duffy, Maureen. *The Erotic World of Faery.* London: Hodder and Stoughton, 1972.

Eliot, George. *Middlemarch.* New York: Oxford University Press, 1990.

Ellsberg, Margaret. *Created to Praise: The Language of Gerard Manley Hopkins.* New York: Oxford University Press, 1987.

Felman, Shoshana. *The Literary Speech Act: Don Juan with J. L. Austin, or Seduction in Two Languages.* Trans. Catherine Porter. Ithaca: Cornell University Press, 1983.

Foucault, Michael. *The Order of Things: An Archaeology of the Human Sciences.* New York: Vintage Books, 1973.

Ford, Ford Madox. *Memories and Impressions: A Study in Atmospheres by Ford Madox Hueffer.* New York: Harper and Brothers, 1911.

Fraser, Hilary. *Beauty and Belief: Aesthetics and Religion in Victorian Literature.* New York: Cambridge University Press, 1986.

Freud, Sigmund. "The Uncanny." In *Collected Papers,* vol. 4. Trans. Joan Riviere. London: The Hogarth Press, 1949.

Gilbert, Sandra, and Susan Gubar. *Madwoman in the Attic: The Woman Writer and the Nineteenth-Century Literary Imagination.* New Haven: Yale University Press, 1979.

Golub, Ellen. "Untying Goblin Apron Strings: A Psychoanalytic Reading of 'Goblin Market.'" *Literature and Psychology* 23, no. 4 (1975): 162–64.

Hardy, Barbara. *The Advantage of Lyric: Essays on Feeling in Poetry.* London: Athlone Press, 1977.

Harrison, Antony H. *Christina Rossetti in Context.* Chapel Hill: University of North Carolina Press, 1988.

Hartman, Geoffrey. "Hopkins Revisited." In his *Beyond Formalism: Literary Essays 1958–1970.* New Haven: Yale University Press, 1970.

Heuser, Alan. *The Shaping Vision of Gerard Manley Hopkins.* London: Oxford University Press, 1958.

Homans, Margaret. " 'Syllables of Velvet': Dickinson, Rossetti, and the Rhetorics of Sexuality." *Feminist Studies* 11, no. 3 (Fall 1985): 569–93.

Hopkins, Gerard Manley. *The Correspondence of Gerard Manley Hopkins and Richard Watson Dixon.* Ed. Claude Colleer Abbott. London: Oxford University Press, 1955.

———. *Further Letters of Gerard Manley Hopkins, Including His Correspondence with Coventry Patmore.* 2d ed., ed. Claude Colleer Abbott. London: Oxford University Press, 1956.

———. *Gerard Manley Hopkins.* Ed. Catherine Phillips. New York: Oxford University Press, 1986.

———. *The Journals and Papers of Gerard Manley Hopkins.* Ed. Humphrey House, completed by Graham Storey. London: Oxford University Press, 1959.

———. *The Letters of Gerard Manley Hopkins to Robert Bridges.* Ed. Claude Colleer Abbott. London: Oxford University Press, 1955.

———. *The Poems of Gerard Manley Hopkins.* Ed. Robert Bridges. London: Humphrey Milford, 1918.

———. *The Poems of Gerard Manley Hopkins.* 4th ed., ed. W. H. Gardner and N. H. Mackenzie. London: Oxford University Press, 1967.

———. *The Sermons and Devotional Writings of Gerard Manley Hopkins.* Ed. Christopher Devlin, S.J. London: Oxford University Press, 1959.

Johnson, Barbara. *A World of Difference.* Baltimore: The Johns Hopkins University Press, 1989.

Kempis, Thomas à. *The Imitation of Christ.* Trans. George F. Maine. London: William Collins, 1957.

Kierkegaard, Søren. *The Concept of Anxiety.* Trans. and ed. Reider Thomte in collaboration with Albert B. Anderson. Princeton: Princeton University Press, 1980.

———. *The Concept of Irony: With Constant Reference to Socrates.* Trans. Lee M. Capel. London: Collins, 1965.

———. *Concluding Unscientific Postscript.* Trans. David F. Swenson. Princeton: Princeton University Press, 1974.

———. *Either/Or.* 2 vols. Trans. and ed. Howard V. Hong and Edna H. Hong. Princeton: Princeton University Press, 1987.

———. *Fear and Trembling / Repetition.* Trans. and ed. Howard V. Hong and Edna H. Hong. Princeton: Princeton University Press, 1983.

———. *Philosophical Fragments, or A Fragment of Philosophy by Johannes Climacus.* Trans. David F. Swenson. Rev. Howard V. Hong. Princeton: Princeton University Press, 1974.

———. *The Point of View for My Life as an Author / A Report to History and Related Writings.* Trans. Walter Lowrie. Ed. Benjamin Nelson. New York: Harper and Row, 1962.

———. *Stages on Life's Way.* Trans. Walter Lowrie. Princeton: Princeton University Press, 1940.

Knoepflmacher, U. C., and G. B. Tennyson, eds. *Nature and the Victorian Imagination.* Berkeley and Los Angeles: University of California Press, 1977.

Lowrie, Walter. *Kierkegaard.* New York: Oxford University Press, 1938.

Loyola, Ignatius. *The Spiritual Exercises of St. Ignatius Loyola: Spanish and English with a Continuous Commentary.* Ed. Joseph Rickaby, S.J. London: Burns, Oates, and Washbourne, 1923.

McGann, Jerome. "Christina Rossetti's Poems: A New Edition and a Revaluation." *Victorian Studies* 23 (Winter 1980): 237–54.

Mackey, Louis. *Kierkegaard: A Kind of a Poet.* Philadelphia: University of Pennsylvania Press, 1971.

———. *Points of View: Readings of Kierkegaard.* Tallahassee: Florida State University Press, 1986.

MacKenzie, Norman H. *A Reader's Guide to Gerard Manley Hopkins.* Ithaca: Cornell University Press, 1981.

Mariani, Paul. *A Commentary on the Complete Poems of Gerard Manley Hopkins.* Ithaca: Cornell University Press, 1970.

Massey, Irving. *The Uncreating Word.* Bloomington: Indiana University Press, 1970.

Mermin, Dorothy. "The Damsel, the Knight, and the Victorian Woman Poet." *Critical Inquiry* 13 (Autumn 1986): 64–80.

Miller, J. Hillis. *The Disappearance of God.* Cambridge: Harvard University Press, 1963.

———. *The Linguistic Moment: From Wordsworth to Stevens.* Princeton: Princeton University Press, 1985.

———. "The Linguistic Moment in 'The Wreck of the Deutschland.'" In Young, *The New Criticism and After,* 47–60.

———. "Nature and the Linguistic Moment." In Knoepflmacher and Tennyson, 440–51.

Milton, John. *Complete Poems and Major Prose.* Ed. Merrit Y. Hughes. Indianapolis: The Odyssey Press, 1980.

Moers, Ellen. *Literary Women: The Great Writers.* New York: Anchor Books, 1977.

Nietzsche, Friedrich. *The Gay Science.* Trans. Walter Kaufmann. New York: Random House, 1974.

Norris, Christopher. *The Deconstructive Turn: Essays in the Rhetoric of Philosophy.* New York: Methuen, 1983.

Nussbaum, Martha. *Love's Knowledge.* New York: Oxford University Press, 1990.

Ong, Walter J., S.J. *Hopkins, the Self, and God.* Toronto: University of Toronto Press, 1986.

Packer, Lona Mosk. *Christina Rossetti.* Berkeley and Los Angeles: University of California Press, 1963.

———, ed. *The Rossetti-Macmillan Letters.* Berkeley and Los Angeles: University of California Press, 1963.

Pater, Walter. *The Selected Writings of Walter Pater.* Ed. Harold Bloom. New York: Columbia University Press, 1974.

Percy, Walker. *The Moviegoer.* New York: Avon Books, 1961.

Pick, John. *Gerard Manley Hopkins: Priest and Poet.* New York: Oxford University Press, 1942.

Plato. *Phaedrus.* Trans. Reginald Hackforth. New York: The Liberal Arts Press, 1972.

Rajan, Tillotama. *Dark Interpreter: The Discourse of Romanticism.* Ithaca: Cornell University Press, 1980.

————. "Romanticism and the Death of Lyric Consciousness." In *Lyric Poetry: Beyond New Criticism,* ed. Chaviva Hosek and Patricia Parker. Ithaca: Cornell University Press, 1985.

Ricoeur, Paul. "Toward a Hermeneutic of the Idea of Revelation." In *Essays on Biblical Interpretation,* ed. Lewis S. Mudge. Philadelphia: Fortress Press, 1980.

Rorty, Richard. *Philosophy and the Mirror of Nature.* Princeton: Princeton University Press, 1979.

Rosenblum, Dolores. *Christina Rossetti: The Poetry of Endurance.* Carbondale: Southern Illinois University Press, 1986.

Rosenthal, M. L., and Sally M. Gall. *The Modern Poetic Sequence: The Genius of Modern Poetry.* New York: Oxford University Press, 1983.

Rossetti, Christina. *The Complete Poems of Christina Rossetti, A Variorum Edition.* 3 vols. Ed. R. W. Crump. Baton Rouge: Louisiana State University Press, 1979–90.

————. *Goblin Market.* Introduction by Germaine Greer. New York: Stonehill Publishing, 1975.

————. *New Poems of Christina Rossetti: Hitherto Unpublished or Uncollected.* Ed. William Rossetti. New York: Macmillan, 1896.

————. *The Poetical Works of Christina Rossetti, with Memoir and Notes by William Michael Rossetti.* London: Macmillan and Co., 1914.

Rossetti, William Michael, ed. *The Family Letters of Christina Georgina Rossetti.* New York: Charles Scribner's Sons, 1908.

Ruskin, John. *The Art Criticism of John Ruskin.* Ed. Robert L. Herbert. Gloucester, Mass.: Peter Smith, 1969.

————. *The Literary Criticism of John Ruskin.* Ed. Harold Bloom. Gloucester, Mass.: Peter Smith, 1969.

Sacks, Peter M. *The English Elegy: Studies in the Genre from Spenser to Yeats.* Baltimore: The Johns Hopkins University Press, 1985.

Schleifer, Ronald, and Robert Markley, eds. *Kierkegaard and Literature: Irony, Repetition, and Criticism.* Norman: University of Oklahoma Press, 1984.

Schneider, Elisabeth W. *The Dragon at the Gate: Studies in the Poetry of G. M. Hopkins.* Berkeley and Los Angeles: University of California Press, 1968.

Seskin, Kenneth. "Job and the Problem of Evil." *Philosophy and Literature* 2, no. 2 (October 1987): 226–41.

Shaw, W. David. *The Lucid Veil: Poetic Truth in the Victorian Age.* Madison: University of Wisconsin Press, 1987.

————. *Tennyson's Style.* Ithaca: Cornell University Press, 1976.

Shelley, Mary. *Frankenstein: Or the Modern Prometheus.* New York: New American Library, 1965.

Smyth, John Vignaux. *A Question of Eros: Irony in Sterne, Kierkegaard, and Barthes.* Tallahassee: Florida State University Press, 1986.

Spanos, William. *Repetitions: The Postmodern Occasion in Literature and Culture.* Baton Rouge: Louisiana State University Press, 1987.

Spivak, Gayatri. "Sex and History in *The Prelude.*" *Texas Studies in Literature and Language* 23, no. 3 (Fall 1981): 324–60.

Sprinker, Michael. *A Counterpoint of Dissonance: The Aesthetics and Poetry of Gerard Manley Hopkins.* Baltimore: The Johns Hopkins University Press, 1980.

Stuart, Dorothy Margaret. *Christina Rossetti.* London: Macmillan and Co., 1930.

———. "Christina Rossetti." The English Association. Pamphlet no. 78, 1931.

Sulloway, Allison. *Gerard Manley Hopkins and the Victorian Temper.* New York: Columbia University Press, 1972.

Taylor, Mark C. *Erring: A Postmodern A/theology.* Chicago: University of Chicago Press, 1984.

———. *Tears.* Albany: State University of New York Press, 1990.

Tennyson, G. B. *Victorian Devotional Poetry: The Tractarian Mode.* Cambridge: Harvard University Press, 1981.

Theresa de Avila. *The Collected Works of St. Teresa of Avila.* Vol. 1. Trans. Kiernan Kavanaugh, O.C.D., and Otilio Rodriguez, O.C.D. Washington, D.C.: I.C.S. Publications, 1976.

Terrien, Samuel. *Job: Poet of Existence.* New York: Bobbs-Merrill, 1957.

Todorov, Tzvetan. *The Poetics of Prose.* Trans. Richard Howard. Ithaca: Cornell University Press, 1977.

Troxell, Janet Camp, ed. *Three Rossettis: Unpublished Letters to and from Dante Gabriel, Christina, and William.* Cambridge: Harvard University Press, 1937.

Woolf, Virginia. *The Second Common Reader.* New York: Harcourt Brace Jovanovich, 1960.

Young, Thomas Daniel, ed. *The New Criticism and After.* Charlottesville: University Press of Virginia, 1976.

Index